Dictionary of
Literature

GEDDES&
GROSSET

This edition published 1999 by Geddes & Grosset, an imprint of
Children's Leisure Products Limited

© 1995 Children's Leisure Products Limited, David Dale House,
New Lanark ML11 9DJ, Scotland

Cover photograph by Steve Cole, courtesy of PhotoDisc

ISBN 1 85534 668 0

Printed and bound in the UK

A

Abbey Theatre an Irish theatre founded in Dublin in 1904 by YEATS and Lady GREGORY. The Abbey quickly became the major venue for new Irish drama, staging plays by, notably, SYNGE, SHAW and O'CASEY as well as by Yeats and Lady Gregory.

Abelard, Peter (1079–1142) French theologian and philosopher. He began lecturing at Notre Dame in Paris in 1115 and soon gained a reputation as a formidable adversary in theological debate. He professed the new doctrine of nominalism, and was condemned for heresy twice, in 1121 and in the year he died. His love affair with his pupil Héloïse (1101–64), whose uncle had him castrated, with its combination of intellectual and physical passion described in their letters to each other, was to haunt the imagination of many poets, notably POPE in his *Epistle of Eloisa to Abelard*.

Absurd, Theatre of the a form of theatre, developed in the 1960s, that characterizes the human condition as one of helplessness in the face of an irrational, 'absurd' universe. BECKETT, PINTER and IONESCO, whose characters communicate with one another in disjointed, inconsequential language, are among the best-known practitioners of the form, whose roots go back to Dadaism and the plays of JARRY. Absurdist drama reacts strongly against the conventions of NATURALISM. However, the only absurdist dramatist to become president of a country, Vaclav HAVEL, has argued that the form is in fact a very efficient vehicle for describing life realistically in a totalitarian society.

Académie française a literary academy founded by Cardinal Richelieu in 1635 to supervise and protect the purity of the French language. The Academy has 40 members ('the immortals') and is frequently quoted as an example of the rigidity or coherence of French culture, in contrast to the looser, less restricted cultures of other nations.

Achebe, Chinua (1930–) Nigerian novelist who became one of the most widely acclaimed African writers of the 20th century. Achebe's novels, e.g. *Things Fall Apart* (1958), have as their central theme the cultural clash between European colonialism and African society. Achebe is a vivid and clever satirist, with a dark and often grim humour.

Acmeist group *see* **Akhmatova, Anna**; **Mandelstam, Osip**.

acrostic a type of poem, in which the initial letters of each line form a word reading downwards. The form was used by Roman poets, and the Elizabethan poet and statesman **Sir John Davies** (1569–1626) devised in *Hymns of Astraea* (1599) 26 verses, each spelling out the name of Elizabeth I ('Elisabetha Regina'). The form was also used by POE and LAMB.

Acton, Sir Harold [Marino Mitchell] (1904–94) English poet, historian and miscellaneous writer. The scion of an aristrocratic Anglo-Italian Roman Catholic family, Acton befriended John BETJEMAN and Evelyn WAUGH at Oxford University. Several characters in the latter's novels, notably Anthony Blanche in *Brideshead Revisited*, are partly based on Acton. Acton's reputation as a dandy and aesthete has tended to obscure the fact that he is both a gifted writer of lucid prose and a perceptive and knowledgeable critic of art and letters. His two volumes of memoirs, *Memoirs of an Aesthete* (1948) and *More Memoirs* (1970), are required reading for anyone interested in the so-called '**Brideshead Generation**'.

Adams, Henry Brooks (1838–1918) American historian, whose nine-volume *History of the United States During the Administration of Thomas Jefferson and James Madison* (1889–91) is a landmark in American historical writing. Adams's great-grandfather, John Adams, was the second US president, and his grandfather, John Quincy Adams, was the sixth. Adams's autobiography, *The Education of Henry Adams* (1907), is an enthralling account of the pitfalls of a progressive mid-19th century education.

Addison, Joseph (1672–1719) English essayist and poet. He achieved public recognition in 1704 with his poem on the battle of Blenheim, *The Campaign*, which earned him a minor government post (a not uncommon reward for politically useful poetry in those days). Addison swiftly demonstrated a fearsome proficiency in many literary fields; his neoclassical tragedy *Cato* (1713) was a huge critical and popular success. It was, however, as an essayist and moralist that Addison was to make his mark. He co-founded *The Spectator* with his old schoolfriend Richard STEELE in 1711, the tone of which is light and often very funny, as in the Sir Roger de Coverley papers, but is always concerned with proclaiming the virtues of reasonableness, common sense and benevolent moderation.

Although Cyril CONNOLLY described Addison (disparagingly) as the first Man of Letters (he made prose 'artful and whimsical') in *Enemies of Promise*, Virginia WOOLF said of him in *The Common Reader*: 'It is due to Addison that prose is now prosaic—the medium which makes it possible for people of ordinary intelligence to communicate their ideas to the world'. His reputation as a moralist has proved less secure. He was unkind to his friend, the gentle Steele, and was foolishly unkind to the ungentle POPE, who hit back in the *Epistle to Dr Arbuthnot*: 'Damn with faint praise, assent with civil leer, / And without sneering, teach the rest to sneer . . . Who must but laugh, if such a man there be? / Who would not weep, if Atticus were he?'

Aelfric (*c*.955–*c*.1020) English monk who wrote works in Old English on the lives of the saints, and translations from Latin homilies and the Bible. He also wrote a Latin grammar which was still being used well into the late Middle Ages. Aelfric has always been highly regarded as a prose stylist.

Aeschylus (524–456 BC) Greek dramatist, who is regarded as the founder of Greek tragedy. Only seven of his plays survive. These include *Seven Against Thebes*, *Prometheus Bound* and the great Oresteia trilogy: *Agamemnon*, *Choephoroe (The Liberation Bearers)* and the *Eumenides*. Aeschylus was regarded by the Greeks as a less sophisticated playwright than the other two great Greek tragedians, EURIPIDES and SOPHOCLES, a judgment that largely prevailed until the Renaissance. SHELLEY was heavily influenced by him, and MARX regarded Aeschylus and SHAKE-SPEARE as the two greatest dramatists of all time.

Aesop (*c*.620–564 BC) supposed Greek author of witty fables in which human characteristics are satirized in the form of dialogues between animals. Aesop's actual existence is dubious; the fables themselves have close parallels in many cultures.

Aesthetic movement a cultural movement which developed in England in the late 19th century, characterized by a very affected and mannered approach to life and the arts, a fondness for orientalism and decadence, archaic language and pseudo-medievalism. The character Bunthorne in GILBERT and Sullivan's comic opera *Patience* (1881) is a conflation of all the features found ridiculous in the movement by contemporaries: 'Though the Philistines may jostle, you will rank as an apostle in the high aesthetic band, / If you walk down Piccadilly with a poppy or a lily in your medieval hand.'

Oscar WILDE is the most prominent literary figure of merit associated with the movement.

Aiken, Conrad Potter (1889–1973) American poet, novelist, short-story writer and critic. Collections of his poems include *Earth Triumphant* (1914) and *A Letter from Li Po* (1955). Novels include *Blue Voyage* (1927) and *A Heart for the Gods of Mexico*

(1939). Aiken was a friend of T. S. ELIOT (his classmate at Harvard), and his work, often autobiographical in content, is regarded as representative of minor 20th-century modernist fiction and poetry.

Akhmatova, Anna [pseud. of Anna Andreyevna Gorenko] (1889–1966) Russian poet who, with MANDELSTAM, was associated with the Acmeist group, a school of Russian poetry which first emerged as a coherent group with the formation of the Poets' Guild in Leningrad in 1911. In part a reaction to the more obscure aspects of SYMBOLISM, the group proclaimed the virtue of clarity of expression. Its founder, Akhmatova's ex-husband, Nikolai Gumilev, was executed by the Bolsheviks in 1921, and her son was arrested and imprisoned several times during Stalin's terror. Her great poem on the suffering of the Russian people under Stalin's rule, *Requiem*, was first published in Munich in 1963. She was denounced by Stalin's odious literary commissar, Zhdanov, as 'a bourgeois relic' and 'half-nun, half-whore'. Akhmatova's poems are among the finest and most important of the 20th century, and she and Mandelstam are now recognized in the USSR as ranking among the greatest Russian poets.

Albee, Edward Franklin (1928–) American dramatist, whose early plays bore resemblances to the Theatre of the ABSURD. His best-known play, however, *Who's Afraid of Virginia Woolf* (1962, filmed 1966) is a semi-naturalistic study of marital breakdown against an academic background, which established him as a very individual voice in American drama, a reputation reinforced by the semi-autobiographical *Three Tall Women* (1994).

Alcott, Louisa M[ay] (1832–88) American novelist. She was an active social reformer and prolific author of novels, but is now remembered chiefly for her hugely successful children's novel, *Little Women* (1868–69), and its sequels, *Jo's Boys* (1886) and *Little Men* (1871).

Aldington

Aldington, Richard (1892–1962) English poet and dramatist. His
most highly regarded novel is *Death of a Hero* (1929), which is a
thinly disguised semi-autobiographical account of the author's
war experiences. His other works include a volume of IMAGIST
poetry, *Images 1910–1915* (1915), and a bitter, debunking biography of T. E. LAWRENCE, *Lawrence of Arabia* (1955).

Aldrich, Thomas Bailey (1836–1907) American poet, novelist
and editor of the *Atlantic Monthly* (1881–90). His most popular
book was the semi-autobiographical novel, *The Story of a Bad
Boy* (1870).

Alfieri, Count Vittorio (1749–1803) Italian poet and tragedian.
His many works, including 21 tragedies, six comedies and an autobiography, display a strong enthusiam for Italian nationalism
and reform.

Alger, Horatio (1834–99) American author of boys' adventure
stories, e.g. *Ragged Dick* (1867) and *From Canal Boy to President* (1881). As the title of the latter book indicates, Alger's
works describe early poverty and adversity being overcome
through manly (or boyish) fortitude.

Algren, Nelson [Nelson Algren Abraham] (1909–81) American
novelist. He wrote four novels, two of which, *The Man with the
Golden Arm* (1949) and *A Walk on the Wild Side* (1956), are classic portrayals of urban American underclass life. His first novel,
Somebody in Boots (1935) is a tediously didactic work inter-
larded with chunks from the Communist Manifesto. His heroes
and heroines are drifters, prostitutes and petty criminals. Algren
was rated highly by his peers; HEMINGWAY believed him to be one
of America's best writers. His main flaw, which has led to his fall
from subsequent critical esteem, is a rather oversentimental view
of his characters (he liked to describe himself as the 'poor man's
Dostoevsky' —*see also* Jim THOMPSON). He had a 17-year-long
love affair with Simone de BEAUVOIR.

8

alienation effect an effect which is supposed to occur upon an audience when the audience is reminded by action, dialogue or song that it is in fact an audience watching a play, and not, for example, waiting for a bus. The intention is to confront the audience with the artificiality of dramatic representation, through devices such as interrupting the action to address the audience, or by bursting into song, or by stylizing the stage set or action. The theory is especially associated with BRECHT, who claimed that his plays created an 'alienating', distancing effect, enabling the audience to resist identifying emotionally with the characters on stage and therefore more capable of absorbing the message of plays, e.g. that traditional notions of morality simply represent 'bourgeois' morality. 'Alienation effects' of the kind described by Brecht have existed in drama since before ARISTOPHANES, and form an important element in the Theatre of the ABSURD. The value of Brecht's formulation and use of the theory, however, is much debated. *See also* GRASS.

allegory a form of narrative in which the characters and events symbolize an underlying moral or spiritual quality, or represent a hidden meaning beneath the literal one expressed. BUNYAN's *Pilgrim's Progress* is the greatest English-language example of a sustained allegory.

Allen, Woody [pseud. of Allen Stewart Konigsberg] (1935–) American writer, actor and film director. His literary works, e.g. *Horse Feathers* (1976), display the obsessions with sex and psychiatry made familiar by his many films, but also show him to be a highly gifted parodist.

Amis, Sir Kingsley (1922–95 English novelist and poet. His first novel, *Lucky Jim* (1953), a witty satire on academic life at an English university (*see* CAMPUS NOVEL), was a great success, its eponymous hero being seen as a type of ANGRY YOUNG MAN. Subsequent novels, e.g. *I Like It Here* (1958) and his one novel with an American setting, *One Fat Englishman* (1963), are seen by some critics as displaying a progression from left-wing anti-Establishment values towards a querulously reactionary position. His novels, however, are too complex and too good to be baldly categorized in this way. *The Anti-Death League* (1966) and *The Green Man* (1969), for example, are profound studies of the nature of death, love and God. (Amis is an avowed atheist, but few other modern novelists have written so passionately on the nature of God.) He is also a great comic writer, and is one of the best parodists in the English language. His *Collected Poems 1944–1979* were published in 1979. *See also* FLEMING.

Amis, Martin (1949–) English novelist, the son of Kingsley AMIS. His first novel, the gruesomely titled *Dead Babies* (1975), is a chilly little fable set in an imaginary England plagued by random killings. This and his later novels, e.g. *London Fields* (1989), are much admired by some critics; others regard them as essays in designer violence.

Anacreon (*fl.* 6th century BC) Greek lyric poet. His poems (mostly on love and wine, and many of doubtful attribution) were translated into French and English in the mid-16th century, and were much imitated, notably by poets of the METAPHYSICAL school.

Andersen, Hans Christian (1805–75) Danish writer. He wrote prolifically in many areas, but is now remembered solely for his fairy tales, such as 'The Ugly Duckling' and 'The Emperor's Clothes'.

Anderson, Sherwood (1876–1941) American novelist and short-story writer. His greatest work is the novel *Winesburg, Ohio* (1919), which, like most of his fiction, focuses on the tragedies of small-town, mid-American life.

Andrewes, Lancelot (1555–1626) English theologian and bishop. He was one of the most distinctive prose writers of his day (T.S. ELIOT quotes him in his poem 'Journey of the Magi'), and was one of the translators of the Authorized Version of the Bible. His sermons combine a scholarly love of classical and scriptural reference with a gift for flowery, not always perfectly clear expression.

Angelou, Maya [pseud. of Marguerite Johnson] (1928–) American dramatist, poet and short-story writer, whose works on her upbringing as a poor black female in St Louis, e.g. *I Know Why the Caged Bird Sings* (1970), have won her a large and appreciative audience.

Angry Young Men a rather imprecise term used in mid–1950s Britain to denote a group of English writers who had little in common apart from vaguely leftish sympathies and a hatred of English provincialism and intellectual pretentiousness ('madrigalphobia'). Other characteristics of Angry Young Men included a liking for jazz, polo-neck sweaters, coffee bars, and compliant women—like their American counterparts, the Beat Generation writers, Angry Young Men regarded women as appendages (although Doris Lessing and Iris Murdoch were sometimes regarded as honorary AYM). Angus Wilson gives a meticulous dissection of the species in his short story 'A Bit off the Map' (1957). Kingsley Amis's *Lucky Jim* and Osborne's Jimmy Porter in *Look Back in Anger* were, like their creators, seen as Angry Young Men.

Anouilh, Jean (1910–87) French dramatist. His first play (in 1944) was an updating of Sophocles's *Antigone*, in which the eponymous heroine becomes a thinly disguised representation of the spirit of France under German occupation. Other notable plays are *The Waltz of the Toreadors* (1952) and *Beckett* (1959). Anouilh's command of the technicalities of theatrical production has been much admired.

antinovel *see* **novel**.

Apollinaire, Guillaume (1880–1918) French art critic and writer of great influence among avant-garde artists and poets at the beginning of the 20th century. A friend of Picasso and a champion of cubism, he published *The Cubist Painters* in 1913. He originated the term SURREALISM in 1917 in a preface to his play *The Breasts of Tirésias*. He was wounded in World War I and subsequently died of Spanish influenza.

Apuleius (2nd century AD) North African Latin author of a romance called *The Golden Ass* (or *Metamorphoses*), a satirical PICARESQUE NOVEL narrated by a man turned into an ass. The novel includes the story of Psyche's love and quest for Cupid, which has been adapted by many other authors, C.S. LEWIS's *Till We Have Faces* (1956) being a remarkable and haunting modern example.

Arabian Nights Entertainments *or* **The Thousand and One Nights** a compilation of stories, the earliest of which probably originated in Persia, that were translated into Arabic in the mid–9th century AD, and have become classics of Arab and world literature. The stories are told by Scheherazade to her husband, a king who has killed each previous bride following the consummation of the marriage. Scheherazade saves her life by keeping the king in suspense, postponing the conclusion of each story until the following night.

Aragon, Louis (1897–1982) French poet, novelist and essayist. Aragon was one of the founders of both Dadaism (*see* TZARA) and SURREALISM. He joined the Communist Party in 1927, after breaking with the Surealists in the early 1930s, and became a forceful exponent of SOCIALIST REALISM. His works include the novels *The Bells of Basel* (1934) and *Residential Quarter* (1936).

Arcadia a region of ancient Greece which became the archetypal setting for rural bliss and innocence in the arts. VIRGIL's *Eclogues* in the 1st century BC established the use of Arcadia as a literary device for this purpose, but the ironic undertone in Virgil's work (Arcadia is largely barren) is usually missing from later writers' use of the myth. Virgil's dark undertone returns to Western culture in the work of several 16th and 17th-century painters, e.g. Poussin, with reference to the phrase *Et in Arcadia Ego* ('And I [i.e. death] also in Arcadia').

Arden, John (1930–) English dramatist. His early plays, e.g. *Live Like Pigs* (1958) and *Serjeant Musgrave's Dance* (1959), were innovative assaults on the evils of social corruption and violence, and were widely praised for their very effective use of song, declamation and harshly poetic dialogue. His later plays are generally regarded as overdidactic, and are not so highly thought of.

Aretino, Pietro (1492–1556) Italian poet and dramatist, whose name became a byword in Elizabethan times for witty licentiousness.

Ariosto, Ludovico (1474–1533) Italian poet. His *Orlando Furioso* (1532), an epic romance in verse set in Charlemagne's time, enjoyed Europe-wide popularity.

Aristophanes (*c.*448–380 BC) Greek comic dramatist. Eleven of his great comedies survive. His work represents an early peak in comic satire that few subsequent dramatists have attained. The objects of his satire ranged from the 'war party' (against the Spartans) in Athens to his fellow dramatists (EURIPIDES being a favourite target). The plays are also a valuable record of the intellectual debates of the day, e.g. the position of women in society and the nature of religious belief. The most popular of his plays in our own day has been *Lysistrata*, in which the women of Athens stage a 'sex strike' against war. Aristophanes's powerful dramatic verse could also rise to great lyric heights, as in the chorus of *The Birds*. *See* COMEDY, GILBERT.

Aristotle (384–322 BC) Greek philosopher. His writings, reintroduced to the Western world in the Middle Ages via Arabian scholarship, had great and occasionally pernicious influence on almost every field of intellectual inquiry until the RENAISSANCE, when his authority ceased to be regarded as infallible. His *Poetics*, however, which resurfaced in fragmentary form during the Renaissance, was to become one of the cornerstones of literary NEOCLASSICISM, particulary in its strictures on the theatrical 'unities'. The plot of Umberto ECO's popular novel *The Name of the Rose* is based on the presence of a lost section of the *Poetics* in a medieval monastery.

Arnold, Matthew (1822–88) English poet and critic. He was the son of the educational reformer **Thomas Arnold** (1795–1842) and became one of the most important commentators on Victorian society. His literary and social criticism was influential on many 20th-century writers, notably T.S. ELIOT, but it is as a poet that he is chiefly remembered. His greatest poems, e.g. 'Dover Beach', reflect the new uncertainties in religion and society created by the new industrial age.

Artaud, Antonin (1896–1948) French actor and theatre director. His essays on the theatre, *The Theatre and Its Double*, were published in New York in 1958 and have had a lasting effect on Western drama. The essays lay down guidelines for what he called a 'Theatre of Cruelty', i.e. a form of theatre which uses non-verbal means of communication such as pantomine, light effects and irrational language, to project the pain and loss fostered by the modern world. His aim was to use drama to subvert the idea of art as a set of concepts separate from real life. An early SURREALIST, he later rejected both that movement and the refuge of Communist ideology into which so many of his fellow Surrealists had fled. He suffered greatly from mental illness in the last 15 years of his life.

Arthur (*fl.* 6th century AD) a possibly mythical Celtic warrior-king of post-Roman Britain, who may have organized resistance against the Saxon invaders. The Arthurian legend, with its tales of brave knights and holy quests, became enormously popular throughout Europe in the early Middle Ages, and its characters and legends have retained their significance in Western culture ever since. Notable users of the Arthurian myth since Sir Thomas MALORY include T. H. WHITE and TENNYSON.

Ascham, Roger (*c.*1515–68) English educationalist and classics tutor to Elizabeth I. His book on education, *The Scholemaster* (1570), which criticizes corporal punishment, is a notable landmark in humanist educational theory.

Ashbery, John (1927–) American poet and critic. Volumes of his poetry include *Some Trees* (1956) and *The Double Dream of Spring* (1970). Ashbery's work is renowned for its vivid imagery.

Asimov, Isaac (1920–92) Russian-born American science fiction author, whose many novels and short stories, e.g. *I Robot* (1950), have been very influential in the science fiction genre.

Atwood, Margaret Eleanor (1939–) Canadian poet and novelist, whose novel *Surfacing* (1972) established her as one of Canada's most important modern writers. Her works explore the common Canadian concern for cultural identity in relation to the US, and also the question of female identity in a male-dominated world.

Aubrey, John (1626–97) English antiquary and biographer. His *Lives of Eminent Men*, brief biographies of (mostly) his contemporaries, was first published in 1813, and is an invaluable and highly entertaining collection of biographical anecdotes, e.g. on SHAKESPEARE and JONSON.

Auden, W[ystan] H[ugh] (1907–73) English poet, who became an American citizen in 1946. His first verse collection, *Poems* (1928), was privately printed in a limited edition by his friend Stephen SPENDER, and is now one of the century's most sought-after first editions. Auden's reputation quickly grew, and by the early 1930s he was recognized as a highly original poet who was also the leading voice of a new generation of young poets, the 'Auden generation' (or, derisively, the 'Pylon School', so-called from their enthusiastic use of industrial imagery). Auden and his followers were concerned to develop a poetic aesthetic that would explain the world in leftest terms. Apart from Auden, the most important figures were Spender, DAY-LEWIS and MACNEICE, followed by a host of lesser poets. (George ORWELL's essay *Inside the Whale* [1940] gives a caustic left-wing appraisal of Auden's politics—*see also* MACDIARMID.) In later years Auden became both a conservative and a Christian, and disowned many of his earlier left-wing poems (including 'Spain', which Orwell had criticized for using the words 'necessary murder').

Austen, Jane (1775–1817) English novelist. Her six great novels were published in the following sequence: *Sense and Sensibility* (1811), *Pride and Prejudice* (1813), *Mansfield Park* (1814), *Emma* (1816), with *Northanger Abbey* and *Persuasion* being published posthumously in 1818. The novels are set firmly within the confines of the society in which Jane Austen lived, the well-bred middle class of Regency England, and usually feature the quest of young women for suitable husbands. Her reputation has increased sharply in the 20th century, and she is now seen as one of the greatest of all English novelists, with her masterly dialogue, finely tuned sense of satire and moral judgment. Even her juvenilia, e.g. the ferociously funny parody of the sentimental novel, *Love and Friendship* [sic], written when she was fourteen, displays a level of talent found in few other writers. Rudyard KIPLING's story 'The Janeites' (1926) provides both the collective noun for her admirers and a perceptive analysis of her appeal. *See also* EPISTOLARY NOVEL.

Austin, Alfred (1835–1913) English poet, notorious for his inept, jingoistic verse. To the astonishment of the literary establishment, he was appointed POET LAUREATE in succession to TENNYSON in 1896. His verse was much parodied by his contemporaries.

Authorized Version *or* **King James Bible** a translation of the Bible published in 1611 in the reign of James I of England. The powerful and poetic language of the Authorized Version has made it perhaps the most influential book on writers in English from the early 17th century on. Although it is often said to be the greatest book ever written by a committee, the work is based for the most part on **William Tyndale**'s (*c*.1495–1536) great translation of 1525.

Ayckbourn, Alan (1939) English dramatist, noted for his often rather dark comedies of middle-class life in suburban England, e.g. *The Norman Conquests* (1974) trilogy, which depicts identical events through the eyes of different characters.

B

Babel, Isaac (1894–1941?) Russian writer, whose semi-autobiographical stories of his life as a Jewish intellectual with the Soviet Red Cavalry in the Russian Civil War, *Red Cavalry* (1923–25), have been highly praised for their portrayal of the harshness of war. Babel was imprisoned in 1939, and is assumed to have died in a Soviet labour camp.

Bacon, Francis (1561–1626) English philosopher and statesman. He served both Elizabeth I and her successor James VI and I in various public offices until his conviction and disgrace for bribery in 1621, shortly after being created Viscount St Albans. Bacon's writings on philosophy and the need for rational scientific method, particularly in *The Advancement of Learning* (1605) and the *Novum Organum* (1620), are landmarks in the history of human thought, particularly in their insistence on argument based on fact and refusal to accept automatically any other authority. Bacon's prose is skilfully authoritative, with good rhetorical touches. This, and the fact that he was extraordinarily learned, gave rise to the theory in the late 19th century that he must have written SHAKESPEARE's plays, as only a genius could have written them. This theory, known as the Baconian heresy, is untenable, and is based purely on snobbery and a peculiar misapprehension of the nature of creative writing.

Bacon, Roger (c.1214–92) English monk and philosopher, known as Doctor Mirabilis by his contemporaries for his wide learning and daring anti-scholastic speculation. Like his later namesake, Francis BACON, he advocated the supremacy of practical experience and experiment over the authority of ancient philosophers such as Aristotle. Bacon acquired the false reputation of being a magician, in which capacity he features in Robert GREENE's play *Friar Bacon and Friar Bungay* (1594).

Bagehot, Walter (1826–77) English social scientist and literary critic, whose works include *The English Constitution* (1867) and *Literary Studies* (1879–95). Bagehot is one of the finest Victorian essayists, and his analyses of such topics as the mystique of the monarchy and the appeal of nature poetry remain as lively and thought-provoking today as when they were first published.

Bainbridge, [Margaret] Beryl (1934–) English novelist. Her novels include *Another Part of the Wood* (1968), *The Dressmaker* (1973), *The Bottle Factory Outing* (1974) and *Young Adolf* (1978). Bainbridge's novels are grim little comedies of ordinary lives disrupted by macabre, and occasionally quite violent, incidents.

Baldwin, James (1924–87) American novelist and essayist, whose works depict the problems of black and homosexual identity in the USA. His novels include *Go Tell it on the Mountain*

(1953) and *Another Country* (1962); his volumes of essays include *Notes of a Native Son* (1955) and *The Fire Next Time* (1963).

ballad a narrative poem or song in brief stanzas, often with a repeated refrain, and frequently featuring a dramatic incident. The songs sold by the vagabond Autolycus in Shakespeare's *As You Like It*, describing battles, public executions and the like, are typical examples of the sort of **broadside ballad** popular with the common people, up to (and a bit beyond) Victorian times. In 1765, the antiquary **Thomas Percy** (1729–1811) published his *Reliques of Ancient English Poetry* (1765), a collection of ancient and not-so-ancient traditional English poems, songs and folk ballads that was to prove immensely influential. Its impact on English poets was deep and long-lasting. Examples of what has been termed the **literary ballad** soon began to appear. Notable examples include COLERIDGE's 'Rime of the Ancient Mariner' and KEATS's 'La Belle Dame sans Merci'.

Among the greatest examples of the form are the **Border ballads**, which stem from the violent world of the English/Scottish Borders from the late Middle Ages to the 17th century. Their merit had been recognized by the great Sir Philip SIDNEY in his *Defence of Poesie* (1595): 'Certainly I must confess mine own barbarousness, I never heard the old song of Percy and Douglas, that I found not my heart moved more than with a trumpet.' Sidney's opinion was to remain very much a minority one until the late 18th century, when the rediscovery of the great ballad heritage coincided with the birth pangs of the ROMANTIC movement, and with enthusiasm for the 'noble' and 'simple' truths of the world of traditional songs throughout Europe (*see also* MACPHERSON). Representative examples of the Border ballads are the laments 'Sir Patrick Spens' and 'The Bonny Earl of Murray', the haunting song of fairyland 'Thomas the Rhymer', and the macabre 'Twa Corbies'.

The most important collection of the Border ballads is that issued (in three volumes) by Sir Walter Scott in 1802–1803, *Minstrelsy of the Scottish Borders*. Many of the ballads here were written down at the dictation of the singers of the old songs themselves, one of whom, James Hogg's mother, complained that they would be spoiled for ever by being written down. As George MacDonald Fraser points out in his history of the Borders, *The Steel Bonnets* (1971), the characteristics of the ballads are those of an earthy, warlike folk: a restless turbulence and melancholy—'Now Liddesdale has ridden a raid/But I wat they had better hae stayed at hame,/For Michael of Winfield he is dead/And Jock o' the Side is prisoner ta'en.'

Balzac, Honoré de (1799–1850) French novelist. His great collection of novels and short stories, written over a 20–year period, describes in masterly prose the lives of French men and women of every class. His collective name for the series, the *Human Comedy*, is meant to invite comparison with Dante's *Divine Comedy*. The series comprises over 90 separate works, whose highlights include *Père Goriot* (1835) and *Cousin Bette* (1847). Balzac was a royalist, a Roman Catholic and a reactionary, and has been hailed by many critics (including Marx) as the greatest of all novelists.

Barker, George [Granville] (1913–91) English poet, noted for his highly dramatic, often surreal verse. Volumes of his poetry include *Thirty Preliminary Poems* (1933), *Eros in Dogma* (1944) and *The True Confession of George Barker* (1950). The persona portrayed in his poems, that of an exuberantly devil-may-care Romantic poet, had a startling and long-lasting effect on Elizabeth Smart.

Barrie, Sir J[ames] M[atthew] (1860–1937) Scottish playwright and novelist. His best-known play is the remarkable fantasy *Peter Pan* (1904), in which human children are taken to Never-

Never Land by Peter Pan. Barrie's critical reputation shrank dramatically within his lifetime, principally in reaction to the sugary whimsy of much of his large output. The best of his work, however, e.g. *Peter Pan*, the strange little supernatural play *Mary Rose* (1920), the novel of class role-reversal *The Admirable Crichton* (1902), and the feminist play *What Every Woman Knows* (1908), are still popular.

Barthes, Roland *see* **Structuralism**.

Basho [Matsuo] (1644–94) Japanese poet, master of the 17–syllable sequential verse form, whose component verses were to become known as *haiku*. A Basho haiku gave Ian FLEMING the title for one of his novels, *You Only Live Twice*.

Beat Generation a term invented by Jack KEROUAC to describe a group of American writers, artists and musicians in the 1950s. Notable beat writers included Kerouac himself, whose novel *On the Road* (1952) became the 'beat bible', the poets **Allen Ginsberg** (1926–97) and Lawrence FERLINGHETTI, and the novelists **Neal Cassady** (1926–68) and William BURROUGHS. The beat writers were anti-Western in their values; they dabbled in communalism, loved modern jazz and took drugs (avidly). The term 'beat' was said to denote (a) the weariness of struggling against materialist society, (b) jazz rhythm, which they tried to capture in their prose, (c) beatitude. The last quality is somewhat dubious, given the callous exploitation of women in which so many of the beats indulged. Ginsberg's poem 'Howl' includes the surprising claim that American society destroyed the 'beat minds' (i.e. the beats) of his generation, a judgment posterity has yet to confirm.

Beaumont, Sir Francis *see* **Fletcher**.

Beauvoir, Simone de (1908–86) French novelist and essayist. Her novels and other writings explore the female predicament from the standpoint of existential feminism. Both her view of the female condition and her literary approach to it derive in large part from her long-standing relationship with SARTRE, which amounted to a lifetime's exercise in damage limitation in terms of ego and libido. Her essay *The Second Sex* (1949) is regarded as a cornerstone of the feminist movement. Her novel *The Mandarins* (1954) includes a thinly fictionalized depiction of her long affair with Nelson ALGREN.

Beckett, Samuel (1906–90) Irish dramatist and novelist. He moved to France in 1932, and subsequently wrote in French as well as English. Beckett described human suffering as the 'main condition of the human experience'; this statement is the main signpost in the bleak territory of Beckett's works, where nothing much occurs except brilliant dialogues or monologues of despair. Beckett has been linked with both EXISTENTIALISM and the Theatre of the ABSURD, with his skill for combining highly sophisticated language with a starkly despairing message, with the occasional startling flash of Irish humour. His best-known play is *Waiting for Godot* (1952), in which two tramps await a third who never appears. Beckett was a friend of James JOYCE, and transcribed *Finnegans Wake* from Joyce's dictation. He was awarded the NOBEL PRIZE for literature in 1969.

Beerbolm, Sir Max (1872–1956) English critic, parodist and caricaturist. His parodies of contemporary writers such as Henry JAMES, KIPLING, H.G. WELLS and SHAW, in such collections as *A Christmas Garland* (1912), are regarded as amongst the finest examples of parody. Shaw, who was often his victim, called him the 'Incomparable Max'.

Behan, Brendan (1923–64) Irish dramatist, noted for his plays based on his experiences as a youthful member of the Irish Republican Army, *The Hostage* (1958) and *The Quare Fellow* (1959), and for his autobiographical account of life in borstal, *Borstal Boy* (1958).

Behn, Aphra (1640–89) English dramatist and novelist. Her most famous play, *Oroonoko* (1688), attacks the horrors of slavery; other works, e.g. *The Forced Marriage* (1670), deal with the oppression of women in society. Her plays were very popular and are still highly regarded.

Bellamy, Edward (1850–98) American novelist. His best-known work, *Looking Backward, 2000–1887* (1888), describes a future America in which capitalism has disappeared and communal values have triumphed. The work was very influential on other 'progressive' writers.

Belloc, Hilaire *see* **Chesterton, G. K**.

Bellow, Saul (1915–) Canadian-born American novelist. Bellow is recognized as a highly gifted writer, the dominant theme of his work being the gradual decay of the spiritual and physical fabric of 20th-century urban life. Representative novels are *The Adventures of Augie March* (1953), *Dr Sammler's Planet* (1969) and *Humboldt's Gift* (1975). He was awarded the NOBEL PRIZE for literature in 1976.

Benét, Stephen Vincent (1898–1943) American poet, whose works include *John Brown's Body* (1928) and the short story 'The Devil and Daniel Webster' (1937). His *Ballads and Poems* (1931) includes the poem 'American Names', in which is his most famous line 'Bury my heart at Wounded Knee'.

Bennett, Arnold (1867–1931) English novelist and dramatist. His most famous novels, e.g. *The Old Wives' Tale* (1908) and *Clayhanger* (1910), are naturalistic narratives of everyday people in the setting of the industrial society of mid-England; the setting being wholly suitable in the eyes of Virginia WOOLF, who dismissed Bennett's work as middle class, middlebrow and of middling morality. His novels are in fact very readable, and display a remarkable gift for characterization and sharp observation of the dilemmas of human life.

Bentley, Edmund Clerihew (1875–1956) English civil servant, noted for his classic detective novel *Trent's Last Case* (1913) and for the invention of the verse form called the *clerihew*. Clerihews have two rhymed couplets of variable length and often encapsulate an unreliable biographical anecdote: 'Mr Michael Foot/Had lots of loot;/He loved to gloat/While petting his stoat.'.

Berger, Thomas (1924–) American novelist, best known for his novels contrasting the American dream with the actual American way of life, e.g. *Reinhart in Love* (1962), and for his remarkable novel of the American West, narrated by an ancient Indian fighter, *Little Big Man* (1963), the film of which is much sentimentalized.

Berryman, John (1914–72) American poet. His verse is intensely personal, self-critical and highly proficient. His work includes *The Dispossessed* (1948) and *Homage to Mistress Bradstreet* (1956).

Betjeman, Sir John (1906–84) English poet, whose nostalgia for pre-20th-century England, coupled with a talent for sharp social satire, made him Britain's most popular poet. He became POET LAUREATE in 1972, by which time he had already achieved the status of a national institution in the UK, his work being very popular with the public yet receiving great acclaim from his peers and the critics. The titles of his collections, e.g. *Continual Dew* (1937), *A Few Late Chrysanthemums* (1954) and *A Nip in the Air* (1972), may give the impression of a slightly fey, eccentric and autumnal character (an impression he assiduously cultivated), but the poems within are often startlingly bleak and despairing. He also wrote widely and wisely on architectural conservation, and published a verse autobiography, *Summoned by Bells* (1960).

Bible, The *see* **Authorized Version**.

Bierce, Ambrose (1842–1914?) American journalist and short-story writer. He was much influenced by POE, but the best of his stories, collected in *In the Midst of Life* (1898), have a macabre flavour all their own. The shocking twist at the end of his Civil War story, 'An Occurrence at Owl Creek .Bridge', has been widely praised and much imitated. His best-known work is *The Devil's Dictionary*, a collection of newspaper pieces first published in book form as *The Cynic's Word Book* (1906).

Bildungsroman (German for 'education novel') a novel that describes the growth of a character (usually based on the author) from youthful naivety to a well-rounded (often rather smug) maturity. The term derives from GOETHE's *Wilhelm Meister's Apprenticeship*. Two notable examples in English are DICKENS's *David Copperfield* and JOYCE's *Portrait of the Artist as a Young Man*.

Blackmore, R[ichard] D[oddridge] (1825–1900) English poet and novelist. The only one of his novels still read is the classic *Lorna Doone* (1869), a tale of love, outlawry and feuding set in 17th-century Exmoor.

Blair, Eric Arthur *see* **Orwell, George**.

Blake, Nicholas *see* **Day-Lewis, Cecil**.

Blake, William (1757–1827) English poet and artist in the tradition of ROMANTICISM. Blake trained as an engraver and scraped a precarious living as a book and magazine illustrator. His first book of poems, *Poetical Sketches* (1783), includes the remarkable lyric 'How Sweet I Roamed', Blake's earliest poem on the themes that haunted his life: the crippling of innocence by cynical experience, and the imprisonment of visionary imagination by materialism. The requirements of his apprenticeship as an engraver led to an interest in church Gothic design and architecture, which inspired his love of precise line and pattern. From 1779 he studied at the Royal Academy, and in the 1780s began to publish his own poems with handwritten text and drawings engraved on one plate in a new colour printing technique. His first engraved 'illustrated poem' was *Songs of Innocence* (1789), a slim, beautifully hand-coloured volume, as were the books that followed, such as *Songs of Experience* (1794), *The Marriage of Heaven and Hell* (1791), and his longest mystical work, *Jerusalem* (1804–20). These works had found a small but highly appreciative band of admirers by the end of his life, as did his no less innovative and lovely watercolours.

Blake is now recognized as one of the greatest of all English poets. His influence on 20th-century poets has been considerable, AUDEN and YEATS being notable admirers of his work.

blank verse a term sometimes used to denote any form of unrhymed verse, but normally applied to unrhymed verse in iambic pentameters, i.e. a line of verse with five short-long 'feet', e.g. the actress Mrs Siddons's reputed remark: 'You brought me water, boy; I asked for beer' (she was known to speak unconsciously in blank verse). The form was developed in English by the Earl of SURREY, and reached its highest peak in SHAKESPEARE's great plays. Other notable works written in blank verse include MILTON's *Paradise Lost* and WORDSWORTH's *The Prelude*.

Blixen, Karen *see* **Dinesen, Isak**.

Bloomsbury Group *see* **Woolf, Virginia**.

Bluestocking an originally disparaging term denoting members of small, mostly female groups in English 18th-century social life, who held informal discussion groups on literary and scholarly matters. The term derives from the blue stockings worn by a male member of the groups, the botanist Benjamin Stillingfleet. Prominent female Bluestockings included Dr JOHNSON's friends Hannah MORE, Elizabeth MONTAGU and Charlotte LENNOX.

Blunt, Wilfrid Scawen (1840–1922) English poet and traveller, who became a staunch anti-imperialist and supporter of Indian and Irish independence movements. His verse collections, e.g.

Sonnets and Songs by Proteus (1875) and *In Vinculus* (1889), reflect his two main interests, women and politics.

Boccaccio, [Giovanni] (1313–75) Italian poet and author, noted particularly for his collection of 100 short tales (*see* NOVELLA), the *Decameron* (1353), in which ten young Florentines, having fled Florence because of a plague, each tell a story to the others every day for ten days. The stories have flashes of occasionally gruesome and licentious wit, and have had considerable influence on English writers, notably CHAUCER.

Böll, Heinrich (1917–85) German novelist, short-story writer and critic. His masterpiece is the novel *The Lost Honour of Katharina Blum* (1975), in which a young woman is hounded by the gutter press. The novel was Böll's response to the same gutter press's attempts to smear him as unpatriotic, his 'crime' being a sharp analysis of postwar German society from a liberal standpoint. Other novels include *Billiards at half-past Nine* (1959) and *The Safety Net* (1979). He was awarded the NOBEL PRIZE for literature in 1972.

Bolt, Robert [Oxton] (1924–95) English dramatist. The best known of his plays is the historical drama *A Man for all Seasons* (1960), which deals with the conflict between Sir Thomas MORE's private conscience as a devout Roman Catholic and his public duty to Henry VIII as Lord Chancellor. In the play, as in life, More accepts martyrdom rather than give up his principles by accepting the monarch's divorce. Bolt's reputation went into partial eclipse during the 1970s, when his work became commonly labelled as 'bourgouis', 'humanist', 'middlebrow' and so forth, despite an often grudging consensus that the plays were skilfully constructed. His central concern, however, the clash between individual morality and public tyranny, remains one of the important issues of the age, and the plays show every sign of outlasting their denigrators. Another important Bolt play is *State of*

Revolution (1977), a study of the effect of power on the leaders of the Bolshevik Revolution.

Bond, [Thomas] Edward (1934–) English dramatist, notable for the extreme violence of his early work, e.g. in *Saved* (1965), in which a baby is stoned in a pram. The great public controversy over such plays as *Saved*, which was banned by the Lord Chamberlain from the stage, led in the end to the abolition of censorship of stage plays in Britain. Bond's other plays include *Bingo* (1974), in which Shakespeare condemns himself for not doing enough to reform society, and *The Fool* (1975), in which John CLARE, in his incarceration in an asylum, is portrayed as a victim of capitalist society. Bond's justification for the violence in his work—that it is needed to expose the rottenness of capitalism—has acquired an increasingly hollow tone over the years, while the plays themselves, like much of the work of his peers HARE and EDGAR, had by the end of the 1980s gathered an eerie aura of period atmosphere.

Booker Prize a prize of £20,000 instituted by the Booker McConnell company that is awarded annually for a work of fiction by a British, Commonwealth or Irish writer.

Book of Common Prayer The once-official book of services for the Church of England, first published in 1549. The most loved version is that of 1662, the language of which, like that of the AUTHORIZED VERSION, has been very influential on English prose and poetry.

Border ballad *see* **ballad**.

Borges, Jorge Luis (1899–1986) Argentinian poet and short-story writer. Borges's (often very short) fiction is renowned for its use of fantastic themes (in a deadpan style), e.g. *Labyrinths* (1953), to make philosophical points—an approach that owes much to CHESTERTON. A favourite symbol is that of the labyrinth or maze, with a plot structure often based on the orthodox machinery of the detective story. Borges had an impish tendency to create imaginary authors, some of whom have found their way into scholarly works of reference.

Borrow, George (1803–81) English novelist and travel writer. His best-known works are semi-autobiographical novels of gypsy life: *Lavengro* (1851) and *The Romany Rye* (1857), and his great travel book, *The Bible in Spain* (1843), which describes his experiences as a Bible distributor.

Boswell, James (1740–95) Scottish lawyer and writer, whose fame largely rests on his *Life of Samuel Johnson* (1791), one of the greatest biographies ever written. Much of Boswell's private writings were suppressed by his descendants until the 20th century, because of their frankness about his sexual encounters. *See* JOHNSON.

Bowdler, Dr Thomas (1754–1825) Scottish physician and editor, who published *Family Shakespeare* in 1818. As the title might suggest, his aim was to produce an edition of SHAKESPEARE suitable for family reading, i.e. with all indecency and blasphemy removed. The work was very successful, and the verb 'to bowdlerize' became part of the English language. Bowdler's censorship was in fact decidedly erratic; many completely inocuous expressions are omitted while he failed to recognize many of Shakespeare's grosser puns.

Bowen, Elizabeth (1899–1973) Anglo-Irish novelist and short-story writer. Her works, e.g. the novels *The Death of the Heart* (1938) and *The Heat of the Day* (1949), have been highly praised for their sharp, witty observation of upper-middle-class life.

Bowles, Paul (1910–) American novelist, short-story writer and composer. His best-known work is the novel *The Sheltering Sky* (1949), a semi-autobiographical account of his marriage to the lesbian novelist **Jane Auer Bowles** (1917–73) and their life in Morocco. Bowles is commonly regarded as the spiritual father of the BEAT GENERATION, but is nonetheless an intriguing and highly skilful writer. His musical compositions include several very fine piano pieces, three operas (including two based on plays by Lorca), and 'Blue Mountain Ballads' (lyrics by Tennessee WILLIAMS).

Boyd, William [Andrew Murray] (1953–) Ghanaian-born Scottish novelist. His highly regarded novels frequently feature expatriate Britons in exotic locations, and include *A Good Man in Africa* (1981), *Stars and Bars* (1984), *The New Confessions* (1987) and *Brazzaville Beach* (1990).

Bradbury, Malcolm [Stanley] (1932–) English novelist and critic. His best-known novels are satirical accounts of academic life, e.g. *Eating People is Wrong* (1959), *Stepping Westward* (1965) and *The History Man* (1975). His critical works include *Possibilities* (1973) and *The Novel Today* (1977).

Bradbury, Ray (1920–) American science fiction novelist and short-story writer. Long regarded as one of the finest writers in the science fiction genre, his works include the novel *Fahrenheit 451* (1959), and a highly original collection of short stories describing the colonization of Mars, *The Martian Chronicles* (1950).

Bradford, Rev. E[dwin] E[mmanuel] (1860–1944) English poet and clergyman. Bradford's collections of verses, e.g. *In Quest of Love* (1914), extol the physical beauty of young boys in a very English manner. AUDEN and BETJEMAN were tongue-in-cheek admirers of his work; Hugh MACDIARMID, however, writing from a mysterious perspective all his own, was quite sincere in his description of Bradford's poems as 'virile, useful work'.

Brady, Nicholas *see* **Tate, Nahum**.

Brecht, Bertolt (1898–1956) German dramatist and poet. His theory of 'epic theatre' was developed in the 1920s, its basis being a loose structure of episodic scenes, connected by speeches or songs, which apply a commentary on the action, intended to demonstrate the falsity of any conclusion incompatible with supposedly Marxist dialectics. The purpose of Brecht's theatrical devices, borrowed from cabaret and popular theatre, is to 'alienate' the audience into a state of objective receptivity to the playwright's message (*see* ALIENATION EFFECT). *The Threepenny Opera* (1928), for which Kurt Weill wrote the music, is an early example of the approach, which was further developed in plays such as *Galileo* (1938), and his best play, *Mother Courage* (1941). He settled in the US during Nazi rule in Germany, returning to East Berlin in 1949, where he founded the Berliner Ensemble theatre. Brecht's main appeal has always been to Western leftwing or liberal audiences. Before the revolutions of 1989 in Eastern Europe, his plays were regarded as too gloomy by the governing commissars of socialist realism, and after, few find the plays to be of any relevance. *See also* GRASS.

Brenton, Howard (1942–) English dramatist. His plays, which are characteristic of 1970s left-wing 'political' theatre, include *The Churchill Play* (1974), *The Romans in Britain* (1980) and (in collaboration with David HARE) a forceful condemnation of the right-wing press, *Pravda* (1985).

Breton, André *see* **Surrealism**.

Brideshead generation *see* **Acton, Sir Harold**; **Waugh, Evelyn**.

Bridges, Robert (1844–1930) English poet. Although very popular in his lifetime and appointed POET LAUREATE in 1913, Bridges's reputation has sunk to the point where he is largely remembered for having encouraged HOPKINS. His last long poem was *The Testament of Beauty* (1929), which he regarded as the summation of his work.

broadside ballad *see* **ballad**.

Brodsky, Joseph (1940–) Russian poet. Brodsky emerged as a major poet in the late 1950s, when many began to see him as following in the path of the great AKHMATOVA. He was arrested by the Soviet authorities in 1964 in the usual manner (for 'parasitism'), was released after international pressure, and settled in the US, becoming an American citizen in 1977. Collections of his work include *Selected Poems* (with a foreword by AUDEN, 1973), and *A Part of Speech* (1980). He was awarded the NOBEL PRIZE for literature in 1987.

Brontë, Anne (1820–49), **Charlotte** (1816–55) and **Emily** (1818–48) English novelists and poets. With their brother **Branwell** (1817–48), the sisters were brought up by their father, an Irish curate, at Haworth parsonage on the bleak Yorkshire moors, their mother having died in 1821. Two elder sisters died in 1825, and ill health dogged the surviving sisters and brother. In 1846, the sisters published a volume of poetry entitled *Poems by Currer, Acton and Ellis Bell*, the pseudonyms repectively of Charlotte, Emily and Anne. The volume attracted little attention, but in 1847 Charlotte's *Jane Eyre*, much of it based on her own experiences at boarding school and as a governess, was published to critical and popular acclaim. Emily's *Wuthering Heights* and Anne's *Agnes Grey* were also published in 1847, and in 1848, the year of Emily's death from consumption, Anne published her second novel, *The Tenant of Wildfell Hall*, in which she drew on the character of Branwell. Charlotte survived her sisters and brother and completed two more novels, *Shirley* (1849) and *Villette* (1853). Of all the Brontës' exceptionally fine novels, *Wuthering Heights* is the greatest: a powerful romance with complex layers of narration and meaning that is quite unlike any other novel. Some of Emily's equally remarkable poems, e.g. 'Cold in the Earth', have the same strange emotional intensity as her great novel.

Brooke, Rupert (1887–1915) English poet, whose patriotic poems on the outbreak of World War I (*1914 and Other Poems*), published posthumously, 1915) were extremely popular during the war. He died of blood poisoning on his way to active service in the Dardanelles.

Brookner, Anita (1938–) English novelist and art historian. Her novels, e.g. *Hotel du Lac* (1984), *Friends from England* (1987) and *Latecomers* (1988), usually feature sensitive and refined heroines in love with men who become entangled with less sensitive and refined women. Her works on art include *Watteau* (1968) and *Jacques-Louis David* (1981).

Browne, Sir Thomas (1605–82) English physician and author. His two most famous works are *Religio Medici* (1642), a meditation on Christian attitudes to life that argues finely for religious toleration, and *Hydriotaphia* or *Urn Burial* (1658), a quirky meditation inspired by burial urns. Browne's ability to convey deep insights in lightly flowing yet grandiloquent prose has been much admired, and is almost impossible to imitate successfully (JOYCE comes close in a section of *Ulysses*).

Browning, Elizabeth Barrett (1806–81) English poet, whose reputation grew rapidly in the early 1840s to the point where she became regarded as a probable successor to WORDSWORTH as poet laureate. She married Robert BROWNING in 1846, against the wishes of her father. The marriage was an idyllic one; they spent 15 happy years together until her death in his arms. Against all precedent, her creative life did not diminish in her husband's shadow. Among the great works that followed their marriage were *Sonnets from the Portuguese* (1850) and *Aurora Leigh* (1857). She also wrote vigorously on social issues ('The Cry of the Children' in her 1844 *Poems* was widely reprinted in campaigns against child labour) and strongly supported Italian independence.

Browning, Robert (1812–89) English poet, husband of Elizabeth Barrett BROWNING. Browning's exuberant and often bizarre poetic language, his gift for narrative, strong sense of realism and innovative experiments in form, established him in his own life-time as one of England's greatest poets. Many of his most an-thologized poems, e.g. 'Pippa Passes', are in his *Bells and Pome-granates* collection (1841–46), His masterpiece is *The Ring and the Book* (1869), a complex psychological study of a 17th-cen-tury murder in Italy. His *Men and Women* (1855) includes his great love poem 'Love Among the Ruins', and the powerfully enigmatic 'Childe Roland to the Dark Tower Came'. His 'A Child's Story, The Pied Piper of Hamelin' (1842), is perennially popular.

Buchan, John, 1st Baron Tweedsmuir (1875–1940) Scottish nov-elist, statesman and Governor-General of Canada 1935–40. Buchan wrote voluminously on many subjects, but is now re-membered chiefly for his adventure novels, such as *The Thirty-nine Steps* (1915), *Greenmantle* (1916) and *Sick Heart River* (1941). The novels often have a haunting, mystical element, par-ticularly in landscape description, that is matched by few other writers.

Buck, Pearl S[ydenstricker] (1892–1973) American novelist. Her most famous work, based on her and her husband's experi-ences as missionaries in China, is *The Good Earth* (1938). She was a highly prolific author (over 80 books, very few of which are now read), and was awarded the NOBEL PRIZE for literature in 1938.

Buckingham, 2nd Duke of *see* **Villiers, George**.

Bulgakov, Mikhail (1891–1940) Russian novelist and dramatist. His novel *The White Guard* (1925) was staged in Moscow in 1926 (as *The Days of the Turbins*) and created a sensation through its sympathetic portrayal of the anti-Bolshevik forces in the Russian revolution. (With a tyrant's whimsy, Stalin protected the author against reprisal.) His masterpiece is the novel *The*

Master and Margarita (published posthumously, 1966), a grimly comic fantasy in which the Devil creates havoc in modern Moscow, and befriends the lover of a sick author who is writing a novel about the Crucifixion, scenes from which are interposed in the main plot.

Bunyan, John (1628–88) English author, whose *Pilgrim's Progress* (1678–84) is perhaps the greatest ALLEGORY in the English language. The book is a Puritan fable in which Christian, a pilgrim, abandons his wife and children to search for the Celestial City of salvation, meeting helpful and unhelpful characters along the way. Bunyan's language (influenced strongly by the AUTHORIZED VERSION) is simple and his vocabulary is restricted to common English words, yet his mastery of dialogue and chartacterization have made his book one of the greatest ever written.

Burgess [Wilson], [John] Anthony (1917–93) English novelist, musician and critic. His output is huge and includes several important (usually satirical) novels, e.g. the nightmarish fantasy, *A Clockwork Orange* (1962) and *Earthly Powers* (1980).

Burke, Edmund (1729–97) Anglo-Irish statesman and philosopher. Burke entered Parliament for the Whig party in 1765 (via a rotten borough), and soon achieved high status within his party for his lively defence of constitutionalism and attacks on government abuses. His wise and prophetic attacks on government policy towards the American colonies established him as the dominant political thinker of the day. He was much admired even by his political enemies, and was a close friend of the strongly Tory Dr JOHNSON. His most important philosophical work is *A Philosophical Inquiry into the Origin of our Ideas of the Sublime and Beautiful* (1756), a work that was highly influential on many ROMANTIC writers and artists throughout Europe, e.g. on GOTHIC novelists such as Mrs RADCLIFFE, and on critics such as Gotthold LESSING. It identified physiological bases for the sublime and beautiful: terror is the source of the sublime, exciting 'the strongest emotion which the mind is capable of feeling'. The source of beauty is oddly defined: an object is beautiful if it has 'the power of producing a peculiar relaxation of our nerves and fibres' (Burke's thinking is often obscure). His most significant political work is *Reflections on the Revolution in France* (1790), a treatise attacking the principles of the French Revolutionaries and their British followers and defending the slow, British approach to constitutional reform, which remains one of the most influential statements of conservative philosophy.

Burney, Fanny [Frances, Madame D'Arbley] (1752–1840) English novelist. Her father, **Dr Charles Burney** (1726–1814), was a composer, author of *General History of Music* (1776–89), and a friend of many of the literary figures of the day, notably Dr JOHNSON, who also became a good friend of Fanny. Her first novel *Evelina* (1778), an EPISTOLARY novel on the usual themes of love and inheritance, was published anonymously and sold very well, as did her following novels, *Cecilia* (1782) and *Camilla* (1796). The novels were extravagantly praised by such figures as BURKE and Johnson, and Jane AUSTEN paid a fine tribute to her in *Northanger Abbey* (1803). She married General D'Arblay, a French refugee, in 1793. Her prose became increasingly tortuous over the years, and her last (five-volume) novel, *The Wanderer* (1814), has long been labelled unreadable. Her tragedy *Edwin and Elgitha* (1795) is an extremely odd work with three bishops among the dramatis personae and a death scene in which the heroine, played by the great actress Sarah Siddons, is brought from behind a hedge to die before the audience then carried back behind the hedge again. The first performance at Drury Lane ended in mass hysterics.

Burns, Robert (1759–96) Scottish poet. His father was a farmer in Ayrshire, where Burns was born. He worked as a farm labourer then an excise officer, and early on developed a reputation as a highly talented poet and convivial drinking companion. It was said of him that he 'loved mankind in general, and women in particular'. His fame rapidly spread after the publication of his first book of poems in 1786, *Poems, Chiefly in the Scottish Dialect*, and the former ploughman became the toast of Edinburgh society. The young Walter Scott, who met him there, described him as having a 'glowing eye', unlike any other he had ever seen. Burns wrote many of his best poems while still in his twenties, e.g. 'The Cotter's Saturday Night', 'The Twa Dogs', 'The Jolly Beggars', and 'To a Mouse'. Apart from the first, these were written in Scots, which remained his best medium for poetry. Most of his poems in the standard vein of 18th-century poetic language (e.g. 'Does Haughty Gaul Invasion Threat') are distinctly unmemorable. Critical opinion is divided as to his erotic collection of verse, *The Merry Muses of Caledonia*: some find them cheerfully bawdy, others wish he had never written them. This collection is still not included in most editions of Burns. His lyrical and satirical verse, however, is ranked with the world's finest poetry. *See also* Clare.

Burroughs, William S[eward] (1914–97) American novelist, who became one of the leading figures of the BEAT GENERATION. His explicit and violent books, e.g. *The Naked Lunch* (1959), are based on his own experiences as a homosexual writer in the rough drug-culture underworld.

Butler, Gwendoline (1922–) English novelist, who has written around 30 crime novels, most notably the series of novels starring Inspector John Coffin, e.g. *Coffin's Dark Number* (1969), *Coffin on the Water* (1986) and *Coffin and the Paper Man* (1990). Butler's work is macabre, witty, and has weirdly offbeat touches: the action of *Coffin Underground* (1988), for example, revolves around a bizarre role-playing game.

Butler, Samuel (1613–80) English poet, author of a splendid satire on Puritan intolerance, *Hudibras* (1663), which achieved instant success in Restoration England. The poem, in three parts and based loosely on the narrative structure of *Don Quixote* (*see* CERVANTES), describes the adventures of a Presbyterian knight, Sir Hudibras, and his 'sectarian' squire Ralpho, with many digressions along the way on such topics as the Civil War, marriage and astrology. Butler's main target throughout, however, is what he sees as the religious intolerance and hypocrisy of the Puritans. *See also* VILLIERS.

Butler, Samuel (1835–1902) English novelist. Like many Victorians, Butler's religious faith was deeply troubled by Charles Darwin's theory of evolution. In later years, he attacked both Darwinian theory and established religion with equal vigour. His best novel is *Erewhon* (1872), a brilliant satire on Victorian hypocrisy in morals and religion, whose title is an anagram of 'nowhere'. His best-known book is *The Way of All Flesh* (published posthumously, 1903), an autobiographical family novel. *See also* HOMER.

Byatt, A[ntonia] S[usan] (1936–) English novelist and critic. Her novels include *The Game* (1967), a study of the relationship between two sisters, one an Oxford don and the other a successful novelist (Byatt's sister is Margaret DRABBLE) and *Possession* (1990).

Byron, Lord George Gordon (1788–1824) English poet. In his own words, 'I awoke one morning and found myself famous', after the publication of his *Childe Harold's Pilgrimage* in 1812, a work that introduced the Byronic hero to the world: a lonely, handsome, melancholy, flawed man, fatally attractive to women, and remarkably similar to his creator. There followed a calamitous few years of great public scandal in which his half-sister Augusta had a child assumed to be his, he married and had a daughter, struggled with debt and public examination of his sanity, and finally left England (and his family) for good in 1816. He stayed with SHELLEY in Geneva for a while, before embarking on a life of romantic intrigue that scandalized Europe. He died of fever in Greece, while preparing to fight for Greek independence from Turkish rule. Byron's romantic verse epics are not now highly regarded, but his superb lyrics, e.g. 'She Walks in Beauty Like the Night', and his great satirical poem *Don Juan* (1819–21) will always be loved. (*Don Juan* contains many biting comments on Byron's contemporaries, e.g. WORDSWORTH and COLERIDGE.)

C

Cabell, James Branch (1879–1958) American novelist, whose mock-courtly novels set in an imaginary medieval French kingdom had a huge following in the 1920s. The novels, e.g. *Jurgen* (1919), are complicated intellectual fantasies in which supernatural and mythological characters feature in bizarre plots of obscure import. Cabell's use of archaic language in the novels is in part a device to help him get away with some quite striking sexual imagery.

Caldwell, Erskine (1903–87) American novelist, whose works, e.g. *Tobacco Road* (1932), are concerned with the lives of poor Whites in the southern US states.

Caliari, Paolo *see* **Veronese, Paolo**.

Calvino, Italo (1923–89) Cuban-born Italian novelist. The style of his work varies from a gruelling realism, e.g. his novel about a child caught up in the guerilla war against Fascism in Italy, *The Path of the Nest of Spiders* (1947), to later, highly complex explorations of fantasy and myth, e.g. *The Non-Existent Knight* (1959), and *Invisible Cities* (1972). *See also* MAGIC REALISM.

Cambridge Platonists *see* **More, Henry**.

Campbell, Roy (1923–57) South African poet. He went to England in 1918 to study, but abandoned Oxford University to concentrate on his poetry. The virile, exuberant language of his first long poem, *The Flaming Terrapin* (1924), an allegory in which post-World War I civilization is seen as Noah's Ark, established his reputation within months of publication. The best of his succeeding verse is bitingly satirical (London literary figures being favourite targets), although he also wrote some fine lyric poetry. He went against the dominant literary current of the day by going to fight for the Fascists in the Spanish Civil War. His *Flaming Rifle* (1939), an unashamedly pro-fascist work, understandably received a chilly reception in the UK and the US. His poem 'Zulu Girl', however, is a wonderfully moving (and prophetic) statement of the dignity and courage of black Africa.

campus novel a NOVEL with a university setting. Such novels are invariably satirical and are equally invariably written by former or practising academics. Early examples are Kingsley AMIS's *Lucky Jim* (1954) and Randall JARRELL's *Pictures from an Institution* (1954). Some novelists, such as David LODGE, whose *Small World* is perhaps the definitive example, have made a speciality of the genre. Another notable example is Malcolm BRADBURY's *The History Man* (1975). American examples tend towards anguish and 'relationships'; the British are more concerned with casting a cold eye on the harsh world of academic politics.

Camus, Albert (1913–60) Algerian-born French novelist, dramatist and essayist. His work has strong links with the Theatre of the ABSURD in its portrayal of the helplessness of humanity in a world of random and brutal forces. The spirit of rebellion, however, is an equally strong element in Camus' work (*see* EXISTEN-

TIALISM). His best-known works are the novels *The Stranger* (usually known in English as *The Outsider*) and *The Plague* (1948), and a very important essay on 20th-century totalitarianism, *The Rebel* (1951). He was awarded the NOBEL PRIZE for literature in 1957.

Canetti, Elias (1905–94) Bulgarian-born German writer, a British citizen from 1952. Of Sephardic Jewish ancestry, Canetti escaped to Britain in 1939. His two best-known works are the novel *Auto da Fé* (1935), an allegory of the collapse of the civilized European mind in the face of the irrational dark forces of the 20th century, and the equally grim sociological study of mass behaviour, *Crowds and Power* (1960). He was awarded the NOBEL PRIZE for literature in 1981.

Capek, Karel (1890–1938) Czech novelist and dramatist. His best-known play is *R.U.R.* (1920), in which robots gain human emotions, rebel against servitude and destroy mankind. The play introduced the word 'robot' into the English language (from the Czech *robota*, 'to work') and spawned a host of imitative science fiction works. With his brother **Josef Capek** (1887–1945), he wrote *The Insect Play* (1921), a prophetic satire on totalitarianism.

Capote, Truman (1924–84) American novelist and socialite. His works include light romances such as *Breakfast at Tiffany's* (1958), and the bleak 'faction' documentary novel *In Cold Blood* (1966), a chilling study of murder.

Carew, Thomas *see* **Cavalier Poets**.

Carlyle, Thomas (1795–1881) Scottish historian and essayist. Strongly influenced by German philosophy and literature, his early works include translations of GOETHE and *Sartor Resartus* (1833–34), a rather odd book which is mainly concerned with philosophical reflections on the appearance of things. This was followed by such works as *Heroes, Hero-Worship and the He-*

roic in History (1841), *Chartism* (1839) and *Past and Present* (1843), and soon many began to hail him as the greatest social critic of the age. Carlyle hated the modern, materialistic age and condemned the exploitation of the poor in the Industrial Revolution. However, his adoration of 'great men' and subsequent hatred of democracy have a sinister undertone for modern readers. His prose style is described by his admirers as exuberant, highly individualistic and dazzlingly eclectic; others subscribe to the critic Dwight Macdonald's view that his prose ('Carlylese') represents the death of the English language in the gutter.

Carroll, Lewis [pseud. of Charles Lutwidge Dodgson] (1832–98) English author, clergyman and mathematician. Educated at Christ Church, Oxford, he took deacon's orders but never priest's, and held a mathematical lectureship at his college until 1881. He published several books on mathematics, e.g. *Symbolic Logic* (1896), but his most famous works are the two remarkable 'Alice' books, *Alice's Adventures in Wonderland* (1865) and *Through the Looking-Glass* (1872), both illustrated by Sir John Tenniel. The books describe the adventures of a young English girl in a bizarre dream world populated by characters such as Humpty Dumpty, the Red Queen and the Cheshire Cat. The works were written for children and have retained their status as classic children's books, but many modern critics see deeper, darker meanings in the text (*see The Annotated Alice*, 1960, by Martin Gardner). A subsequent book, *The Hunting of the Snark: an Agony in Eight Fits* (1876), a fantasy narrative in verse, did not gain the popularity of the 'Alice' volumes.

Cartland, Dame Barbara (1901–) English romantic novelist. Over 500 million copies of her upwards of 500 published novels have been sold, making her one of the bestselling authors of all time. The novels have one basic theme: an innocent, virginal heroine in distress is rescued from her plight by a handsome stranger with a 'past'. She has explained her worldwide appeal as being due to the fact that 'East of Suez everyone wants a virgin.' From this perspective, critical disdain for her works may perhaps be seen as a form of cultural snobbery.

Carver, Raymond (1939–88) American poet and short-story writer. His collections of stories include *What We Talk About When We Talk about Love* (1981) and *Cathedral* (1983); volumes of poetry include *Where Water Comes Together With Other Water* (1985) and *In a Marine Light: Selected Poems* (1988). Carver's work is primarily concerned with the transient nature of American life, which is mirrored in the drifting, temporary relationships of his characters.

Cassady, Neal *see* **Beat Generation**.

Cather, Willa Sibert (1876–1947) American novelist, whose novels of immigrant life on the American plains, e.g. *O Pioneers!* (1913) and *My Antonia* (1918), were based on her childhood experiences in Nebraska, and have been widely acclaimed for their realism.

Cavalier poets a loose grouping of lyric poets associated with the court or cause of Charles I during his clashes with the English Parliament and the ensuing Civil War. (Poets such as MARVELL and MILTON who supported the Parliament cause, however, are not known as Roundhead poets.) The most notable Cavalier poets are HERRICK, SUCKLING, **Thomas Carew** (*c*.1595–1640) and **Richard Lovelace** (1618–*c*.1658). The latter's witty and graceful 'To Althea' is perhaps the most loved of the Cavalier poems.

Caxton, William (*c*.1422–91) English printer and translator. His *Recuyell of the Historyes of Troye* (printed at Bruges, 1475) is the first book to be printed in English. Soon afterwards, he began printing books at Westminster in London, with *Dictes or Sayengis of the Philosophres* (1477) being the first dated book to be printed in England.

Cervantes [Saavedra], Miguel de (1547–1616) Spanish novelist, dramatist and poet. His satirical masterpiece, *Don Quixote de la Mancha* (first part 1605, second part 1615) describes the PICARESQUE adventures of the simple-minded gentleman Don Quixote, his more wordly squire Sancho Panza, and his horse Rosinante, in the course of which we are given the famous chivalric image of the elderly knight tilting at windmills, mistakenly believing them to be giants. Cervantes also wrote other very fine works, notably the short stories in *Exemplary Tales* (1613).

Chandler, Raymond Thornton (1888–1959) American novelist, educated in England, whose detective novels, e.g. *Farewell, My Lovely* (1940), have been widely praised for their sharp, wisecracking dialogue. Most of his novels have been filmed, and his private detective hero, Philip Marlowe, the incorruptible loner, has become the most famous of the genre.

Chatterton, Thomas (1752–70) English poet, whose pseudo-medieval poems (which he claimed were written by an imagined 15th-century poet, Thomas Rowley) were published posthumously in 1777. Chatterton's manner of death—he committed suicide while in distress—probably had more influence on Romantic literature (e.g. WORDSWORTH and BLAKE) than his poetry had, although it does show remarkable powers.

Chaucer, Geoffrey (*c*.1343–1400) English poet whose great narrative skill is displayed at its finest in *The Canterbury Tales* (*c*.1387). This masterpiece of wit and humour is set in a London inn, and consists of short stories, mostly in rhyming couplets, told to each other by various pilgrims from all social strata on their way to Canterbury. *See also* BOCCACCIO.

Cheever, John (1912–82) American short-story writer and novelist. Short-story collections include *The Enormous Radio and Other Stories* (1953), *The Brigadier and the Golf Widow* (1964) and *The World of Apples* (1973). His four novels are *The*

Wapshot Chronicle (1957), *The Wapshot Scandal* (1964), *Bullet Park* (1969) and *Falconer* (1977). The main theme of Cheever's work, using his own comfortable background as a source, is the isolated discontent of life in affluent American suburbia, observed with a knowing, ironic and occasionally very funny eye. *The Stories of John Cheever* (1978) won the Pulitzer Prize in 1979.

Chekhov, Anton Pavlovich (1860–1904) Russian dramatist and short-story writer. Chekhov's great plays deal with the lives and problems of the Russian middle classes. Summaries of their content, characterized by moods of indecision, helplessness and loss, can give only a faint impression of the universal appeal of their dramatic power, wit, and even occasional knockabout humour. Some famous examples are *Uncle Vanya* (1900), *Three Sisters* (1901), and *The Cherry Orchard* (1904). Chekhov regarded his plays as comedies, but many critics see the tragic element as uppermost. As well as being one of the world's great dramatists, he was also one of its great short-story writers, his best being 'My Life' (1896) and 'The Lady with the Little Dog' (1899).

Chesterton, G[ilbert] K[eith] (1874–1936) English essayist, novelist, critic and poet. He was a highly prolific writer who acquired a remarkable facility for writing well in many modes during his early journalistic days. With his friend and collaborator **Hilaire Belloc** (1870–1953)—their partnership was called the 'Chesterbelloc', 'two buttocks of one bum'—he became known as a gifted disputant for what he saw as the glory of old, agricultural Roman Catholic England, as opposed to the new, industrial, cosmopolitan world, a position which unfortunately also led to his adoption of Belloc's unsavoury anti-Semitism. Chesterton's novels and detective stories, e.g. *The Innocence of Father Brown* (1911), and his weirdly anarchic *The Man Who was Thursday: a Nightmare* (1908), are highly entertaining in their paradoxical complications.

Christie, Dame Agatha [Clarissa Mary] (1890–1976) English detective-story writer, whose ingeniously plotted novels, e.g. *The Murder of Roger Ackroyd* (1926), established her as the finest writer in the field of the so-called 'genteel' English murder mystery. Her two best-loved creations are the Belgian detective Hercule Poirot and the elderly amateur sleuth Miss Marple. Another recurring character worth noting is the crime novelist Ariadne Oliver, a figure clearly representing Christie herself (and with a good authorial joke: Oliver doesn't know why her detective is Finnish and a vegetarian, and wishes her readers wouldn't ask her why).

Highlights of Christie's work include *Murder on the Orient Express* (1934) and *The ABC Murders* (both Poirot, as is *The Murder of Roger Ackroyd*), and *The Murder at the Vicarage* (1930) and *Murder is Easy* (1939) (both Miss Marple, and sharing a quite horrific atmosphere of outward respectability and actual corruption). The most famous of her works is probably the unfortunately named (and diabolically clever) *Ten Little Niggers* (1939). This latter work is the only one of the many Christie works renamed for the American market with a better title than the original: *And Then There Were None*. Critical opinion as to the merit of Christie's novels varies widely: her popularity with the reading public, however, is unrivalled; her books have sold over a billion copies in English, and another billion in 44 other languages.

Cibber, Colley *see* **poet laureate**.

Clare, John (1793–1864) English poet. While working as a labourer, he acquired a wide following in the 1820s and 1830s with such volumes as *The Shepherd's Calendar* (1827). As with Burns, Clare's popularity derived from his poems on rural life, and the fashionable appeal of the unlettered 'ploughman poet' image (one much closer in reality to Clare's social status than

Burns'). Clare spent most of his life in insane asylums from 1837 on, where he wrote many of the highly original and beautiful poems on which his reputation rests.

Cleland, John (1709–89) English hack writer and novelist, notable for his novel *Memoirs of a Woman of Pleasure* (1748–49), now known universally as *Fanny Hill*. This is a graphically detailed account of a prostitute's life in her supposed own words, which achieved huge underground sales in the 18th century and has appeared in countless (until our own times, illicit) editions since then. *Fanny Hill* is of interest for three reasons: (a) until modern times, it has been ignored by standard histories of English literature despite being one of the longest-running bestsellers in the language; (b) its status as either erotica or pornography is relevant to the seemingly unresolvable modern debate over what, if anything, constitutes pornography; (c) it is, in parts, an enjoyable read, despite (or perhaps because of) Fanny's occasional indignant and entirely spurious moral observations (a technique perfected by Cleland that lives on in the world of tabloid journalism).

Clemens, Samuel Langhorne *see* **Twain, Mark**.

Clerihew *see* **Bentley, Edmund Clerihew**.

Clough, Arthur Hugh (1819–61) English poet. Like many Victorian poets (e.g. Matthew ARNOLD), Clough was much troubled by religious doubt and scepticism as to the worth of 19th-century civilization. His *Amours de Voyage* (1858) is a fascinating (and often very funny) exploration of the uneasy intellectual attitudes of the age, and his short poem 'The Latest Decalogue' (published posthumously, 1862) remains the definitive assault on the citadel of Victorian hypocrisy. 'Say not the struggle nought availeth' (also 1862) is his most famous title, if not poem.

Cobbett, William (1763–1835) English essayist and political reformer. His best-known work is *Rural Rides* (1830), a polemical collection of essays describing the poverty of the English country-side. Cobbett's prose has been much admired (even by his political enemies) for its lucidity and strength.

Coleridge, Samuel Taylor (1772–1834) English poet. With his friend William WORDSWORTH he published *Lyrical Ballads* in 1798, one of the most significant volumes in the history of English poetry. The authors rejected the notion of a special 'poetic' language, and believed that poetry should be clear and accessible. Coleridge's main contribution to *Lyrical Ballads*, 'The Rime of the Ancient Mariner', a highly dramatic and nightmarish account of a doomed sea voyage, is a typical product of ROMANTICISM and contrasts vividly with Wordsworth's poems of everyday life (a contrast the authors intended). From being an early sympathizer with revolutionary ideas, Coleridge became an active proponent of conservatism, and, with Wordsworth and SOUTHEY, was attacked for this by BYRON. His literary criticism was heavily influenced by German philosophy to the point of incomprehensibility but has flashes of brilliant insight into the creative process.

Collins, [William] Wilkie (1824–89) English novelist, noted particularly for his remarkable and very influential detective novel *The Moonstone* (1868), one of the earliest and greatest examples of the genre, which introduced the first English fictional detective, Sergeant Cuff.

comedy a form of drama, usually of a light and humorous kind and frequently involving misunderstandings that are resolved in a happy ending. The first major examples known, those by ARISTOPHANES, are still among the greatest, and became known as old comedy. The roots of Aristophanes's work are ancient, based on fertility rituals, and often involve ferocious attacks on named individuals, e.g. EURIPIDES and SOCRATES. The outrage caused by Aristophanes's plays led to the Athenians banning the ridicule of named individuals on stage. The so-called **new comedy** that then developed in Greece, e.g. in MENANDER's plays, is known to us largely through adaptations of lost Greek originals by the Roman dramatists TERENCE and PLAUTUS. It is this new comedy, based upon ARISTOTLE's opinion that the business of Comedy is with people of no significance (who can be safely ridiculed), that was to prevail on the stage until the advent of CHEKHOV, IBSEN and STRINDBERG, with their downbeat comedies of middle-class life. These latter comedies may loosely be described as **tragicomedies**, although the term is normally reserved to denote those plays of the Jacobean period, such as Beaumont and FLETCHER's *Philaster* (1609) and *A King and No King* (1611), and SHAKESPEARE's 'dark comedies', e.g. *Measure for Measure* (1604), in all of which the action seems to be leading inexorably towards a tragic ending, but resolves itself (more or less) happily at the end, after trials, tests and tribulations. Fletcher defined the form thus: 'A tragicomedy is not so called in respect of mirth and killing, but in respect it wants deaths, which is enough to make it no tragedy, yet brings some near it, which is enough to make it no comedy, which must be a representation of familiar people, with such kind of trouble as no life be question'd; so that a god is as lawful in this as in tragedy, and mean [i.e. "common"] people as in a comedy' (from the Preface to *The Faithful Shepherdess*, 1610, which may be defined as a romantic pastoral with tragicomic elements).

Other notable forms of comedy include the comedy of HUMOURS, the COMEDY OF MANNERS, SENTIMENTAL COMEDY and COMMEDIA DELL'ARTE. *See also* MELODRAMA, MOLIÈRE; *compare* TRAGEDY.

comedy of humours *see* **humours, theory of**.

comedy of manners a form of COMEDY that features intrigues, invariably involving sex and/or money, among an upper region of society. The central characters are usually witty sophisticates, and there is often much mockery of characters from inferior stations who try to imitate the behaviour of their betters, e.g. a merchant trying to live the lifestyle of a gallant. The form is associated particularly with RESTORATION dramatists such as CONGREVE, ETHEREGE and WYCHERLEY. The finest of these Restoration Comedies is Congreve's *The Way of the World* (1700).

commedia dell'arte a form of Italian COMEDY, popular from the Renaissance until the 18th century, that used stock farcical characters (such as Harlequin and Columbine) and plots as a basis for improvisation. Actors wore masks representing their particular characters, and were often skilled acrobats. The commedia dell'arte form was given new life by GOLDONI. *See also* MEYERHOLD.

Compton-Burnett, Ivy (1884–1969) English novelist. Her 19 novels are composed almost entirely of dialogue and are mainly concerned with the traumas and dismal hypocrisies of upper-middle-class family life. Some critics regard her as a major novelist, others regard her works as oddities (a common complaint is that the dialogue is stylized to an exasperating degree). Her rather haughty criticisms of other novelists, e.g. of TOLSTOY, have not helped her reputation. The novels include *Brothers and Sisters* (1925), *Manservant and Maidservant* (1947) and *The Present and the Past* (1953).

Congreve, William (1670–1729) English dramatist, whose comedies (*see* COMEDY OF MANNERS) are notable for their witty dialogue and sharp observation of social behaviour in Restoration England. His main theme was love (or its lack) and marriage. *The Way of the World* (1700), with its two evenly matched lovers, Mirabell and Millamant, is his best play.

Connolly, Cyril [Vernon] (1903–74) English critic, who edited the literary magazine *Horizon* (founded with SPENDER and another in 1939), one of the most discussed and influential magazines of the 1940s, in which several important works were first published, e.g. Evelyn WAUGH's *The Loved One*. Connolly's own works include a novel, *The Rock Pool* (1936), collections of essays such as *Enemies of Promise* (1938), and his best-known work, *The Unquiet Grave* (1944), a gloomy, faintly decadent 'Word Cycle' of aphorisms and reflections on Western culture (the final issue of *Horizon* in 1950 includes the much quoted comment that 'It is closing time in the gardens of the West and from now on an artist will be judged only by the resonance of his solitude or the quality of his despair.') Connolly features as 'Everard Spruce' in Waugh's *Sword of Honour* trilogy. The portrayal of Connolly and his magazine (*Survival*, a 'cultural beacon which blazed from Iceland to Adelaide') is a sardonic one, but also displays a wary respect for Connolly's sharp critical judgment.

Conquest, [George] Robert (1917–) English poet, historian and critic. His works include Poems (1955) and, with Kingsley AMIS, a highly entertaining comedy of sexual intrigue, the novel *The Egyptologists* (1965). He has also edited, with Amis, several important anthologies of science fiction stories. His most important work, however, is his study of Stalin's murderous policies in the Soviet Union in the 1930s, *The Great Terror* (1968, revised edition 1990).

Conrad, Joseph (1857–1924) Polish-born English novelist. English was Conrad's third language, after Polish and French. He qualified as a master mariner in the British marine service in 1894, and his first novels, *Almayer's Folly* (1895) and *The Outcast of the Islands* (1896), set the main pattern of his work: isolated (often outcast) characters tested to their limits in doom-laden exotic settings. His masterpiece is the great novella *Heart of Darkness* (1902), which describes the corrupting and destructive effects of European colonialism in Africa on both exploited and exploiter. (The story was used by Francis Ford Coppola as the basis for his Vietnam war film *Apocalypse Now*.)

Constructivist theatre *see* **Meyerhold, Vsevolod**.

Cooper, James Fenimore (1789–1851) American novelist. Although most of Cooper's 33 novels are now almost completely unreadable, the series of five novels comprising the 'Leatherstocking Tales' represents a major landmark in American fiction. The novels, e.g. *The Last of the Mohicans* (1826) and *The Deerslayer* (1841), describe the adventures of frontiersman Natty Bumpo (also known as Deerslayer, Leatherstocking, Hawkeye, Pathfinder). The dialogue within the books is strange to modern readers: the upper and middle classes speak in stilted, formal sentences, the lower classes in barbarous frontier jargon, while the Indians deliver sententious metaphor-laden speeches of solid teak. Once the language conventions are accepted, however, the novels can be read and enjoyed for what they are, the first lengthy fictional study of the frontier myth that continues to haunt the American mind.

Corneille, Pierre (1606–84) French dramatist. The best known of Corneille's 33 plays are the tragedies *Le Cid* (1637), *Horace* (1640), *Cinna* (1641) and *Polyeucte* (1643). Corneille is regarded as the main founder of the form of French neoclassical tragedy (*see* NEOCLASSICISM), a form that reached its peak in the tragedies of RACINE. *Le Cid*, in particular, was enormously popular with the public, but the nefarious Cardinal Richelieu persuaded the ACADÉMIE FRANÇAISE to condemn the play for violating the Unities. Corneille's work was very influential on the course of English drama during the Restoration, particularly on DRYDEN's plays.

Cornwell, David John *see* **Le Carré, John**.

Cotton, Charles (1630–87) English poet, best known for his contribution (a dialogue) to the 5th edition of Walton's *The Compleat Angler* (1676), and for a translation of MONTAIGNE's

Essays (1685). Cotton was also a fine poet, whose charming landscape poems, e.g. *The Wonders of the Peak* (1681), were much admired by WORDSWORTH, COLERIDGE and LAMB.

Coward, Sir Noel [Pierce] (1899–1973) English dramatist, actor and songwriter, best known for his witty 'sophisticated' comedies of life on the fringes of English upper-middle-class society, e.g. *Private Lives* (1930) and *Blithe Spirit* (1941), and musicals such as *Bitter Sweet* (1929). Coward's dry, cynical wit has only slightly dated, but his 'patriotic', uplifting works, e.g. the play *Cavalcade* (1931) and the film *In Which We Serve* (1942), are now only of note as period pieces. His languid skill as an actor is seen at its best in the film version (1959) of Graham GREENE's novel *Our Man in Havana*.

Cowley, Abraham (1618–67) English poet. His most important works are *The Mistress* (1647), a collection of DONNE-inspired METAPHYSICAL love poems, 'Davideis', a Scriptural epic in rhymed couplets on the story of David, and several PINDARIC odes, e.g. *Ode, upon the Blessed Restoration* (1660), which were very influential on later 17th-century poets, notably DRYDEN.

Cowper, William (1731–1800) English poet. Cowper was best known in his own day as an engaging satirist and nature poet, but his darker religious poems, mostly written during periods of mental instability, e.g. 'The Castaway' (1799, published posthumously, 1803), are now seen as of more lasting importance. Cowper is also now regarded as an important transitional figure between the 18th century and the romantic era.

Crabbe, George (1754–1832) English poet. His poem *The Village* (1783) presents a bitter and true picture of rural poverty in England. The work is a scathing riposte to the more idyllic portrayal of village life given by writers such as GOLDSMITH, and was published with the help of Dr JOHNSON and Edmund BURKE. The 'Peter Grimes' section of his poem *The Borough* (1810) inspired

Benjamin Britten's great opera (1945) of the same name. Although he wrote mainly in standard 18th-century rhymed couplets, Crabbe's social indignation and subject matter place him, like COWPER, as a bridge between the 18th century and the romantic era.

Crane, [Harold] Hart (1899–1932) American poet. He published only two volumes of verse, *White Buildings* (1926), a series of poems on life in New York City, and *The Bridge* (1926), a WHITMAN-inspired epic series of poems on the 'Myth of America', exemplified in such figures as Pocahontas and Rip Van Winkle, with Brooklyn Bridge as the unifying symbol.

Crane, Stephen [Townley] (1871–1900) American journalist, poet and novelist. Crane's greatest work is *The Red Badge of Courage* (1895), a study of the shattering impact of the Civil War upon a young soldier. His volume of poems, *The Black Riders and Other Lines* (1895), draws on Emily DICKINSON's verse in American poetry.

Crashaw, Richard (1613–49) English poet. He converted to Roman Catholicism around 1645, and his often highly florid and elaborate 'baroque' imagery was inspired by his reading of Spanish mystical writers. His main work is *Steps to the Temple* (1646), which includes the much derided description of Mary Magdalene's eyes (in 'The Weeper') as 'two portable fountains'.

Cruelty, Theatre of *see* **Artaud, Antonin**.

Cudworth, Ralph *see* **More, Henry**.

cummings, e[dward] e[stlin] (1894–1962) American poet, novelist and artist. His autobiographical novel *The Enormous Room* (1922), which describes his wrongful three-month imprisonment for treason in France, won him international recognition, and his subsequent experimental free verse and distinctive use of typography was to prove of great influence. His name is given above in the lower-case form he preferred.

Cunninghame Graham, Robert Bontine (1852–1936) Scottish travel and short-story writer, essayist and politician. The son of a Scottish laird and a half-Spanish mother, he ranched in Argentina and married a Chilean poet in 1879. Graham's remarkable political career included service as a Liberal MP, imprisonment after a demonstration against unemployment (Bloody Sunday, 1887), and the first presidency of the Scottish Labour Party. His travel books include *Mogreb-el-Acksa* (1898), a description of exploration in Morocco that inspired George Bernard SHAW to write *Captain Brassbound's Conversion*. His many other books include *Thirteen Stories* (1900), *Scottish Stories* (1914) and *The Horses of the Conquest* (1930). His friend Joseph CONRAD used him as the model for Charles Gould in *Nostromo*.

Cyrano de Bergerac, Savinien (1619–55) French soldier, poet and dramatist. His works include two fantasies, *Comical History of the States and Empires of the Moon* (1656) and *Comical History of the States and Empires* (1661), satires on contemporary social customs which were influential on both SWIFT and VOLTAIRE. He is most famous for having an enormous nose, and for reputedly fighting around a thousand duels. *See also* ROSTAND.

D

Dahl, Roald (1916–90) English author (of Norwegian parentage), who is known primarily for his entertaining and unpatronizing children's stories, such as *Charlie and the Chocolate Factory* (1964), *Danny, Champion of the World* and several brutally funny collections of poems for children (often illustrated by Quentin Blake). His collections of short stories (definitely not for children), e.g. *Over to You* (1946), *Kiss, Kiss* (1960) and

Switch Bitch (1974), include several suberbly macabre tales, and a few haunting air-war stories (Dahl served as an RAF fighter pilot during World War II).

Dante [Alighieri] (1265–1321) Italian poet, whose earliest work, *Vita Nuova* (1290–94), tells of his love for 'Beatrice', probably Bice Portinari, a girl whom he hardly knew but who became for him a symbol of beauty and purity. Expelled from his native Florence for political reasons, Dante wrote his masterpiece, the *Divine Comedy*, during 20 years of wandering exile. It is an allegorical description in three parts of the poet's journey through Hell, Purgatory and Paradise. He is guided by VIRGIL through Hell to the summit of Purgatory from where his idealized earthly love Beatrice, a representative of the divine, conducts him to the presence of God. One of the world's great poets, his influence was enormous, and he was responsible for making Tuscan the language of literary Italy.

D'Arblay, Madame *see* **Burney, Fanny**.

Davenant *or* **D'Avenant, Sir William** (1606–68) English dramatist. None of his plays, with the possible exception of the comedy *The Wits* (1633) is of much interest. Davenant is worthy of note, however, for (a) evading the Puritan ban on plays with an early English opera (*see* HEROIC TRAGEDY), *The Siege of Rhodes* (1656); (b) introducing women actors on to the public stage (and more elaborate, movable scenery); (c) the possibility that Shakespeare may have been his real father, a rumour current amongst his contemporaries that Davenant himself encouraged. He succeeded to JONSON's unofficial position of POET LAUREATE, and to his pension, in 1638.

Davies, Sir John *see* **acrostic**.

Davies, [William] Robertson (1913–95) Canadian novelist, playwright, literary critic and essayist. Educated at Oxford, Davies worked as an actor, journalist and teacher and was professor of English at the University of Toronto. Davies has gained acclaim for the scale and quiet humour of his work, starting with his first trilogy, *The Salterton Trilogy* (*A Mixture of Frailties*, *Leaven of Malice* and *Tempest-Tost*). Subsequent works include *The Deptford Trilogy* (*Fifth Business*, 1970; *The Manticore*, 1972; and *World of Wonders*) and *The Cornish Trilogy* (*The Rebel Angels*, which, according to Anthony BURGESS made Davies NOBEL PRIZE material; *What's Bred in the Bone* (1985) and *The Lyre of Orpheus*) and *Murther and Walking Spirits* (1991), the title of which is a quotation from Samuel BUTLER.

Davies, W[illiam] H[enry] (1871–1940) Welsh poet. He emigrated as a young man to the US, but after losing a leg in an accident returned to England where he survived as a tramp, managing to scrape together enough money to publish a volume of poems, *The Soul's Destroyer*, which attracted financial support from SHAW. His best-known prose work is *The Autobiography of a Super-Tramp* (1908).

Day-Lewis, Cecil (1904–72) Irish-born English poet. In the 1930s he belonged to the 'AUDEN generation' of left-wing poets, and proclaimed the glories of revolutionary socialism in such volumes as *The Magnetic Mountain* (1933), with a rather bloodthirsty enthusiasm. As with most of his peers, his socialist ideas gradually eroded over the years; he became POET LAUREATE in 1968. He also wrote highly regarded detective novels under the pseudonym 'Nicholas Blake', e.g. *A Question of Proof* (1935).

Deconstruction *see* **Structuralism**.

Defoe, Daniel (1660–1731) English novelist and pamphleteer. Embroiled in many controversies, Defoe was a skilled and prolific propagandist for whichever political faction was paying his wages at the time. His tract *The Shortest Way with the Dissenters* (1702), which argues with deadly irony for the ruthless extirpation of all religious dissenters (he was one himself), was taken at face value by the authorities and he was pilloried and imprisoned. His two greatest novels are marvellously detailed first-person narratives: *Robinson Crusoe* (1719), which has been described as the first real novel (also the first survivalist manual), and *Moll Flanders* (1722), in which an ex-prostitute describes her misadventures in English low life and her eventual happy settlement in Virginia.

Dekker, Thomas (*c.*1570–*c.*1632) English dramatist and pamphleteer. His best-known play, *The Shoemaker's Holiday* (1600), in which a shoemaker becomes Lord Mayor of London, is typical of his work in its sympathetic and uncondescending treatment of the lives of ordinary people. His great tragedy, *The Honest Whore* (1604–1605), was written in collaboration with MIDDLETON.

De la Mare, Walter (1873–1956) English poet and novelist. The best of his work, e.g. *The Listeners* (1910), *The Return* (1910) and *Memoirs of a Midget* (1921), has a delicately eerie quality that is quite unlike any other writer's work. Much of his work was written for children, e.g. the poetry collection *Peacock Pie* (1913), and the loss of childhood innocence and happiness is the dominant theme in his fiction and poems.

De Quincey, Thomas (1785–1859) English essayist and critic. His best-known work is his *Confessions of an English Opium Eater* (1822), which describes his opium addiction and poverty in the London slums. His essays are among the most entertaining in the English language, and include such gems as 'On Murder Considered as One of the Fine Arts' and 'On the Knocking on the Gate in "Macbeth"'.

Derrida, Jacques *see* **Structuralism**.

deus ex machina a Latin term meaning 'god from the machine', i.e. a god introduced into the action of a play to resolve some intractable situation in the plot. The device was used commonly in both Greek and Roman drama. In Greek drama, the intervention took the form of the god being lowered on to the stage via some kind of stage machinery. EURIPIDES seems to have been particularly fond of the device, but it was rarely used by AESCHYLUS and SOPHOCLES. The term has come to denote any twist in a plot which resolves or develops the action in an unexpected way. The device became an extremely common feature of Victorian literature and drama, in the form of legacies from long-lost relatives enabling otherwise impossible marriages to take place and foiling innumerable wicked schemes. The device has been rarely used in modern serious literature, except for ironic effect, as at the end of David LODGE's novel *Nice Work*.

Dickens, Charles (1812–70) English novelist. He achieved immediate popularity with *The Posthumous Papers of the Pickwick Club* (1836–37), the first of his 14 great novels, most of which were published in instalments in periodicals. His popularity with the reading public in both Britain and America was quite remarkable, with, for example, crowds of New Yorkers waiting at the docks for the latest instalment of *The Old Curiosity Shop* (1840–41); the news of Little Nell's death sent a tidal wave of grief across the country. Dickens's critical reputation has grown steadily since the 1930s. His faults were always apparent: an often ludicrous adulation of women ('the angel in the house') and occasional gross wallows in sentiment; however, his narrative skill, characterization, dialogue and social analysis place him firmly in the first rank of all novelists. The novels include *Oliver Twist* (1837), *Martin Chuzzlewit* (1843–44, which includes a section set in America with some caustic comments on American culture and society), the semi-autobiographical *David Copperfield* (1849–50), *Bleak House* (1852–53, a stunning panorama of English life), *Great Expectations* (1860–61) and *Our Mutual Friend* (1864–65).

Dickinson, Emily (1830–86) American poet. A virtual recluse
from her late twenties onward, only seven of her *c.*2,000 poems
were printed in her lifetime. Editions of her poetry began to appear in the 1890s, and the startling originality and worth of her
work gradually became recognized. Her strange aphoristic lyrics
with their individualistic punctuation—with dashes—and a
highly personal imagery derived from inner, obliquely described
torment—are among the greatest produced in the US.

Diderot, Denis (1713–84) French philosopher. With others, he
edited the great *Encyclopédie*, 17 volumes of which appeared
under Diderot's overall direction between 1751 and 1772, despite attempts on the part of reactionary elements, including the
Church, to suppress its publication. Diderot's other works include several rather dull 'bourgeois' plays, e.g. *The Father of the
Family* (1758), which show the influence of LILLO, several novels and *Rameau's Nephew* (1761), an intriguing philosophical
tract in the form of a dialogue between Diderot and the composer
Rameau's nephew, in which the moralistic ideas of the former
are opposed to the latter's sensuality, with each party gradually
becoming aware of the validity of the other's argument and/or of
the dualism of man's nature (it is also a wide-ranging satire on
contemporary intellectuals).

Dinesen, Isak [pseud. of Baroness Karen Blixen] (1885–1962)
Danish short-story writer. Her elaborate fantasy stories, e.g.
Seven Gothic Tales (1934) and *Winter's Tales* (1942), with their
tone of aristocratic amusement and vaguely decadent air, have an
occasionally almost 1890s atmosphere about them. Her autobiographical account of life on a Kenyan coffee farm, *Out of Africa*
(1937), was made into a very successful film in 1985.

Disraeli, Benjamin [1st Earl of Beaconsfield] (1804–81) British
statesman and novelist. His father, **Isaac Disraeli** (1766–1848)
wrote several notable works, including *Curiosities of Literature*

(1813). Benjamin was baptized a Christian at 13, but remained proud of his Jewish ancestry and heritage throughout his life. His political novels, e.g. *Coningsby* (1844) and *Sybil* (1845), were written as manifestoes for 'Young England' Toryism, and show a strong sympathy for the plight of the poor in the 'two-nation' society created by the Industrial Revolution. He became prime minister of the United Kingdom in 1868 and 1874–80.

Dodgson, Charles Lutwidge *see* **Carroll, Lewis**.

domestic tragedy a form of TRAGEDY that appeared in the Elizabethan period, which focuses on the crises of middle-class domestic life in an unpatronizing and sympathetic manner. Early examples include the anonymous *Arden of Faversham* (1592) and HEYWOOD's *A Woman Killed with Kindness* (1607). LILLO's *The London Merchant* (1731), which was much admired and very influential throughout Europe (*see* Gotthold LESSING), established the genre as a highly popular (and profitable) one. The form is closely related to SENTIMENTAL COMEDY, and was influential on the development of MELODRAMA.

Donleavy, J[ames] P[atrick] (1926–) American-born Irish novelist. His works include *The Ginger Man* (1955), a comedy of undergraduate life in Dublin, and *The Beastly Beatitudes of Balthazar B* (1968).

Donne, John (1572–1631) English poet and divine. Brought up a Roman Catholic, he converted to Anglicanism in the mid–1590s. The pattern of most of his life, as with most ambitious men of his age, is an unsettled one, punctuated by occasional hazardous adventures such as accompanying Sir Francis Drake on his raid on Cadiz (1596). He became dean of St Paul's in 1621 and was one of the most popular preachers of his time. His poetry is regarded as amongst the finest METAPHYSICAL verse, and displays a love of paradox and self-questioning doubt with regard to spiritual and philosophical beliefs. Few other poets have his ability to take a metaphorical description to its limits, e.g. his comparison of his mistress's body with a landscape in 'Going to Bed', without being ridiculous.

Dos Passos, John (1896–1970) American novelist. His masterpiece is his great trilogy of American life, *U.S.A.*, comprising *The 42nd Parallel* (1930), *1919* (1932) and *The Big Money* (1936).

Dostoevsky, Fyodor (1821–81) Russian novelist. Like many Russian intellectuals, he was a revolutionary in his youth but converted to a mystical faith in Russian Orthodoxy and the 'slav soul' while exiled for his beliefs in Siberia. His exile was preceded by a macabre mock execution by firing squad, an encounter with death that affected him deeply. His novels are profound explorations of sin and redemption through suffering. They include *Crime and Punishment* (1866), *The Idiot* (1868), *The Possessed* (1872) and *The Brothers Karamazov* (1880).

Douglas, Lord Alfred *see* **Wilde, Oscar**.

Doyle, Arthur Conan (1859–1930) Scottish physician, novelist and short-story writer. His most famous creation is the amateur detective Sherlock Holmes, who solves mysteries by a mixture of deduction and intuitive perception. The stories have been translated into practically every major language, and were collected in various volumes, e.g. *The Adventures of Sherlock Holmes* (1892) and *The Hound of the Baskervilles* (1902).

Drabble, Margaret (1939–) English novelist. Her novels, which frequently feature the dilemmas and life crises of intelligent, married career women, are often snootily dismissed as 'old-fashioned', 'middlebrow' or 'traditional', but have many admirers. The novels include *The Millstone* (1965), *The Ice Age* (1977) and *The Middle Ground* (1980). She also edited the long-awaited fifth edition of *The Oxford Companion to English Literature* (1980), which is now established as the essential reference guide to the subject. *See also* BYATT.

Drayton, Michael (1563–1631) English dramatist and poet. Little of his huge and wide-ranging output is now read, except for a few fine short poems, notably the sonnet beginning 'Since there's no hope, come let us kiss and part', and 'Agincourt', whose first line is 'Faire stood the wind for France'. His plays were often written in collaboration with other dramatists, e.g. MIDDLETON.

Dreiser, Theodore (1871–1945) American novelist. Dreiser was a naturalistic novelist with an ultra-mechanistic view of human nature as defined and governed by the natural laws of biology and social conditioning, a view expressed with stolid conviction in such novels as *Sister Carrie* (1904). His later novels, and non-fiction documentary works such as *America is Worth Saving* (1941), are more optimistic, reflecting his transition from nihilism to socialism. His masterpiece is *An American Tragedy* (1925), a doom-laden narrative in which a factory worker is inexorably led by fate to drown his girlfriend.

Dryden, John (1631–1700) English poet, dramatist and critic. Dryden was the most important literary figure of late 17th-century England, as well as a highly significant contributor to the political and religious controversies of the day. His verse satires, e.g. *Absalom and Achitophel* (1681), the social comedies, e.g. *Marriage à-la-Mode* (1672), and the verse tragedies, e.g. *All for Love* (1678), are among the finest of their respective genres. He was also the first great English critic, and a poet of great stature. He became POET LAUREATE in 1668 but lost the post in 1688 in the political upheaval surrounding the replacement of King James II by William and Mary.

Dumas, Alexandre [*Dumas père*] (1802–70) French novelist and dramatist, whose entertaining romantic novels, e.g. *The Three Musketeers* (1844) and *The Count of Monte Cristo* (1845) achieved instant and lasting popularity. His illegitimate son, also called **Alexandre Dumas** [*Dumas fils*] (1824–95), also wrote novels and plays, his masterpiece being the play *Camille*, an adaptation of his own novel (1848), which caused a sensation when it was staged in 1852, and was the basis for Verdi's opera *La Traviata* (1853).

Du Maurier, Dame Daphne (1907–89) English novelist and short-story writer. Several of her very popular stories and novels have been filmed, e.g. *Jamaica Inn* (1939), *Rebecca* (1940) and 'Don't Look Now' (1973). Once dismissed as a writer of superficial interest, the critical reputation of her work is steadily growing. Her gift for creating an atmosphere of supernatural menace (as in 'Don't Look Now') is especially good.

Dunbar, William (*c*.1465–*c*.1530) Scottish poet and divine, noted mainly for his very fine poem 'Lament for the Makaris' (*c*.1507), an elegy primarily for his fellow dead poets (makar is the Scots word for 'poet').

Dunsany, Edward, 18th Baron (1878–1957) Anglo-Irish novelist, dramatist and short-story writer. He was acquainted with YEATS, who encouraged him to write for the ABBEY THEATRE. The best of his work, e.g. the fantasy stories in *The Book of Wonder* (1912), is rated above the ruck of the 'Celtic Twilight' fantasy of some of his Irish contemporaries. His readership and critical reputation increased sharply with the growth of the fantasy market in the 1960s.

Duoduo [pseud. of Li Shizheng] (1951–) Chinese poet. Duoduo (the name is that of his dead daughter) is regarded as a unique figure in modern Chinese poetry, in that he is a strong admirer of Western poets such as Dylan THOMAS and Sylvia PLATH and has assimilated their influence in his work, yet is still very much a traditional Chinese poet, albeit one working in the modernist vein. His poems, e.g. those in *Looking Out From Death* (1989), are characterized by a restrained yet impassioned intensity. He has lived in exile since the Tiananmen Square Massacre of 1989.

Durrell, Lawrence (1912–90) English poet, novelist and travel writer. His most famous work is the series of novels comprising the *Alexandria Quartet*, i.e. *Justine* (1957), *Balthazar* and *Mount Olive* (both 1958), and *Clea* (1960). The quartet is typical of Durrell's work in its use of lush, baroque language and complex sexual intrigue. Durrell was an admirer of Henry MILLER, with whom he exchanged letters of extravagant mutual admiration.

E

Eco, Umberto (1932–) Italian critic and novelist. Eco first made his mark as a writer on semiotics, in such works as *A Theory of Semiotics* (1972). His best-known work of fiction is *The Name of the Rose* (1981, filmed 1987), a best-selling medieval detective story overladen with theological and language puzzles, in which an English monk, appropriately named William of Baskerville, solves a series of murders in a monastery. *See also* ARISTOTLE.

Edgar, David (1948–) English dramatist. His two most important works are *Destiny* (1976), a long, absorbing and cold-eyed study of fascism and British society that remains one of the few worthwhile plays on the subject, and his adaptation of DICKENS's *The Life and Adventures of Nicholas Nickleby* (1980), which achieved huge critical and popular success, and is remembered with great affection by many people. Edgar's work differs from that of fellow left-wing dramatists of his time, such as BOND and HARE, in that he has a much superior gift for characterization, and, perhaps more notably, has a sense of the ridiculous, e.g. in his short sketch *Ball Boys* (1975).

Edgeworth, Maria (1768–1849) Irish novelist. Her many works include a treatise on education, children's stories and romantic novels, but her greatest and most influential works were her historical novels of Irish life, notably *Castle Rackrent* (1800), which with its exuberant, realistic dialogue and concern for social harmony and justice, set a pattern that was to be followed by other historical novelists, such as SCOTT. Her books were much admired by her contemporaries, and are highly readable.

Edwards, Jonathan (1703–58) American divine, whose rigidly predestinarian writings, e.g. *The Freedom of the Will* (1754), had a strong and somewhat depressing influence on many 18th- and 19th-century writers, e.g. HAWTHORNE.

Ehrenburg, Ilya Grigoryevich (1891–1969) Russian war correspondent and novelist. His greatest novel is *The Thaw* (1954), which is the first major work published in the USSR to address the horrors of the Stalin era.

Eliot, George [pseud. of Mary Ann Evans] (1819–80) English novelist. Eliot's novels deal with the problems of ethical choice in the rapidly changing rural environment of 19th-century England, and are regarded as amongst the finest in the language. Her novels include *Adam Bede* (1869), *The Mill on the Floss* (1860), and her masterly study of 1830s English life *Middlemarch* (1871–72), which was described by Virginia WOOLF as 'one of the few English novels written for grown-up people'. *See also* REALISM.

Eliot, T[homas] S[tearns] (1888–1965) American-born British poet and critic, whose early work was heavily influenced and shaped by his friend Ezra POUND. His early volumes of poetry, notably *Prufrock and Other Observations* (1917) and *The Waste Land* (1922), are concerned with what Eliot saw as the breakdown of civilization and its values in the cultural 'Jazz Age' disarray of the post-World War I era. The poems struck an immediate and responsive chord throughout Europe and America, and by the time he became a British subject in 1927, he was established as the most influential poet of the age. He also attempted to revive the art of verse drama, in such works as *Murder in the Cathedral* (1935) and *The Family Reunion* (1939). Eliot's work has been attacked as being over-replete with often highly recondite allusions and a fashionably slick despair, but he remains one of the most important poets in the language. His critical works, e.g. *The Sacred Wood: Essays on Poetry and Criticism* (1920), are equally important landmarks in the field of criticism. He converted to High Anglicanism in the late 1920s, and was regarded as a pillar of the British establishment for the rest of his life. He was awarded the NOBEL PRIZE for literature in 1948.

Ellis, Alice Thomas [pseud. of Anna Haycraft] (1932–) Anglo-Welsh novelist, regarded by many critics as one of the wittiest modern British writers. Her novels include *The Sin Eater* (1977), *The Birds of the Air* (1980) and *Unexplained Laughter* (1985). Ellis's work is fey, witty and often hauntingly sad, with occasional supernatural elements. Her collection of articles from *The Spectator* magazine, *Home Life* (issued in four volumes 1986–90), is virtually unique among such compilations in not being depressingly twee.

Ellison, Ralph (1914–94) American writer, whose KAFKAesque and partly autobiographical novel *Invisible Man* (1952) describes the alienated life of a young black man in New York.

Emerson, Ralph Waldo (1803–82) American philosopher, essayist and poet. He was an exponent of Transcendentalism, a characteristically American philosophy compounded of cloudy, generalized mysticism (showing the influence of CARLYLE) and optimism. He was much revered by contemporaries such as THOREAU, who saw him as one of the greatest 19th-century thinkers. His ideas are contained in his early work *Nature* (1836) and *Essays, First and Second Series* (1841, 1844).

Empson, Sir William (1906–84) English poet and critic. His *Seven Types of Ambiguity* (1930, written while he was studying mathematics at Cambridge) is a modern classic of literary criticism that has been much enjoyed for its witty insights into the language used by writers such as DONNE and SHAKESPEARE.

Engels, Friedrich *see* **Marx, Karl**.

epic theatre *see* **Brecht, Bertolt**.

Épinay, Louise Florence Pétronille, Madame d' (1726–83) French writer. In 1748 she became acquainted with ROUSSEAU and gave him a cottage where he lived for some time. Her *Conversations d'Émilie* (1774) is a companion volume to Rousseau's *Émile*. She also wrote her memoirs.

epistolary novel a novel in the form of a series of letters written to and from the main characters, sometimes presented by the author in the anonymous role of 'editor'. The form flourished in the 18th century, examples including RICHARDSON's *Pamela* (1741) and BURNEY's *Evelina* (1778). The best parody is Jane AUSTEN's *Love and Friendship* (written when she was 14), closely followed by FIELDING's (much larger) *Shamela Andrews* (1741). Jane Austen toyed for a while with the form: *Lady Susan* (written 1793–94), a minor work by her own high standards, ends with a lovely send-up of the form's conventions in the 'Conclusion', and the first draft of *Sense and Sensibility* (1797–98), entitled *Elinor and Marianne*, was originally in epistolary form, but the form was too weak for what she planned to write.

Erasmus, Desiderius (1467–1536) Dutch scholar, one of the greatest of the Renaissance and Reformation period. A humanist rather than a reformer or theologian, he took no direct part in the Reformation (being reproached by Martin Luther for his lukewarmness) but he waged war on ignorance and supersition and always promoted the cause of truth. He edited various classics and the first edition of the Greek Testament, but his best-known work is *Encomium Moriae* (*In Praise of Folly*, 1509, written while he was staying in London with Thomas MORE).

Erckmann-Chatrian [combined pseud. of Émile Erckmann (1822–99) and Alexandre Chatrian (1826–90)] French Alsatian fiction writers. They formed their literary partnership in 1847, but their first success did not occur until 1859 with the publication of the novel *L'Illustre Docteur Mathéus*, the first of many novels, including *Waterloo* (1865). Their plays included *Le Juif polonais* (1869, which was made famous in England by Sir Henry Irving under the name of *The Bells*) and *L'Ami Fritz* (1876).

Etherege *or* **Etheredge, Sir George** (*c.*1635–92) English dramatist, whose play *The Comical Revenge* (1664) established the main pattern of RESTORATION comedy, i.e. witty, cynical characters in the amoral world of fashionable society. His best play in this vein is *The Man of Mode* (1676).

Ettrick Shepherd, The *see* **Hogg, James**.

Euripides (480–406 BC) Greek dramatist, the youngest of the three great Greek tragedians, the others being AESCHYLUS and SOPHOCLES. His popularity lasted until well into the Byzantine era, and 19 of his (perhaps 92) plays are extant, the most notable being *Alcestis, Medea, Orestes* and *The Trojan Women*, the last of which describes the fate of the captive Trojan women after the Greek victory over Troy. It has had several major productions since the end of World War II, resonant as it is with the aftermath of holocaust. Euripides adopted a more rationalist, questioning approach to the gods and their divine affairs than his great predecessors, and was clearly more concerned with the business of everyday human beings, for which he was mercilessly satirized by ARISTOPHANES.

Eusden, Laurence *see* **poet laureate**.

Evans, Mary Ann *see* **Eliot, George**.

Evelyn, John (1620–76) English author and diarist. His diary was first published in 1818, and first published in full in 1955. Like the diary of his friend PEPYS, it is full of valuable details of domestic and social life in 17th-century England.

existentialism a philosophical position based on a perception of life in which man is an actor forced to make choices in an essentially meaningless universe that functions as a colossal and cruel Theatre of the ABSURD. The main writers associated with Existentialism are French, notably SARTRE and CAMUS, and the bilingual BECKETT. The roots of Existentialism are complex; one important source is NIHILISM, the influence of which is apparent in Camus' great novel *The Outsider* (1942), described by its author as 'the study of an absurd man in an absurd world'. Another important source is the Danish theologian **Søren Kierkegaard** (1813–55), who observed that life must be lived forwards, but can only be understood backwards. Life is therefore a continual act of faith in which choices are made for a series of actions, the consequences of which must remain unclear.

Camus' quest for meaning in life and art led him to an accommodation with Christianity, detailed in his great anti-totalitarian essay *The Rebel* (1951), whereas Sartre came to an uneasy alliance with Marxism; Beckett, however, kept on ploughing his unique and lonely furrow, free of political or religious comfort, until his death.

Discussion about Existentialism in the Arts tends to degenerate into bad-tempered squabbles about the motivation, meaning and effect of the particular piece under examination, a process complicated by the often pervasive role of violence in works labelled 'Existentialist'. Thus, the film director Sam Peckinpah was probably sincere in describing his films as Existentialist dramas in the quasi-Marxist mode of Sartre; for most viewers, however, they are simply glorifications of violence.

F

Farquhar, George (1678–1707) Irish dramatist. His plays are the best of the late Restoration comedies. They are also the most good-natured, without lacking any satirical bite, and there have been many successful modern productions of them. His best plays are *The Recruiting Officer* (1706) and *The Beaux' Strategem* (1707), both of which are important transitional works between the witty bawdiness of Restoration comedy and the more decorous, moralistic plays of the 18th century.

Farrell, J[ames] G[ordon] (1935–79) English novelist. He spent much of his childhood in Ireland, and the political problems of the 1920s there provided the background to his first major novel, *Troubles* (1970), leading him on to a continued interest in novels concerning the end of the British Empire, e.g. *The Siege of Krishnapur* (1973), *The Singapore Grip* (1978), and *The Hill Station* (published posthumously 1981). The last was unfinished at the time of his accidental death by drowning while on a fishing trip, shortly after he had moved to Ireland.

Farrell, J[ames] T[homas] (1904–79) American novelist. Most of his work is set in the Irish slums of Chicago, where Farrell was brought up. His best-known work is the *Studs Lonigan* trilogy, a grim saga (in the naturalistic mode) of the life of a small-time hoodlum in Chicago: the three novels are *Young Lonigan* (1932), *The Young Manhood of Studs Lonigan* (1934) and *Judgment Day* (1935).

Faulkner, William (1897–1962) American novelist. His first novel, *Soldier's Pay* (1926), was written with Sherwood ANDERSON's encouragement. His next two novels, *Sartoris* and *The Sound and the Fury* (both 1929), began the famous series of works dealing with the history of a fictional Mississippi county, Yoknapatawpha, which ended with *The Reivers* (1962). The series deals with the political, social, racial and sexual tensions created in the South in the aftermath of the Civil War. The critical reputation of Faulkner's work has grown considerably since the 1940s, and is now seen as a significant examination of the crisis of the fragmentation of American society. He was awarded the NOBEL PRIZE for literature in 1949.

Feige, Albert Otto Max *see* **Traven, B**.

Ferlinghetti, Lawrence (1919–) American poet and publisher, whose City Lights Bookshop in San Francisco was a breeding ground for BEAT GENERATION writers, of whom he is a typical example, in the 1950s. His own works also include the more lyrical *A Coney Island of the Mind* (1958).

Feuchtwanger, Lion (1884–1958) German novelist. His best-known work is the historical novel *Jew Süss* (1925), which describes the rise and fall of a Jewish politician in 18th-century Germany. Being Jewish, a pacifist and a socialist, Feuchtwanger fled Nazi Germany to Vichy France, from where he escaped to the US. He was a friend of Bertolt BRECHT, with whom he collaborated on several plays.

Feydeau, Georges (1862–1921) French dramatist. The son (by a prostitute) of the novelist **Ernst Aimé Feydeau** (1821–73) whose major work was the novel *Sylvie*, Georges quickly turned to the field of farce, his plot lines usually involving a frantic chase in the near-discovery of adultery. His farces, e.g. *A Flea in Her Ear*, are frequently revived.

Fielding, Henry (1707–54) English novelist and dramatist. His satirical plays, e.g. *Pasquin* (1736) and *The Historical Register for 1736* (1737), both of which were cruelly funny attacks on the Walpole administration, provoked the British Government into passing the strict Licensing Act of 1737 to censor stage plays.

Fielding then continued his attack on corruption and hypocrisy by turning to novel writing. His first novel, *Joseph Andrews* (1742) was a very successful send-up of Samuel RICHARDSON's *Pamela* in which the conventions of male and female virtue are reversed; the second, *Jonathan Wild* (1743), re-assails the British Government by presenting the career of a criminal as an allegory of political vice; and his greatest work, *Tom Jones* (1749), surveys the whole of English society with masterly insight, humour and compassion. He is one of the great innovators of the novel, and his works remain hugely entertaining. In his last novel, *Amelia* (1751), the most sombre and realistic of his books, Fielding once again stood convention on its head by having the eponymous heroine disfigured—he was concerned to show that outer and inner reality did not always match up. He also wrote many important tracts on social problems, and worked tirelessly as a magistrate to improve judicial standards.

Firbank [Arthur Annesley] Ronald (1886–1926) English novelist. His weirdly exotic works bear the stamp of the AESTHETIC MOVEMENT, but are unlike any others in the language in their oblique, flickering dialogue and fantastic characters. Typical examples are *Valmouth* (1919) and *Concerning the Eccentricities of Cardinal Pirelli* (1926). He influenced, among others, WAUGH and HUXLEY.

Fitzgerald, Edward (1809–83) English poet. His best-known work is his very free translation of *The Rubaiyat of Omar Khayyám* (1859). This enormously successful work is one of the most quoted poems in the language, although Fitzgerald's version is more resonant of Victorian doubts and fears than of the bright scepticism of the 12th-century Persian Omar.

Fitzgerald, F[rancis] Scott [Key] (1896–1940) American novelist and short-story writer. His works are moralistic fables of extravagance and glamour set against the background of Fitzgerald's own world of 1920s 'Jazz Age' High Society. *The Great Gatsby* (1925), the story of a mysterious financier, and *Tender is the Night* (1934), a fictional reworking of Fitzgerald's own problems (his wife Zelda became mentally ill), are his best-known works.

Fitzgerald, Penelope (1916–) English novelist. Her novels include *The Bookshop* (1978), *Human Voices* (1980) and *The Gate of Angels* (1990). *Human Voices*, a very funny yet moving account of life at the BBC during the Blitz, is perhaps her most representative novel.

Flaubert, Gustave (1821–80) French novelist. His masterpiece is his first published novel, *Madame Bovary* (1857), one of the greatest of all 19th-century novels, a story of romantic self-deception, adultery and suicide in rural France. Flaubert's meticulous concern for finding exactly the right word, and for objective, impersonal narrative, a fluid style and artistic integrity, have earned him a niche all of his own in world literature.

Flecker, James Elroy (1884–1915) English poet and dramatist. The title poem in his collection *The Golden Journey to Samarkand* (1913) is his best-known work, although his verse play *Hassan* (1922) was staged in 1923, with music by Delius.

Fleming, Ian [Lancaster] (1908–64) English journalist and novelist. His series of novels featuring the secret agent James Bond, e.g. *Live and Let Die* (1954) and *Goldfinger* (1964), were enormous popular successes and have all been filmed. The novels have been attacked for their slick treatment of sex and violence; Kingsley AMIS gave a spirited defence of them in his *The James Bond Dossier* (1965), but, characteristically, managed to point out all Fleming's lapses in taste along the way.

Fletcher, John (1579–1625) English dramatist. Fletcher was one of the most popular dramatists of his day, and frequently collaborated with other dramatists, most notably **Sir Francis Beau-**

mont (1584–1616), from 1606 to 1613. Their best-known works are the tragicomedies (a genre they had a significant influence on) *The Maid's Tragedy* (1610–11) and *A King and No King* (1611) (*see* COMEDY). Fletcher also collaborated with SHAKE-SPEARE on *The Two Noble Kinsmen* (first published 1634) and *Henry VIII* (1613), the firing of a cannon during the production of the latter causing the burning down of the Globe Theatre.

Flirts and Straights a distinction between authors who specialize in showing off to their readers (flirts) and those whose main concern is getting on with telling the story (straights). A flirt will play with conventions and expectations, and disrupt the narrative with disquisitions on the meaning of life or on what the author had for breakfast. A straight will, for the most part, maintain the agreed conventions between author and reader. A writer of detective stories, in which genre the conventions are fairly rigorous, is almost always a straight, though inferior crime writers will make their heroes secret readers of PROUST or NIETZSCHE. Many writers combine both elements: George ELIOT is a straight in character development, but a flirt in digression.

Florio, John (*c*.1553–1625) English author. His father was an Italian Protestant refugee who settled in London. He compiled an Italian-English dictionary, *A World of Words* (1598). His translation of MONTAIGNE's *Essays* (1603) was of great influence (Shakespeare quotes from them in *The Tempest*).

Fo, Dario (1926–) Italian dramatist and director. Fo's satirical farces, e.g. *Accidental Death of an Anarchist* (1970), have as their target such social issues as police corruption and the oppression of women. He was awarded the Nobel prize for literature in 1997. Influences on Fo include BRECHT, COMMEDIA DELL'ARTE and Mayakovsky (*see* FUTURISM).

Foote, Samuel (1720–77) English actor and dramatist, whose plays and performances frequently satirized his contemporaries.

A representative work is *The Minor* (1760), an anti-Methodist satire.

Ford, Ford Madox (1873–1939) English novelist, editor and critic. His most important works are the novels *The Good Soldier* (1915) and the tetralogy *Parade's End* (published in one volume 1950). Ford had great influence on his contemporaries in his role of editor and critic (he founded the *Transatlantic Review* in 1924 and was a generous source of encouragement to many writers), and the reputation of his own writings (greatly revered by Graham GREENE) is steadily growing.

Ford, John (1585–*c*.1639) English dramatist, notable for such REVENGE TRAGEDIES as *'Tis Pity She's a Whore* and *The Broken Heart* (both 1633). Ford's bleak, objective vision of human suffering and his command of blank verse were highly praised by T.S. ELIOT.

Forster, E[dward] M[ontagu] (1879–1970). English novelist and critic. His novels, e.g. *The Longest Journey* (1907) and *Howards End* (1910), are mainly concerned with moral and ethical choices and personal relationships within groups of educated, middle-class people. His best-known work is *A Passage to India* (1924), which describes the clashes and prejudices between the British and Indians under the British Raj.

Fowles, John [Robert] (1926–) English novelist. The film rights to his first book *The Collector* (1963), a creepy psychological study of a butterfly collector turned kidnapper, were sold while the book was still in proof stage. His next novel, *The Magus* (1966), in which an English schoolteacher on a Greek island is subjected to a series of sinister 'happenings' by a god-like millionaire, and his third, *The French Lieutenant's Woman* (1969), a quasi-historical narrative written for the most part in pastiche Victorian prose, and with two separate endings, have established him as one of the major novelists of our time.

Frame, Janet [Janet Paterson Frame Cluthal] (1924–) New Zealand novelist and short-story writer. Frame spent eight years in a psychiatric institution after being labelled as schizophrenic, and only narrowly escaped being leucotomized thanks to the publication of her collection of short stories, T*he Lagoon: Stories* in 1952. Her work includes ten highly regarded novels, e.g. *Owls Do Cry* (1957) and *Intensive Care* (1970). Her autobiographical volumes, *To the Island* (1982), *An Angel at my Table* (1984) and *The Envoy from Mirror City* (1984), are, like her novels, moving explorations of the anarchic borderlands between sanity and mental breakdown.

France, Anatole [pseud. of Jacques Anatole Thibault] (1844–1924) French novelist, who specialized in social and political satire. His best-known work is *Penguin Island* (1908), an allegory of the evolution of society. He was awarded the Nobel prize for literature in 1921.

Franklin, Benjamin (1706–90) American author, scientist and statesman. He helped draft the Declaration of Independence, and played an active role in American political life for most of his long life. His best-known works are *Poor Richard's Almanack* (1733–58), a witty blend of common-sense philosophy and satire, and his masterpiece, the highly entertaining *Autobiography* (first published in England in 1793, and in America in 1818).

Frayn, Michael (1933–) English dramatist and novelist, noted for his dry, sardonic humour. Representative novels include *The Tin Men* (1965), a satire on robotics and computers, and *A Very Private Life* (1968), a futuristic, anti-Utopian fantasy. His plays include *Noises Off* (1982), which uses the conventions of farce to send up theatrical life.

Frazer, Sir James George (1854–1941) Scottish scholar and anthropologist. His study of religious customs and myth, *The Golden Bough* (1890–1915), was a major influence on many 20th-century writers, notably T. S. ELIOT and JOYCE, and his belief that faith and ritual must be set in the context of religions influenced FREUD's theories.

free verse *or* **vers libre** any form of verse without traditional metrical or stanzaic form. It is usually characterized by the use of rhythmic 'natural speech' cadences, is dependent on alliteration and the subtle placing of syllabic stresses, and can be rhymed or unrhymed. T.S. ELIOT described free verse as not a liberation from form, but a 'revolt against dead form'. The SYMBOLIST MOVEMENT placed great emphasis on free verse, which has a very long ancestry. The 'Song of Songs' in the AUTHORIZED VERSION is in free verse, as is Milton's *Samson Agonistes*. Whitman's huge epic poem *Song of Myself* (1855) is another notable example.

Freud, Sigmund (1856–1939) Austrian psychiatrist, who founded psychoanalysis. His works, which include *The Interpretation of Dreams* (1900) and *The Ego and the Id* (1923), have been of enormous influence in the 20th century. Freudian literary criticism is the study of literature according to the precepts and insights of Freud's theories on the hidden imperatives of the unconscious (Freud's own writings on literature, e.g. on Hamlet and Oedipus in *The Interpretation of Dreams*, are of great value). *See also* FRAZER, JUNG.

Frost, Robert Lee (1874–1963) American poet. Frost's work is concerned mainly with the people and landscape of New England; his best poems, e.g. 'The Death of the Hired Man' and 'Stopping By Woods on a Snowy Evening', have a quiet, lyrical quality that won him many admirers. Later critics, such as Lionel TRILLING, have pointed out the dark, enigmatic nature of much of his symbolism. Representative volumes include *A Boy's Will* (1913), *North of Boston* (1914)—both these volumes being first published in the UK, where Frost lived 1912–15—*A Witness Tree* (1942) and *In the Clearing* (1962).

Fry, Christopher [Harris] (1907–) English dramatist, whose verse dramas such as *A Phoenix too Frequent* (1946) and *The Lady's Not for Burning* (1949) were popular with both critics and the public, and are frequently revived.

Fugard, Athol (1932–) South African dramatist, whose plays explore the tragedy of racial tension caused by apartheid in South Africa. His works include *The Blood Knot* (1961), *Boesman and Lena* (1968), *Sizwe Bansi is Dead* (1972) and *Master Harold . . . and the Boys* (1982). He has also written film scripts and a novel, *Tsotsi* (1980), the latter being a study of a young black criminal's growing social and moral awareness.

Futurism a movement of writers and artists, originating in early 20th-century Italy, that extolled the virtues of the new, dynamic machine age, which was reckoned to have rendered the aesthetic standards of the past redundant. The founding document of the movement is the poet **Filipo Marinetti**'s (1876–1944) *Futurist Manifesto* of 1909, which, in literature, called for the destruction of traditional sentence construction and the establishment of a 'free verse in free words' (*parole in libertà*) owing nothing to the literary standards of the past (*see* TZARA); the new relationship between words was to be in terms of analogy alone. The English variant of Futurism is Vorticism, which included writers such as Wyndham LEWIS and Ezra POUND. The Russian variant, Russian Futurism, was led by the poet **Vladimir Mayakovsky** (1893– 1930), whose curious love affair with the Soviet dictatorship ended with his suicide (Lenin described him as 'incomprehensible'; once he was safely dead, Stalin lauded him as a great Bolshevik poet).

Futurism became a spent force by the 1930s, largely because of its close association with Fascism and the establishment of the Futurist hero Mussolini's dictatorship in Italy (Marinetti's vision of war as 'the hygiene of the world' is also Mussolini's). The relationship between Italian Fascism, Soviet Communism, and Futurism, it should be noted, was actually a very close one. The Italian critic (and founder of the Italian Communist Party) **Antonio Gramsci** (1891–1937), praised Marinetti and his cronies for their destructive onslaught on traditional culture ('clearly revolutionary . . . absolutely Marxist'), as did the Soviet cultural commissar Anatoly Lunacharsky, who described Marinetti as 'the one intellectual revolutionary in Italy', while the Soviet avant-garde journal *Lef* asserted that 'In Italy Mayakovsky would have been Marinetti, and in Russia Marinetti would have been Mayakovsky' (*see* Igor Golomstock's *Totalitarian Art*, 1990, for an extended analysis of the unsavoury relationship between such banalities and 20th-century totalitarianism). *See also* REALISM.

G

Galsworthy, John (1867–1933) English novelist and dramatist. His plays, e.g. *Strife* (1909) and *Justice* (1910), are realistic, hard-hitting campaigning works designed to expose social injustice (the furore over *Justice* resulted in UK prison reform). His plays are excellently constructed, recognize the complexity of human motivation, and there have been several successful revivals. His most lasting achievement, however, is his *Forsyte Saga* trilogy, *The Man of Property* (1906), *In Chancery* (1920) and *Awakening* (1920). The trilogy is centred on the life of Soames Forsyte, a suburban London solicitor, and examines the brutality beneath the veneer of seemingly civilized middle-class life. An adaptation of the *Forsyte Saga* by the BBC in 1967 achieved remarkably high viewing figures throughout the world. He was awarded the NOBEL PRIZE for literature in 1932.

Galt, John (1789–1839) Scottish novelist. He described his novels as 'theoretical histories' of the changing social patterns of Scottish country life. His best novel is *Annals of the Parish* (1821), in which a clergyman, with much unconsciously funny deadpan detail, describes incidents in the humble lives of his parishioners (the philosopher J.S. Mill took the term 'utilitarian' from this book).

Garrick, David (1717–79) English actor and dramatist. He was a pupil of Dr JOHNSON at Lichfield, and accompanied him to London in 1737. He made his mark as an actor within a few years, his performance as Richard III in 1741 making particular impact. He dominated the English theatre for the rest of his life, and was actor-manager of Drury Lane Theatre from 1747 to 1776. The farces he wrote are now of little interest, but his letters (published 1831–32) provide fascinating portraits of his contemporaries, who were in no doubt as to his acting genius: the actress Kitty Clive said of him, 'Damn him, he could act a gridiron!'

Gaskell, Mrs Elizabeth (1810–65) English novelist. Her novels about English country life, e.g. *Mary Barton* (1848) and *North and South* (1855), are often concerned with the injustices of the 'two-nation' society (*see* DISRAELI) of 19th-century England. Her most popular novel, however, was (and is) *Cranford* (1851–53), a gentle and entertaining study of life in a small village. She became a friend of Charlotte BRONTË, whose biography she wrote (1857).

Gay, John (1685–1732) English dramatist and poet. His masterpiece is *The Beggar's Opera* (1728), a ballad opera based upon an observation by his friend SWIFT that a 'Newgate pastoral' might make an 'odd pretty sort of thing'. The work was a huge success, its popularity due in part to the fact that characters and incidents in the play are drawn from real life—notably, from the life of the prime minister, Walpole, who gritted his teeth on this occasion but banned the play's sequel, *Polly* (1729). The play was said to have made Gay rich, and the producer John Rich gay. BRECHT's *Threepenny Opera* is based on Gay's play.

Genet, Jean (1910–86) French dramatist and novelist. His best-known novel, *Our Lady of the Flowers* (1943), describes homosexual life in prison in loving detail, and, like all of his novels, was banned in the US until the 1960s. His plays, e.g. *The Maids* (1947) and *The Balcony* (1957), are remarkable examples of the Theatre of the ABSURD, and suffered much from censorship.

Gerhardie, William (1895–1977) English novelist. Gerhardie was highly thought of by his contemporaries, notably WAUGH. The novels, especially *The Polyglots* (1925), are full of strange characters and events which are often straight renderings of incidents in Gerhardie's own rather bizarre life.

Gibbon, Edward (1737–94) English historian. His masterpiece is his *History of the Decline and Fall of the Roman Empire* (1776–88), a work which, in breadth of narrative and erudite analysis, remains one of the greatest of all historical studies. Gibbon's sceptical and ironical tone while describing the rise and establishment of Christianity gave much offence to many of his contemporaries.

Gibbon, Lewis Grassic [pseud. of James Leslie Mitchell] (1901–35) Scottish novelist. His masterpiece is his trilogy *A Scots Quair*, i.e. *Sunset Song* (1932), *Cloud Howe* (1933) and *Grey Granite* (1934), which charts the progress of Chris Guthrie, a Scottish farm girl, through broken marriages and parenthood to life in the city. The underlying philosophy of the trilogy is a bizarre blend of Scottish nationalism, Marxism (the structure is based on MARX's 'progressive' theory of history, and Chris's son joins the Communist Party) and an elemental mysticism that faintly echoes Emily BRONTË's *Wuthering Heights* (the work ends with Chris apparently becoming one with the land). Gibbon was much influenced by MACDIARMID.

Gide, André (1860–1951) French novelist. Brought up under a strict Protestant family regime, Gide early on developed a strong but confused moral sense, and decided he was a homosexual after reading Oscar WILDE. His novels, e.g. *Fruits of the Earth* (1897) and *Strait is the Gate* (1909), are usually short and are fascinating studies of sexual and social self-deception. He flirted with communism for a while, but condemned the horrors of the Soviet system in his *Return from the U.S.S.R.* (1936), a work which, in its integrity and lack of bigotry, is one of the key political books of the 1930s. He was awarded the NOBEL PRIZE for literature in 1947.

Gilbert, Sir W[illiam] S[chwenck] (1836–1911) English dramatist and librettist. His collaboration with the composer Sir Arthur Sullivan (1842–1900) resulted in the 'Savoy operas', e.g. *Trial by Jury* (1875) and *The Gondoliers* (1889), of which there are 13 in all. The operas are such fun, and the tunes so good, that the extreme sharpness of social comment and essential impropriety of much of the dialogue, tends to be missed. Gilbert is probably the only dramatist to have operated at the same level of satire as ARISTOPHANES, and the enormous popularity of the operas with the Victorian middle classes remains something of an enigma. Gilbert was also one of the finest English parodists, and wrote much excellent light verse. *See also* AESTHETIC MOVEMENT.

Gill, [Arthur] Eric [Rowton] (1882–1940) English typographer, writer, sculptor and engraver. He converted to Roman Catholicism in 1913, and his religious beliefs were profoundly influential in his work. His type designs include Perpetua and Gill Sansserif, his sculpture the *Prospero and Ariel* sculpture for Broadcasting House (1931), and his books *Art* (1934) and *Autobiography* (1940).

Ginsberg, Allen *see* **Beat Generation**.

Gissing, George (1857–1903) English novelist. His novels are unrelentingly grim works designed to expose the horrors of social injustice and often have as their central character an artist or hack writer (like Gissing himself) struggling to survive in a sea of indifference and poverty. His two best-known novels are *New Grub Street* (1891), a bitter portrayal of the literary world's underclass, and *The Private Papers of Henry Ryecroft* (1903).

Glasgow, Ellen (1873–1945) American novelist. Her novels are usually set in her native Virginia and are closely observed dramas of social and political tension. Representative examples include *Virginia* (1913) and *Barren Ground* (1925).

Goethe, Johann Wolfgang von (1749–1832) German poet, dramatist, novelist, philospher, scientist and statesman. He was one of the most learned and influential figures of his time. His novel *Die Leiden des jungen Werthers* (*The Sorrows of Young Werther*, 1774) is a morbid tale of unrequited love that supposedly inspired a wave of suicides of oversensitive young men throughout Europe (*see also* MACPHERSON). Other great works include the novel *Die Wahlverwandtschaften* (*Elective Affinities*, 1809), the verse drama *Egmont* (1788) and much great poetry. His masterpiece, the verse drama *Faust*, was published in two parts in 1808 and 1832.

Gogarty, Oliver St John (1878–1957) Irish poet and novelist, remembered principally for being the model for the rumbustious Buck Mulligan in James JOYCE's *Ulysses*, and for *As I was Going Down Sackville Street* (1937), a valuable memoir of Dublin's literary world.

Gogol, Nikolai (1809–52) Russian short-story writer, dramatist and novelist. His two great works are the play *The Government Inspector* (1836), a scathing satire on Russian bureaucracy and obsequiousness, and *Dead Souls* (1842), a novel in which the names of dead peasants are bought by a young man scheming for an inheritance. He also wrote some exceptionally fine stories, e.g. 'The Nose' and 'The Overcoat', in which his favourite theme of confusion between appearance and reality is used to wildly comic effect.

Golding, Sir William (1911–93) English novelist. His first novel, *Lord of the Flies* (1954), describes the reduction to primal brutality of a party of British schoolboys stranded on a desert island; his second, *The Inheritors* (1955), a savage fable of man's origins, established him as a master of dark allegories concerning man's propensity for evil. He was awarded the NOBEL PRIZE for literature in 1983.

Goldoni, Carlo (1707–93) Italian dramatist. He wrote over 250 plays (in French as well as Italian), and some operas. Around 150 of his plays are comedies, invariably set in his native Venice and frequently featuring satirical attacks on the aristocracy. Goldoni's comedies are generally seen as adapting the form of COMMEDIA DELL'ARTE to a more realistic approach with greater appeal to the tastes of the middle-class audiences of the mid-to-late 18th century.

Goldsmith, Oliver (1730–74) Irish poet, essayist and novelist. He settled in London in 1756, where he became a hack reviewer and writer for periodicals. His two greatest works are the novel *The Vicar of Wakefield* (1764), a cunningly structured blend of virtue and humour that became one of the most popular of all 18th-century novels, and his hugely successful play *She Stoops to Conquer* (1773), which is one of the most popular of all English comedies.

Gopaleen, Myles na *see* **O'Brien, Flann**.

Gorenko, Anna Andreyevna *see* **Akhmatova, Anna**.

Gorky, Maxim (1868–1936) Russian novelist, dramatist and short-story writer. He was born into poverty, self-educated, and his works deal with the plight of the poor and society's outcasts in Czarist Russia. His best-known works are *The Mother* (1906–

1907), a story of awakening political consciousness, the autobiographical trilogy *Childhood* (1913), *Among People* (1915) and *My Universities* (1923), and his great play *The Lower Depths* (1902). His works were later used as templates by many practitioners of socialist realism, a doctrine he helped formulate in the 1930s (*see* MARX). The best of his former colleagues were killed by the Soviet regime in the 1930s.

Gothic novel a type of NOVEL that was enormously popular in the late 18th century, combining elements of the supernatural, macabre or fantastic, often in wildly RADCLIFFE settings, e.g. ruined abbeys or ancient castles. The heroes and/or heroines, whether medieval or modern, for the most part speak in a formal, stilted language curiously at odds (for the modern reader) with the appalling situations they find themselves in. Horace WALPOLE's *The Castle of Otranto* (1764) and Ann RADCLIFFE's *The Mysteries of Udolpho* (1794) are among the best-known examples of the genre. Jane AUSTEN's *Northanger Abbey* (1818) remains the definitive parody.

Grahame, Kenneth (1859–1932) Scottish author of the classic children's stories *The Golden Age* (1895), *Dream Days* (1898), and (his masterpiece) *The Wind in the Willows* (1908). Grahame became Secretary of the Bank of England, writing his stories in his spare time to entertain his only son.

Gramsci, Antonio *see* **Futurism**.

Granville-Barker, Harley (1877–1946) English dramatist, producer, critic and actor. The best of his plays are the naturalistic dramas *The Voysey Inheritance* (1905) and *Waste* (1907). His productions, especially those of SHAKESPEARE, broke new ground in their concern for textual authenticity and disdain for overelaborate sets. His *Prefaces* to Shakespeare's plays were published in four volumes, 1927–45, and are the first major study of Shakespeare from the viewpoint of a drama producer.

Grass, Günter [Wilhelm] (1927–) German novelist, dramatist and poet. His best-known novel is *The Tin Drum* (1959), a grimly comic satire on the collapse of Hitler's Third Reich, as seen through the eyes of a dumb boy. His plays include *The Plebians Rehearse the Uprising* (1966), a satire on BRECHT's dramatic and political theories, set during the Berlin workers' rebellion against the East German dictatorship. Grass's own political views are staunchly socialist but democratic, with a consistent and wholly admirable opposition to totalitarianism of all varieties.

Graves, Richard (1715–1804) English clergyman and author of *The Spiritual Quixote* (1773), an entertaining PICARESQUE NOVEL that describes the experiences of a dissenter travelling through England. The work satirizes the 'enthusiastic' preaching and conduct of the more extreme Methodists, particularly George Whitefield, who is disowned in the book by John Wesley himself.

Graves, Robert [von Ranke] (1889–1985) English poet, novelist and critic. His great autobiography, *Goodbye to all That* (1929), was one of the first accounts of World War I soldiering to make a major impact from an antiwar standpoint. In his poetry, Graves developed a highly idiosyncratic voice based on his belief in a primal matriarchal principle that had been suppressed by rational, superficial, patriarchal values, a view in which he was influenced by the American poet **Laura Jackson Riding** (1901–91), with whom he lived from 1927 to 1939. He describes his beliefs in *The White Goddess* (1948). His poems were extensively revised by him throughout his life (five collected editions between 1938 and 1975). His two great historical novels, *I, Claudius* and *Claudius the God* (both 1934) are very highly regarded.

Gray, Thomas (1716–71) English poet. His best-known poem is

'Elegy Written in a Country Churchyard' (1751), a meditation on the graveyard at Stoke Poges, which is one of the most quoted from poems in the language.

Green, Henry [pseud. of Henry Vincent Yorke] (1905–73) English novelist. His strange, highly original novels have been much praised by his peers, notably UPDIKE and WAUGH. His most remarkable quality is his fluid and confident use of the rhythms and expressions of ordinary speech. The novels include *Living* (1929), *Loving* (1945) and *Back* (1946).

Greene, Graham (1904–91) English novelist, who is regarded as one of the greatest modern novelists. He converted to Roman Catholicism in 1926, and his religious beliefs (or disbeliefs: his 'faith' is indistinguishable from atheism for many) play an important part in his fictional world, the so-called 'Graham Greeneland', a seedy, often exotic world of spiritually tainted not-quite heroes. His wartime experiences as a British Intelligence Agent in Africa during World War II, a role ideally suited to Greene, also shaped his fiction. Greene's division of his novels into 'entertainments', e.g. *Brighton Rock* (1938), and works to be classed as more serious, e.g. *The Heart of the Matter* (1948), is generally disregarded by both readers and critics.

Greene, Robert (*c.*1558–92) English poet, dramatist and pamphleteer. Greene's tracts on the Elizabethen underworld are valuable for their descriptions of criminal life and language. He is also noted for his attack on SHAKESPEARE in his 'Groat's Worth of Wit' (1592), in which he warns his fellow university-educated dramatists against the 'upstart Crow' Shakespeare. The publisher of the tract apologized publicly for the remark.

Gregory, Lady Augusta (1852–1932) Anglo-Irish dramatist. She was a founder and director of the ABBEY THEATRE and a close friend of, and collaborator with, YEATS. Her plays, many of which are based on Irish legends, include *The Kiltartan Molière*

(1910) and *Irish Folk History Plays* (1912). Her memoir, *Our Irish Theatre* (1913), is a vivid and very entertaining account of the spectacular ego clashes of Anglo-Irish literary life.

Grieve, Christopher Murray *see* **MacDiarmid, Hugh**.

Grossmith, George (1847–1912) *and* **Weedon** (1852–1919) English theatricals and authors of *A Diary of a Nobody* (text by both, illustrations by Weedon), which first appeared (to immediate acclaim) in *Punch* magazine in 1892. The diary solemnly recounts the humdrum experiences, and small triumphs and disasters, of Charles Pooter, a lower-middle-class clerk, in suburban London. The work is generally regarded as a classic of English humour.

H

Haggard, Sir H[enry] Rider (1856–1925) English novelist. He wrote 34 adventure novels, of which *King Solomon's Mines* (1886) and *She* (1887) are the best known. The novels are exciting, well-constructed narratives, and occasionally display a strong empathy with African culture.

Haiku *see* **Basho**.

Hall, [Marguerite] Radclyffe (1883–1943) English novelist. Her novel *The Well of Loneliness* (1928) was one of the first significant works of fiction to describe lesbianism openly and sympathetically; it was banned in the UK until 1949, but not in the US. She also published four volumes of poems and seven other novels, notably *Adam's Bread* (1926).

Hallam, Henry (1777–1859) English historian. Contributions to the *Edinburgh Review* were followed by his *View of the State of Europe during the Middle Ages* (1818) and *The Constitutional History of England* (1827) to establish his reputation for solid learning, patient research, accuracy and impartiality. His *Introduction to the Literature of Europe* (1837–39) is a useful survey of literary history. His eldest son, **Arthur Henry Hallam** (1811–33), a youth of high promise who died suddenly at the age of twenty-two, is the subject of TENNYSON's poem *In Memoriam*.

Hammett, [Samuel] Dashiell (1894–1961) American novelist. Like Raymond CHANDLER (whom he influenced), he wrote tough 'hard-boiled' realistic crime novels, that are based on his own experiences as a Pinkerton detective and that won a wide following. Examples include *The Maltese Falcon* (1930), which featured the laconic private eye Sam Spade, and *The Thin Man* (1932), whose hero was the contrastingly urbane Nick Charles.

Hamsun, Knut (1859–1952) Norwegian novelist, poet and dramatist. His best-known novel is *Hunger* (1890), a vivid, almost surreal autobiographical work narrated by a starved clerk, which includes scenes set in the US, where Hamsun had worked as a tram conductor in Chicago. Other works, e.g. *Pan* (1894) and *Growth of the Soil* (1917), display a mystical absorption in nature that darkened in later years to support for the irrational, occult aspects of Nazism. He was awarded the NOBEL PRIZE for literature in 1920.

Hardenberg, Friedrich Leopold von *see* **Novalis**.

Hardy, Thomas (1840–1928) English novelist, short-story writer and poet. His novels are set for the most part in his native Dorset (the 'Wessex' of the novels). The greatest of the novels are *Far from the Madding Crowd* (1874), *The Return of the Native* (1878), *The Mayor of Casterbridge* (1886), *Tess of the D'Urbervilles* (1891) and *Jude the Obscure* (1896). Hardy was the first major English novelist to suffer from censorship; editors of the magazines in which many of the novels were originally published (in parts) often demanded cuts on the ground of propriety, which Hardy would later restore in volume form. Hardy's novels are generally characterized as gloomy studies of doomstruck characters struggling in vain against a hostile fate in an uncaring environment, and they usually end in death ('the President of the Immortals . . . had ended his sport with Tess'). The merits of the novels have been constantly debated since they were published; Henry JAMES, for example, described *Tess* as full of 'faults and falsity'. Few other novelists, however, have written prose that displays a more deeply moving empathy with all living creatures, an empathy that produced in his later years some of the greatest English poetry, e.g. *Wessex Poems* (1898), *Time's Laughing-stocks* (1909), *Satires of Circumstances* (1914) and *Winter Words* (1928). The *Collected Poems* (1930) contains more than 900 poems produced over a period of 60 years, poems of a quite remarkable variety of form, but all alike in their strange, dignified and lyrical descriptions of humankind and our tortured relationship with other forms of life and the environment. He is now ranked as one of the three great poets in English of the 20th century, the others being YEATS and ELIOT.

Hare, David (1947–) English dramatist. His plays include *Slag* (1970), *Knuckle* (1974), *Teeth 'n' Smiles* (1975), *Plenty* (1978), and 'films for television', *Licking Hitler* (1978) and *Dreams of Leaving* (1980). A recurring theme in Hare's work is the proposition that Britain lost a unique opportunity at the end of World War II for creating a genuinely egalitarian society. *See also* BOND, BRENTON.

Harington, Sir John (1561–1612) English writer. A godchild of Queen Elizabeth I, he was excluded from court in 1596 on account of his book *The Metamorphosis of Ajax*, written in the manner of RABELAIS and containing the first design for a water closet, but was allowed to return. He translated ARIOSTO's *Orlando Furioso* (1591) in heroic verse.

Harris, Frank (1856–1913) Irish-born Anglo-American writer and editor, whose best-known work is his autobiography *My Life and Loves* (1922–27), an entertaining, sexually explicit and thoroughly unreliable autobiography describing Harris's life as, among other things, a cowboy in the West and a literary editor in London. He edited the *Saturday Review* from 1894 to 98, and his friends (who usually became ex-friends) included WILDE, SHAW and WELLS.

Harris, Joel Chandler (1848–1908) American writer, whose Aesop-like 'Uncle Remus' stories, e.g. *Uncle Remus and Br'er Rabbit* (1906), are based upon a deep and sympathetic knowledge of the folklore of Southern Blacks.

Harris, Thomas (*c.*1940–) American novelist. His gripping thrillers, *Red Dragon* (1983) and *The Silence of the Lambs* (1988), are superbly plotted psychological studies of serial killers and their FBI hunters. *The Silence of the Lambs* was described by Roald DAHL as the 'best novel for years', and by another reviewer as a 'literary nasty'. The central character of these haunting studies of 'children of a nightmare' is the psychotic psychiatrist Dr Hannibal Lecter, a monstrous comic/macabre creation who has been described as a cross between Dracula and Sherlock Holmes.

Harte, [Francis] Bret[t] (1836–1902) American poet and short-story writer, noted especially for his shrewdly observed stories of Californian gold miners in *The Luck of Roaring Camp and Other Stories* (1870). The best of his humorous verse, e.g. 'Plain Language from Truthful James' (1870) is still highly regarded.

Hartley, L[eslie] P[oles] (1895–1972) English novelist. His novels include the *Eustace and Hilda* trilogy, i.e. *The Shrimp and the Anemone* (1944), *The Sixth Heaven* (1946), and *Eustace and Hilda* (1947). His best-known work is *The Go-Between* (1953), a subtle portrayal of social and sexual intrigue in Edwardian England.

Hasek, Jaroslav (1883–1923) Czech novelist and short-story writer. His masterpiece is *The Good Soldier Svejk* (1925), a brilliantly mordant PICARESQUE novel based on Hasek's own experiences as a soldier in the Austro-Hungarian army. Svejk's cunning talent for extracting himself from difficult situations resulted in him becoming an unofficial national symbol in 20th-century Czechoslovakia. Hasek's own improbable career included service in the Bolshevik Red Army as a political commissar.

Havel, Vaclav (1936–) Czech dramatist and statesman. Havel's plays of the 1960s and 1970s, e.g. *The Garden Party* (1963), used the techniques of the Theatre of the ABSURD to satirize the brutality and corruption of Czech communism, with an ORWELLian-like emphasis on the corruption of language under totalitarianism. Like KUNDERA and other Czech writers, he enjoyed a brief spell of artistic expression during the 'Prague Spring', but was imprisoned for several years after the Soviet invasion of 1968. In one of the most astonishing turnarounds in literary, political, or any careers, Havel was elected President of Czechoslovakia in 1990. *See also* IONESCO.

Hawthorne, Nathaniel (1804–64) American novelist and short-story writer. He was born in Salem, Massachusetts, where his ancestors had helped persecute the so-called 'Salem witches', and his consciousness of the dark side of New England Puritanism (*see also* EDWARDS) profoundly shaped his life and work. His masterpiece is *The Scarlet Letter* (1850), a psychological novel on the guilt-ridden consequences of adultery in 17th-century New England. Other notable novels include *The House of the Seven Gables* (1851), which also explores the dark recesses of his sense of ancestral guilt, *The Blithesdale Romance* (1852), a sardonic reworking of his experiences at the Brook Farm Transcendentalist colony, and *The Marble Faun* (1860), a historical novel set in Renaissance Italy. His short-story collections include *Twice-Told Tales* (1837) and *Mosses from an Old Manse* (1846). He also wrote comparatively light-hearted stories for children, e.g. *Tanglewood Tales* (1853).

Hazlitt, William (1778–1830) English essayist and critic. Highly influential in his own day, Hazlitt remains one of the most important literary critics, especially valued for his essays on his contemporaries and on SHAKESPEARE. His works include *Characters of Shakespeare's Plays* (1817), *Lectures on the English Comic Writers* and *Political Essays* (both 1818) and *The Spirit of the Age* (1825). His personal relations with his great contemporaries, e.g. WORDSWORTH, were often strained because of his impulsive nature and high opinion of the critic's worth.

Heaney, Seamus [Justin] (1939–) Irish poet and critic, regarded by many critics as the finest Irish poet since YEATS. Heaney's collections include *Eleven Poems* (1965), *Death of a Naturalist* (1966), *Wintering Out* (1972) and *Station Island* (1984). Brought up a Roman Catholic in Northern Ireland, Heaney now lives and works in the Republic of Ireland. The two dominant themes of his poetry are the recurring patterns of 'tribal revenge' rooted in Irish culture and the decay of traditional Irish country life.

Heine, Heinrich (1797–1856) German poet and critic. His masterpiece is his *Book of Songs* (1827), which includes some of the greatest lyric poems ever written, many of which have been set to music, notably by Schubert. One of his great achievements as a poet was to combine high lyricism with a dry sense of irony, as in 'The Lorelei'. He had a cautious friendship with MARX, who observed of Heine that poets were a breed apart. Although strongly radical in his politics, Heine had an equally strong (and prophetic) distrust of the intolerance and anti-Semitism of German radicalism.

Heliodorus (*fl.* 3rd–4th century AD) Greek romance writer born in Syria. His romance *Aethiopica* (so called because its opening and closings scenes are set in Ethiopia), also called *The Loves of Theagenes and Chariclea*, is written in poetic prose and has a well-managed plot, well-drawn characters and abounds in scenic descriptions and vivid portrayals of manners and customs. It had a considerable influence on the writings of later authors such as CERVANTES.

Heller, Joseph (1923–) American novelist. His experiences as a USAF bombardier during World War II formed the factual basis for his first remarkable novel, *Catch–22* (1961), a grim, surrealist satire on military life and logic. His other novels include *Something Happened* (1974) and *Good as Gold* (1979).

Héloïse *see* **Abelard, Peter**.

Hemingway, Ernest (1899–1961) American novelist and short-story writer. His first important work was *The Sun also Rises* (1926), a novel set among what his friend Gertrude STEIN called the 'lost generation' of expatriate American writers and artists in 1920s Paris. His laconic narrative style, with its 'tough guy' dialogue and macho values, made a big impression on his contemporaries, an impression consolidated by his next novel, *A Farewell to Arms* (1929), a tragic love story set on the Italian Front during World War I (in which Hemingway served as an ambulance driver). His subsequent collections of short stories, *Men Without Women* (1927) and *Winner Take Nothing* (1933), were also highly acclaimed. He supported the Republican government during the Spanish Civil War, his reporting experiences there forming the basis for his great novel *For Whom the Bell Tolls* (1940). He settled in Cuba in 1945 and was sympathetic to Castro's revolution of 1959 (Castro won first prize in a 1960 fishing competition; Hemingway presented him with it). He committed suicide in the US in 1961. His influence on other American writers, both in prose and lifestyle, has been immense but often pernicious. He was awarded the NOBEL PRIZE for literature in 1954.

Henley, W[illiam] E[rnest] (1849–1903) English poet, critic and editor. Henley was an interesting minor poet with a talent for unusual rhymes. Some of his poems, e.g. 'Invictus', will always retain their popularity, but his role as a mentor to younger writers is more significant. Both KIPLING and STEVENSON (the latter based Long John Silver in *Treasure Island* on Henley) spoke feelingly of Henley's support and encouragement.

Henry, O *see* **O Henry**.

Herbert, George (1593–1633) English Anglican priest and poet. Herbert's poems were published posthumously as *The Temple: Sacred Poems and Private Ejaculations* (1633) and are among the greatest devotional poems in the language. He described his poems as 'a picture of the many spiritual conflicts that have passed betwixt God and my soul'. The poems display the characteristics of METAPHYSICAL POETRY in their subtle, paradoxical exploration of spiritual themes. The simple piety of Herbert's life and the intellectual power of his poetry makes him one of the most appealing of all English poets. The popularity of his work with both Puritans and High Anglicans in late 17th-century England was quite unusual.

heroic tragedy a form of TRAGEDY that became very popular during the RESTORATION. Such tragedies were usually written in bombastic rhymed couplets, and featured the adventures in love and war of improbably noble characters in exotic locations, past and present. The characteristic conflict at the heart of such plays was the clash between the equally imperious commands of love and duty. The first appearance of the form was DAVENANT's 'opera in the manner of the ancients', *The Siege of Rhodes*, in 1656. The form was used by dramatists of the stature of DRYDEN and OTWAY, but eventually collapsed under the satirical onslaught of VILLIERS' *The Rehearsal* in 1671.

Herrick, Robert (1591–1674) English Anglican priest and poet.

His sacred and secular poems were collected in a joint volume published during the Commonwealth period, *Hesperides* and *Noble Numbers* (both 1648). Many of the poems are surprisingly direct in their sympathy for the traditional (virtually pagan) customs of English country life. The delicate sensuality of his poems places him high among the English lyric poets. *See also* JONSON.

Hesse, Hermann (1877–1962) German-born Swiss novelist, short-story writer and poet. Hesse's fiction reflects his fascination with oriental mysticism, spiritual alienation and worldly detachment. In the 1960s, he was seen as a major prophet of 'alternative' culture values. His novels include *Steppenwolf* (1927), *Narziss and Goldmund* (1930) and *The Glass Bead Game* (1943). He was awarded the NOBEL PRIZE for literature in 1946. His works were blacklisted by the Nazis in 1943, but (as with JUNG, who influenced him) controversy remains active over his relationship with Nazism.

Heywood, Thomas (*c*.1574–1641) English dramatist. His two best-known plays are the DOMESTIC TRAGEDY *A Woman Killed with Kindness* (1603), once described as the first 'bourgeois tragedy', and an uproarious adventure comedy, *The Fair Maid of the West* (1600–1603). Charles LAMB described him as 'a sort of prose Shakespeare'.

Higgins, George V[incent] (1939–) American novelist and short-story writer. His experiences as a reporter and assistant district attorney in Boston form the background to Higgins's highly acclaimed crime fiction. Notable works include the novels *The Friends of Eddie Coyle* (1972) and *Impostors* (1986). Higgins's masterly low-life dialogue has no equal, and his sense of irony and fate has been compared to that of the great Greek tragedians.

Highsmith, Patricia (1921–95) American novelist. Her most famous creation is the charming villain Tom Ripley (virtually a psychopath), who features in such novels as *The Talented Mr Ripley* (1956) and *Ripley's Game* (1974).

Hill, Reginald (1936–) English novelist. His series of detective novels featuring the Yorkshire policemen Dalziel and Pascoe, e.g. *A Clubbable Woman* (1970) and *Bones and Silence* (1990), have been much admired for their skilful plotting, characterization, and sharp social comment on modern Britain.

Hilton, Walter *see* **Julian of Norwich, Dame**.

Hobbes, Thomas (1588–1679) English philosopher, whose materialist views were strongly influential on his contemporaries. He was born in the year of the Armada, and once noted that he and 'fear came into the world at the same time'. Hobbes's most notable work is *Leviathan* (1651), a study of society, observing that the life of man outside the constraints of civilized society is 'poor, nasty, brutish and short', and concluding that men live best under strong leadership (Cromwell became Lord Protector in 1653). A great deal of subsequent political theory, continuing into our own time, consists of attempts either to refute or accommodate Hobbes's bleak conclusions on human nature. Hobbes's prose is very fine, with a sure feel for the telling image: 'The Papacy is not other than the Ghost of the deceased Roman Empire, sitting crowned upon the grave thereof.' He wrote his autobiography in Latin verse when he was 85. *See also* Henry MORE.

Hochhuth, Rolf (1931–) German dramatist. The best known of his plays are *The Deputy* (1963), an attack on Pope Pius XII for his supposed unwillingness to condemn the Nazis' mass murder of the Jews during World War II, and *Soldiers* (1967), which, with no basis, implied that Winston Churchill was involved in assassinating the Free Polish leader, General Sikorski, who died in an air crash in 1943. The plays have little merit but are of interest as examples of the 'drama documentary' of the 1960s and 1970s.

Hoffmanstahl, Hugo von (1874–1929) Austrian poet, dramatist, and librettist for six of Richard Strauss's operas, e.g. *Elektra* (1909) and *Rosenkavalier* (1911). His works were rooted in a deep Roman Catholic faith and display a concern for artistic integrity and a growing concern for social issues. His plays, e.g. *The Tower* (1925), were highly praised by T.S. ELIOT.

Hogg, James (1770–1835) Scottish novelist and poet. Hogg was a self-educated shepherd (nicknamed the 'Ettrick Shepherd' by his contemporaries), who rapidly became a leading light of Edinburgh's literary world from 1810. Sir Walter SCOTT (who gave him early encouragement), and WORDSWORTH were among his friends. Hogg produced some quite remarkable works, including (his masterpiece) the novel *The Private Memoirs and Confessions of a Justified Sinner* (1824), a macabre study of religious mania and murder that has gained sharply in reputation this century, and *The Three Perils of Man* (1822), a bizarre and highly entertaining precursor of the 'sword and sorcery' genre. He also wrote some marvellous parodies of his fellow poets.

Holmes, Oliver Wendell (1809–94) American essayist, noted especially for the light, humorous discourses of *The Autocrat of the Breakfast Table* (1858) and its sequels, e.g. *The Professor at the Breakfast Table* (1860).

Holub, Miroslav (1923–98) Czech poet, critic and scientist. Widely regarded as one of Europe's greatest living poets, Holub's work combines a scientifically rigorous approach to observation with a vivid poetic imagination. Like that of all important East European poets after World War II, much of his work had to be published abroad until the 1989 Revolution. He published many volumes of verse and several important collections of essays, e.g. *The Dimension of the Present Moment and other Essays* (1990). His scientific works include *The Immunology of Nude Mice* (1989).

Homer (*c*.800 BC) Greek poet, author of the two great epic poems, *The Iliad*, the story of the Greek war against Troy, and *The Odyssey*, which describes the adventures of the Greek hero Odysseus (known to the Romans as Ulysses) on his voyage home from the war. The characters and events of the poems have had a profound influence on Western literature. Homer was reputedly blind, and born on the island of Chios, but nothing about him is known for certain, not even his existence—or sex; Samuel BUTLER (1835–1902) believed Homer was a woman.

Hood, Thomas (1799–1845) English poet. His humorous verses, e.g. *Odes and Addresses to Great People* (1825), were very popular in their day, and Hood is still recognized as a master of light, satirical, skilfully punning verse, as in 'Faithless Sally Brown'. Some of his serious poems, e.g. 'The Song of the Shirt', which exposed the appalling working conditions of seamstresses, and 'The Dream of Eugene Aram', a nightmarish study of a murderer, also achieved great popularity.

Hooker, Richard (*c*.1554–1600) English divine. His *Laws of Ecclesiastical Polity* (1593–97), written in response to Puritan attacks on Anglican moderation, remains the most readable theological work of its size in English, thanks to Hooker's beautifully constructed prose and humane tolerance.

Hopkins, Gerard Manley (1844–89) English Jesuit priest and poet. Hopkins converted to Roman Catholicism in 1866. His poems frequently express the keen conflict he felt between his desire to serve God as both priest and poet, and his deeply felt inadequacies, particularly in the 'Dark Sonnets' of the mid–1880s, e.g. 'No worst, there is none'. Other well-known poems are 'The Wreck of the Deutschland', inspired by the death of nuns in a shipwreck, and 'The Windhover', a spiritually charged celebration of a falcon hovering.

Horace [Quintus Horatius Flaccus] (65–8 BC) Roman poet and satirist. Like his friend VIRGIL, he looked to the literature of Greece for inspiration, but the sardonic, realistic and tightly controlled language of his poems' language is wholly Roman. His *Odes*, *Satires* and *Epistles* have been much imitated by poets of all ages, e.g. POPE.

Household, Geoffrey (1900–1988) English novelist and short-story writer. The typical Household narrative is an adventure story, frequently involving a lengthy pursuit or duel, written in the first person, and with revenge as the most common motivation. His masterpiece is *Rogue Male* (1939), in which the narrator sets out to assassinate Hitler; the sequel, *Rogue Justice*, following 42 years later. One of Household's most unusual gifts is his ability to create an atmosphere of conflict that borders chillingly on the supernatural, as in *The Dance of the Dwarfs* (1968). Also of note is his superb collection of short stories, *The Europe That Was* (1979), a masterly evocation of vanishing (or vanished) patterns of European life.

Housman, A[lfred] E[dward] (1859–1936) English poet and neo-classical scholar. Housman's poetic output was small: *A Shropshire Lad* (1896), *Last Poems* (1922), and *More Poems* (1936) are all slim volumes containing short, elegiac lyrics expressing a pessimistic outlook on life. The poems often describe young labourers or soldiers meeting an untimely end. He also spent 27 years of his life (1903–30) preparing an authorized five-volume edition of a very minor Roman poet, Manilius, a project that baffled his colleagues. His criticism of his fellow scholars' work could be extremely cutting, and is often very funny.

Howard, Henry, Earl of Surrey *see* **Surrey, Earl of**.

Howells, William Dean (1837–1920) American novelist, critic and editor. He wrote 35 novels of which the best known are *A Modern Instance* (1882), *The Rise of Silas Lapham* (1885) and *A Hazard of New Fortunes* (1890). The novels show a general progression towards a kind of Tolstoyan socialist idealism. He was very influential in his role as associate editor of *Harper's Magazine* (1886–91), and encouraged, among others, Mark Twain and Henry James.

Hudson, W[illiam] H[enry] (1841–1922) Argentinian-born British novelist and naturalist. His nonfiction works include *The Naturalist in La Plata* (1892), *Idle Days in Patagonia* (1893), and his fascinating account of his childhood, *Far Away and Long Ago* (1918). His masterpiece is the novel *Green Mansions* (1904), a strange tale of love and death set in the Venezuelan jungle.

Hughes, James Langston (1902–67) American poet. He is best known as a chronicler of the sufferings of poor urban Blacks. His works include *The Weary Blues* (1926) and *One-Way Ticket* (1949).

Hughes, Ted [Edward James Hughes] (1930–98) English poet, noted for his violent poetic imagery drawn from the natural world in such collections as *The Hawk in the Rain* (1957) and *Crow* (1970). Most of his poems about animals have bloody conclusions, which led one critic to conjecture that he would eventually run out of animal subjects. His appointment as POET LAUREATE in 1984 following the death of BETJEMAN was greeted with some surprise (his work, however, is no more death-haunted than Betjeman's). He married Sylvia PLATH in 1956, whose suicide in 1963 led to Hughes becoming the target of a peculiarly nasty campaign of vilification by self-appointed guardians of Plath's memory. His last collection of poems, *Birthday Letters* (1998) is concerned with that mariage and won the Whitbread Prize posthumously.

Hugo, Victor (1802–85) French novelist, dramatist and poet. The production of his play *Hernani* (1830), a highly romantic and unconventional poetic drama, was marked by inflamed squabbles between supporters and opponents of the new formally looser and more socially challenging drama. The ensuing controversy established Hugo as the leader of French literary romanticism. His best-known novels are *The Hunchback of Notre Dame* (1831) and *Les Misérables* (1862).

humours, theory of (in medieval medical theory) Any of the four body fluids: blood, phlegm, yellow (choleric) bile, and black (melancholic) bile. This theory is the basis for the comedy of humours, notably Ben Jonson's *Every Man in his Humour* (1598), in which the characters have names and behaviour appropriate to their eccentrically dominant 'humour' or personality trait. For humour in the modern sense, *see* WIT.

Hunt, [James Henry] Leigh (1784–1859) English poet and essayist. With his brother **John Hunt** (1775–1848), he founded in 1808 a very successful weekly paper called *The Examiner*, which promoted reformist politics. Hunt also produced some charming light verse, e.g. 'Jenny Kissed Me', and the two ingenious sonnets 'To a Fish' and 'A Fish Replies'. He published BYRON and SHELLEY when other editors regarded them as beyond the pale, and was very encouraging to KEATS. DICKENS used his less attractive characteristics as the basis for the character Harold Skimpole in *Bleak House*.

Huxley, Aldous [Leonard] (1894–1963) English novelist, short-story writer and essayist. His early novels and stories, e.g. *Crome Yellow* (1921) and *Mortal Coils* (1922), are sardonic, waspish satires on the brittle post-World War I world of English intellectual life. These and succeeding works, e.g. *Antic Hay* (1923) and *Point Counter Point* (1928), often feature thinly disguised portraits of Huxley's friends and associates, e.g. D. H. LAWRENCE and the critic **John Middleton Murry** (1889–1957), the latter seriously contemplating challenging Huxley to a duel over his portrayal as 'Burlap' in *Point Counter Point*. Huxley's masterpiece is *Brave New World* (1932), a chilling fable of a future totalitarian state based on a scientifically contrived caste system. Huxley's later works, e.g. the Utopian novel *Island* (1962), are rather more optimistic in tone. His nonfiction works include *The Doors of Perception* (1954) and *Heaven and Hell* (1956), in which he records the spiritual insights he claims to have received as a result of taking hallucinogenic drugs. *See also* Sir Thomas MORE.

I

Ibsen, Henrik (1828–1906) Norwegian dramatist. Ibsen's great plays fall into three groups: the early verse dramas, which culminated in *Brand* (1866) and *Peer Gynt* (1866); the plays of social realism dealing with such issues as venereal disease, municipal corruption and female emancipation, e.g. *A Doll's House* (1879), *Ghosts* (1881), and *An Enemy of the People* (1882); the late symbolic plays, e.g. *The Wild Duck* (1884), *The Master Builder* (1892), and *John Gabriel Borkman* (1896), in which the realism of the middle period is mixed with an introspective, disturbing symbolism which draws upon folk traditions. *Hedda Gabler* (1890) marked a powerful return to realism in its depiction of the menace of intellectual arrogance. Ibsen's plays have been heavily influential upon 20th-century drama. He particularly influenced SHAW, whose *Quintessence of Ibsenism* (1891) is a lively summation of Ibsen's achievement.

imagism a poetry movement of the early 20th century which advocated using everyday language and precise representation of the image of the subject discussed. Imagist poems were short and to the point, anti-ROMANTIC and anti-Victorian in tone, and could be on any subject under the sun (as in William Carlos WILLIAMS's

'The Red Wheelbarrow'). Prominent Imagists included Williams, Ezra POUND and Amy LOWELL, whose *Tendencies in Modern American Poetry* (1917) has the best introduction to the movement. Ford Madox FORD, who is sometimes described as an Imagist, had a row with Amy Lowell at a fund-raising Imagiste dinner, after which he claimed that no one really knew what an Imagist was.

Innes, Michael *see* **Stewart, J.I.M**.

interior monologue *see* **Richardson, Dorothy**.

Ionesco, Eugène (1912–94) Romanian-born French dramatist of the ABSURD. His plays include *The Old Soprano* (1950), *The Lesson* (1951) and *Rhinoceros* (1959), all of which have become firm favourites in the theatrical repertoire. Ionesco's passionate hatred of both left and right totalitarianism and his distrust of political didacticism have made him a rather isolated figure in French intellectual circles. When President HAVEL visited Paris in 1990, Ionesco pointed out (with great relish) that Havel was now being feted by the very intellectuals who had denounced his plays as giving ammunition to the right; a true absurdist situation.

Iron, Ralph *see* **Schreiner, Olive**.

Irving, Washington (1783–1859) American essayist and short-story writer. His best-known stories are 'Rip Van Winkle' and 'The Legend of Sleepy Hollow', both of which are included in *The Sketch Book of Geoffrey Crayon* (1820). He also wrote a five-volume biography of George Washington (1855–59).

Isherwood, Christopher (1904–86) English-born American novelist and dramatist. His best-known works are the novels *Mr Norris Changes Trains* (1932) and *Goodbye to Berlin* (1939), the latter forming the basis for the film *Cabaret* (1972). He also wrote works in collaboration with his friend AUDEN, e.g. the verse drama *The Ascent of F6* (1936).

J

Jacobean tragedy a development of REVENGE TRAGEDY in the Jacobean period. The distinction between 'Jacobean' and 'revenge' tragedy is a disputed one, hinging on the supposed wave of cynicism and pessimism that is alleged by some historians to have accompanied the accession of James VI of Scotland to the English throne, and the end of the Elizabethan era. The debate is a complex one, but it is undoubtedly the case that tragedies such as SHAKESPEARE's *Hamlet*, TOURNEUR's *The Revenger's Tragedy*, MIDDLETON's *The Changeling*, and WEBSTER's *The White Devil* and *The Duchess of Malfi*, are obsessed with political and sexual corruption to a virtually pathic degree. The language of these plays is highly sophisticated, ironic, and coldly brilliant.

Jacobs, W[illiam] W[ymark] (1863–1943) English novelist and short-story writer. Many of his stories are humorous, but he is particularly noted for the macabre little story 'The Monkey's Paw', in *The Lady of the Barge* (1902).

James, Henry (1843–1916) American-born British novelist, short-story writer and critic. James settled in England in 1869 and became a British citizen in 1914, after the outbreak of World War I. His works fall into three main groups: the first deals with the contrast between American innocence and brashness, and the older, more cynical European culture, e.g. *Daisy Miller* (1879) and *Washington Square* (1880); the second group examines, with often obsessive detail, the minutiae of English upper-class social life and character, e.g. *The Spoils of Poynton* (1897) and *The Awkward Age* (1899); the third group, e.g. *The Ambassadors* (1905) and *The Golden Bowl* (1904), returns to the American/European contrasts of the first period. (An alternative grouping of the works was said to be James the First, James the Second, and the Old Pretender.) James also wrote over 100 short stories, including the classic ghost story, *The Turn of the Screw* (1898). James's meticulous concern for finding exactly the right word to convey his precise meaning has often been ridiculed, but his concern for personal integrity and for making the right choice between right and wrong actions, and his profound understanding of the moronic nature of evil, e.g. in *What Maisie Knew* (1897), make him one of our greatest writers.

James, M[ontague] R[hodes] (1862–1936) English scholar and ghost-story writer. His stories, e.g. *Ghost Stories of an Antiquary* (1904) and *More Ghost Stories of an Antiquary* (1911), have a unique atmosphere: a mix of dry, scholarly wit (his protagonists are invariably old-fashioned, donnish gentlemen) with a horrifically reticent undertone of supernatural terror. His story 'Casting the Runes' was memorably filmed by Jacques Tourneur in 1957 as *The Night of the Demon*.

James, P. D. [pseud. of Phyllis Dorothy James White] (1920–) English novelist. Her crime novels, particularly those starring her poet/policeman Inspector Adam Dalgleish, have acquired a wide and appreciative following. The novels include *A Mind to Murder* (1963), *The Black Tower* (1975), *Death of an Expert Witness* (1977) and *A Taste for Death* (1986). The last, a sombre piece which is as much about religious faith as traditional detection, has been hailed as her masterpiece.

James, William (1842–1910) American philosopher, brother of Henry JAMES. His *The Varieties of Religious Experience* (1902) includes the phrase 'stream of consciousness', which has been adapted by literary critics to denote a fluxive method of narration in which characters voice their feelings with no 'obtrusive' authorial comment and with no orthodox dialogue or decription. The term has particular reference to the work of JOYCE and WOOLF.

Jarrell, Randall (1914–65) American poet, critic and author of a satirical novel on the piranha bowl of academic life, *Pictures from an Institution* (1954), which, like Kingsley AMIS's *Lucky Jim*, is an early example of the so-called CAMPUS NOVEL. His volumes of poetry include *Losses* (1948) and *The Woman at the Washington Zoo* (1960).

Jarry, Alfred (1873–1907) French dramatist of the ABSURD. The first performance of his anarchic farce *Ubu Roi* (1896), a savage and surreal version of *Macbeth*, is memorably described by YEATS in *The Trembling of the Veil* (1926). Supporters and opponents of Jarry's work came to blows as an actor impersonated an opening door. Jarry's subversive, extravagant and often brutal work has had much influence on modern drama.

Jeffers, [John] Robinson (1887–1962) American poet. The dominant theme in his poetry is his doctrine of 'Inhumanism', in which mankind is portrayed as being of little significance in the great wheel of uncaring natural forces. His works include *Roan Stallion* (1925) and several influential adaptations of Greek tragedies, e.g. *Medea* (1947).

Jerome, Jerome K[lapka] (1859–1927) English dramatist, essayist and novelist. His most enduring work is *Three Men in a Boat* (1889), a light-hearted tale of three men and a dog on a rowing holiday, which is regarded as a classic of humorous writing.

Johnson, Marguerite *see* **Angelou, Maya**.

Johnson, Dr Samuel (1709–84) English critic, lexicographer and poet. One of the greatest literary figures of the 18th century, his works include the *Dictionary of the English Language* (1755), a highly important edition of *Shakespeare* (1765), *Lives of the Most Eminent Poets* (1779–81), several wonderful essays, e.g. in *The Rambler* (1750–52), and the great verse satires *London* (1738) and *The Vanity of Human Wishes* (1749). In 1763 he met James BOSWELL. Johnson was the great moralist of the age, a devout Christian tormented by self-doubt, an English Tory with Jacobite sympathies, who once drank a toast to the 'next slave rebellion in the West Indies'; Boswell was dissolute, a rapacious sexual predator, associated with radicals, and was a Whiggish Scot who saw slavery as a necessary part of life. An unlikely friendship was formed, and Boswell began recording Johnson's conversations. After Johnson's death, Boswell published the greatest biography in the English language, his *Life of Samuel Johnson, L.L.D.* (1785). In 1773, Johnson and Boswell travelled to the Scottish Hebrides, the tour resulting in two books, Boswell's *Journal of the Tour of the Hebrides* (1785), and Johnson's *Journey to the Western Isles* (1775). Johnson's only novel, *Rasselas* (1759), is a melancholic little fable which sums up its author's philosophy thus: 'Human life is everywhere a state in which much is to be endured, and little to be enjoyed'. *See also* GARRICK, VOLTAIRE.

Johnston, Jennifer (1930–) Irish novelist. Her first (and best) novel, *The Captains and the Kings* (1972), a remarkable study of the doomed relationship between an old, haunted Anglo-Irishman and a young boy, has been very highly praised for its skilfully crafted blend of pathos and humour. Johnston's other novels include *The Gates* (1973), *Shadows on our Skin* (1977) and *The Invisible Worm* (1991).

Jonson, Ben[jamin] (*c.*1572–1637) English dramatist and poet. After a turbulent early life, in which he 'trailed a pike' in the Flanders campaign, and killed a fellow actor in a duel, Jonson settled down to writing the 'comedies of HUMOURS' (i.e. plays featuring characters who personify a particular quality or vice) that established him as one of the great dramatists. The plays are especially noted for their satirical dialogue. The most frequently staged examples are *Volpone* (1616), *The Alchemist* (1616) and *Bartholomew Fair* (1614). He was appointed the first POET LAU-

REATE in 1616, in which year he published a folio edition of his poetic and dramatic works, setting a highly important precedent: his friend SHAKESPEARE's first folio followed in 1623. Jonson was much admired by the younger generation of poets, such as HERRICK, who called themselves the 'Sons of Ben'.

Joyce, James [Augustine Aloysius] (1882–1941) Irish novelist and short-story writer. Educated in Jesuit schools and at Dublin University, he left Ireland in 1902, returning briefly twice, once for his mother's death and burial, and once to oversee the publication of his short stories. Their publication was suppressed from (justified) fear of libel, the collection finally appearing as *Dubliners* (1914) in London. (His first published work had been a collection of slight but charming lyrics, *Chamber Music*, in 1907). His first great novel, *Portrait of the Artist as a Young Man*, in which the hero, Stephen Dedalus, is based on Joyce himself, appeared in 1914–15. By the time his masterpiece, *Ulysses* (1922), was published in Paris, he was widely seen as a world-class writer. *Ulysses* was banned in the US until 1933, and in the UK until 1936. The novel describes the experiences of two men in Dublin during one day, 16 June 1904: Leopold Bloom, a Jewish advertisement salesmen, who represents the common man, and Stephen Dedalus, who reappears to represent the artist. The supposed 'difficulty' of the book has been much exaggerated. The structure is based on HOMER's *Odyssey*, and the text is saturated with literary references from Joyce's wide reading, but the book can be read and enjoyed with no recourse to scholarly explanation. The same cannot really be said of *Finnegans Wake* (1939), which uses a vast repertoire of difficult, punning and alliterative language to create an effect of all actual and possible human experience. The best way into it is to listen to Joyce's own recording of the 'Anna Livia Plurabelle' section of the wake. *See also* BECKETT, Dorothy RICHARDSON.

Julian of Norwich, Dame (*c*.1342–*c*.1413) English anchorite. Her *Sixteen Revelations of Divine Love* (1393) examines the contradiction between her mystical revelations of the proximity of Christ to her, and the chasm between Christ and man caused by the sins of humanity. T.S. ELIOT quoted her thoughts on the mystery of sin and redemption in his *Four Quartets* ('Little Gidding'): 'Sin is behovely [i.e. necessary], but all shall be well and all shall be well and all manner of things shall be well.' Julian was one of a number of 14th-century English mystical writers, notably the Augustinian **Walter Hilton** (d.1396), the hermit **Richard Rolle** (*c*.1300–1349); **Margery Kempe** (*c*.1373–*c*.1439), and the anonymous author of the much admired *Cloud of Unknowing*.

Jung, Carl Gustav (1875–1961) Swiss psychiatrist, who began his career as a follower of FREUD, but split with him after challenging Freud's concentration on the sex impulse. His theory of the 'collective unconscious', a sort of reservoir in the unconscious mind filled with memories and instincts common to all humans, and his use of the term 'archetype' to denote an image or symbol drawn from this store, have had a great influence on many writers, e.g. HESSE and PRIESTLEY. Jung also wrote some very interesting literary criticism, notably on SHAKESPEARE and JOYCE. Jung's relationship with the Nazi regime in Germany during the 1930s is still a matter of intense debate.

K

Kafka, Franz (1883–1924) Prague-born German novelist and short-story writer. His novels *The Trial* (1925) and *The Castle* (1926), and several of his short stories, notably 'Metamorphosis', are established classics of 20th-century literature. The atmosphere of his fiction, in which characters are often trapped in bureaucratic totalitarianism, is oddly prophetic of the era of the dictators; many of his family were to die in Hitler's camps. His unfinished novel, *Amerika* (1927), is a surprisingly light-hearted Chaplinesque affair set in the US (which he never visited).

Kalidasa (*fl.* 5th century) Indian poet and dramatist. One of the greatest of Indian dramatists, his *Sakuntala* ('The Fatal Ring'), when first translated into English in 1789 at once aroused interest in Sanskrit literature in Europe. He was also the author of two other plays—*Vikramorvaci* ('The Hero and the Nymph') and *Malavika and Agnimitra*—while two epics and other works are ascribed to him.

Keats, John (1795–1821) English poet. He abandoned his apprenticeship as an apothecary to concentrate on poetry in 1816, the year he met Leigh HUNT, who published the young poet's work in *The Examiner*. He also became friendly with many of Hunt's friends, notably SHELLEY. His poems were savagely attacked by *The Examiner*'s literary and political rivals; Keats seems to have been deeply affected by the criticism, which was based purely on class spite and cultural snobbery (the 'Cockney School' of poetry was one sneering description). Keats, who was never in good health, died of tuberculosis in Rome, where he is buried. Most of his great poems, e.g. 'The Eve of St Agnes' and 'To a Nightingale', are included in *Lamia and Other Poems* (1820).

Kemal, Yashar (1923–) Turkish (Kurdish) novelist and short-story writer, whose exhilarating tales of blood feuds, banditry and social change in rural Turkey have been labelled, with some justice, as Tolstoyan in characterization and landscape description (Kemal's paternal forebears were feudal lords, his mother's were brigands; at the age of five, he saw his father murdered). The novels include *Memed, my Hawk* (1955), *The Lords of Akchasaz* (1974) and *The Saga of a Seagull* (1976).

Kemble, 'Fanny' [Frances Anne Kemble] (1809–93) English writer and actress. A member of a remarkable theatrical dynasty, she made her debut at the age of twenty as SHAKESPEARE's Juliet. She retired on her marriage to an American plantation owner in 1834, but after their divorce in 1848 she returned to England and the stage. Her writings include plays, e.g. the tragedy *Francis I* (in which she acted the part of Louis of Savoy), autobiographical writings, e.g. *Journal of a Residence on a Georgia Plantation*, and works on the theatre, e.g. *Notes on Some of Shakespeare's Plays*.

Kempe, Margery *see* **Julian of Norwich, Dame**.

Keneally, Thomas (1935–) Australian novelist. His novels include *The Chant of Jimmie Blacksmith* (1972), a grim, bloody tale of a young aborigine's violent response to the shabby ambiguities of his role in white society; *Confederates* (1979), an American Civil War saga; and *Schindler's Ark* (1982), his remarkable nonfictional study of the unlikeliest Scarlet Pimpernel in history, Oskar Schindler, a German businessman whose Cracow factory became a place of refuge for imprisoned Jews. It was filmed (1996) by Steven Spielberg under the book's American title, *Schindler's List*.

Kennerly Jr, Thomas *see* **Wolfe, Tom**.

Kerouac, Jack (1922–69) American novelist. One of the best known of the BEAT GENERATION, his most popular work is the semi-autobiographical novel *On the Road* (1957), a typically meandering, episodic account of the ramblings across America of a young writer and his friend. His other works include *The Dharma Bums* (1958) and volumes of poetry.

Kierkegaard, Søren *see* **Existentialism**.

King James Bible *see* **Authorized Version**.

Kinglake, Alexander William (1809–91) English historian. Trained as a lawyer, he abandoned the law in 1856 after establishing a literary career with *Eothen* (1844), a journal of his travels in the east. He observed the Crimean War, and his monumental *History of the War in the Crimea* (8 vols 1863–87) established his reputation as a fine historian.

Kingsley, Charles (1819–75) English clergyman and novelist. His works include historical novels such as *Westward Ho!* (1855) and *Hereward the Wake* (1866), and reformist-orientated novels of industrial society such as *Alton Locke* (1850). His masterpiece, however, is his children's story *The Water Babies* (1863), a bizarre fantasy about a young chimney sweep's adventures in an underwater world (apparently after drowning). The work is popular with both children and FREUDians.

Kinsella, Thomas (1928–) Irish poet. His collections include *Another September* (1958), *Downstream* (1962) and *Peppercanister Poems: 1972–1978* (1979).

Kipling, Rudyard (1865–1936) Indian-born English short-story writer, poet and novelist. Born in Bombay, he was sent home to be educated, then returned to India where he rapidly made a name for himself as a superb journalist and caustic observer of Anglo-Indian society. He returned to England in 1889, where he achieved celebrity status with his poems of army life, *Barrack-Room Ballads* (1892), which established him as an unofficial spokesman for the (then much despised) British soldier and for the British Empire. From this period until his death, Kipling's reputation was to vary according to the political climate. In the 1940s, however, both T.S. ELIOT and George ORWELL, who differed widely in their politics, wrote essays giving high praise to his work, and subsequent critics have tended to agree with their opinions of his worth. The poems and short stories are particularly good, the best of which, e.g. the poems 'Gethsemane' and 'The Buddha at Kamakura', and the stories 'The Wish House' and 'They', have a strange, occasionally quite eerie beauty all their own. His most enduringly popular works are his children's books, e.g. *The Jungle Book* (1894) and *Just So Stories* (1902). He was awarded the NOBEL PRIZE for literature in 1907.

Kirkup, James (1923–) English poet and travel writer. The publication in 1977 of his poem 'The love that dares to speak its name' (describing the physical love of a centurion for Christ) in the British homosexual periodical *Gay News*, resulted in the first prosecution for blasphemous libel for half a century (*Gay News* was fined and its editor given a suspended prison sentence). His most highly regarded work is the title poem of *A Correct Compassion* (1952), a wonderful celebration of a masterly surgeon working 'with proper grace/Informing a correct compassion'. His autobiographical novel, *The Only Child* (1957), based on his working-class childhood, is a rarity among such works in being a largely happy one. He has also written widely on Japan, where he has taught for many years.

Koestler, Arthur (1905–83) Hungarian-born British author and journalist. A former Communist, he wrote widely on a range of interests, but his masterpiece, and one of the greatest of all political novels, is *Darkness at Noon* (1940), which describes the trial and execution (under Stalin's regime) of an old Bolshevik called Rubashov, who is a fictional composite of several real victims of Stalin, notably Nikolai Buhkarin, former head of the Communist International. A believer in the right to euthanasia, Koestler and his wife died in a suicide pact.

Kundera, Milan (1929–) Czech novelist. His novels include *The Unbearable Lightness of Being* (1985), which is set against the background of repression that followed the Soviet invasion of Czechoslovakia in 1968, and *Immortality* (1991).

Kyd, Thomas (1558–94) English dramatist. His most important work is his REVENGE TRAGEDY *The Spanish Tragedy* (1588–89), which was very popular on the early 17th-century stage and very influential on the work of many dramatists, most notably on

SHAKESPEARE, whose *Titus Andronicus* (1592–93) is modelled on the Kyd play. (Kyd may also have written a lost *Hamlet*, on which it is suggested Shakespeare's play was based.)

Kyd's history is a curious one. With Shakespeare, he was attacked by Robert GREENE in Greene's *Groats-worth of Wit* (1592) as one of a new breed of non-university educated dramatists who were subverting the livelihood of their betters. He became closely associated with Christopher MARLOWE, with whom he lodged for a while, and was arrested and tortured in 1593 following the discovery of some papers, attributed to Marlowe by Kyd, denying the divinity of Christ. Kyd was released a month after Marlowe's murder in the same year, and died in poverty the following year; his parents refused to administer his estate.

L

Lacan, Jacques *see* **Structuralism**.

Lamb, Charles (1775–1834) English essayist and critic. Lamb was a much loved friend of HAZLITT, Leigh HUNT, WORDSWORTH and COLERIDGE, and many of his writings display the great charm his friends describe. With his sister **Mary Anne Lamb** (1764–1847), he wrote a prose version for children of SHAKESPEARE's plays, *Tales from Shakespeare* (1807), which has retained its popularity. In 1796, in a fit of insanity, Mary killed their mother, and Charles looked after her until his death. His *Specimens of English Dramatic Poets* (1808) was an important contribution to the reasessment of Shakespeare's contemporary dramatists.

Lampedusa, Giuseppe di (1896–1957) Italian novelist. His most famous work is *The Leopard* (1958), which describes the decline of aristocratic society in Sicily following the island's annexation by Garibaldi in 1860 during his unification of Italy.

Lancaster, Sir Osbert (1908–86) English cartoonist and author of several satirical studies of British architectural history, e.g. *Progress at Pelvis Bay* (1936) and *Draynfleete Revealed* (1949). Lancaster's reputation as one of the deadliest and wittiest critics ever of architectural folly is secure. His two autobiographies, *All Done from Memory* (1953) and *With an Eye to the Future* (1967), are minor classics of the genre. His aesthetic tastes largely matched those of his friends BETJEMAN and WAUGH.

Landor, Walter Savage (1775–1864) English poet and essayist, noted for his classically inspired lyrics and epigrams, and for his *Imaginary Conversations* (1824–29), a collection of around 150 imagined dialogues between such people as Francis BACON and Richard HOOKER, and DANTE and Beatrice. DICKENS used him as the model for the bad-tempered yet lovable eccentric Boythorne in *Bleak House*. *See also* SPENSER.

Lang, Andrew (1844–1912) Scottish scholar, essayist and poet, remembered chiefly for his anthropological works, e.g. *Myth, Ritual and Religion* (1887), which FREUD drew from, and his fairy stories for children, e.g. *The Blue Fairy Book* (1889).

Langland, William (*c*.1332–*c*.1400) English poet, reputed author of the allegorical religious poem *Piers Plowman*. Virtually nothing is known of Langland for certain. The poem, written in alliterative verse, is one of the greatest works in medieval literature and contains passages of great beauty.

Lanier, Sidney (1842–81) American poet, noted for his study of the connection between music and poetry, *The Science of English Verse* (1880), and for his verse collection, *Poems* (1877), which experiments with metrical forms that resemble musical forms.

Lardner, Ring (1885–1933) American journalist and short-story writer, whose stories of American low life, e.g. *What of It?* (1925), are noted for their cynical wit.

Larkin, Philip [Arthur] (1922–85) English poet. His early verse e.g. *The North Ship* (1945), shows the influence of YEATS. His later, far greater poems, owe more to the influence of HARDY, but Larkin's later voice, as became apparent in *The Less Deceived* (1955), is all his own: a dark, sardonic lyricism combined with disconcertingly colloquial turns of phrase. Two further important volumes followed: *The Whitsun Weddings* (1964) and *High Windows* (1972), establishing him as the greatest of all postwar English poets. Larkin's poetry is wryly observant of social change, e.g. 'Sexual intercourse began in 1963/Somewhere between the end of the Lady Chatterley ban,/And the Beatles' first LP' (from 'Annus Mirabilis'), and is often very bleak. Larkin also wrote two novels, *Jill* (1946) and *A Girl in Winter* (1947); a collection of essays on jazz, *All What Jazz?* (1970); and edited *The Oxford Book of Twentieth Century Verse* (1971), an exhilaratingly offbeat anthology.

Law, William (1686–1761) English divine. His masterpiece is *A Serious Call to a Holy and Devout Life* (1728), which uses sharply drawn portraits ('characters') to illustrate how the Christian life should be lived (and how it should not). Law's beautifully simple prose, and gentle, undogmatic tone, have been highly and deservedly praised.

Lawrence, D[avid] H[erbert] (1885–1930) English novelist, poet and short-story writer. Brought up in a poor mining community in Nottingham, he attended university there with the aid of a scholarship. His novels, e.g. *Sons and Lovers* (1913), *The Rainbow* (1915) and *Lady Chatterley's Lover* (1928), caused much controversy for their frank treatment of sex, the last book not being published in its full four-letter form until 1960, when it was the subject of an unsuccessful prosecution for obscenity. Opinions about Lawrence's novels are sharply divided: his stirringly eloquent attack on the damage done to human relations by industrial society, his desire for a closer union between man and nature, most movingly expressed in his poems, e.g. *Birds, Beasts and Flowers* (1923), and for sexual honesty have been widely praised, but others are repelled by his CARLYLE-like worship of elemental forces and exaltation of the darker impulses within us. His dialogue can often be wildly (but unintentionally) comic in his novels, a fault not evident in his collection of short stories, e.g. *The Prussian Officer* (1914). Lawrence and his wife Frieda spent most of their married life outside England, and he wrote several fine travel books, notably *Etruscan Places* (1932).

Lawrence, T[homas] E[dward] (1888–1935) English soldier, scholar and writer, known as 'Lawrence of Arabia' for his role as a leader of irregular Arab forces in the war against the Turks (1916–18). His masterpiece is *Seven Pillars of Wisdom* (1926), which blends reminiscences of the war with an account of his spiritual growth. Opinions of Lawrence's character vary dramatically, from Winston Churchill's 'one of the greatest beings alive in our time', to Lawrence DURRELL's 'disgusting little thing'. *See also* RATTIGAN.

Lear, Edward (1912–88) English poet and painter. An accomplished watercolourist (he gave drawing lessons to Queen Victoria), he travelled widely and published accounts of his travels, e.g. *Illustrated Excursions in Italy* (1846), but he is particularly noted for his ingenious and amusing nonsense verse, especially in limerick form, e.g. *Book of Nonsense* (1846) and *Botany and Alphabets* (1871) which includes 'The Owl and the Pussycat'.

Leavis, F[rank] R[aymond] (1895–1978) English literary critic, who, with his wife **Q[ueenie] D[orothy] Leavis** (1906–81), made a major impact on literary criticism from the early 1930s on, through such works as *New Bearings in English Poetry* (1932) and *The Great Tradition* (1948). Their critical journal *Scrutiny* (1932–53) lambasted the modern age of mass culture and advertising, which they saw as destructive of the true 'organic' culture of Old England. The Leavises promoted the close 'practical' study of the texts of a severely limited group of authors, principally Jane AUSTEN, George ELIOT, Henry JAMES, Joseph CONRAD, and, latterly, Charles DICKENS, as charts for a moral 'serious' way of living. Unfortunately, they argued their case in a vicious, intolerant and egoistic manner that tended to negate their case for the humanizing influence of great literature.

Le Carré, John [pseud. of David John Cornwell] (1931–) English novelist. Le Carré's novels are sombre anti-romantic narratives of Cold War espionage, and usually have as their chief protagonist a disillusioned, cynical spy, e.g. *The Spy Who Came in from the Cold* (1963) and *Smiley's People* (1980). Many of his novels have been filmed.

Le Guin, Ursula K[roeber] (1929–) American novelist and short-story writer, who is regarded as one of the leading 20th-century science fiction and fantasy authors. Her works include the 'Hainish' or 'Hain' series of novels, e.g. *The Left Hand of Darkness* (1969), an exploration of human sexuality through alien eyes, and *The Dispossessd* (1974), an intriguing study of political systems. Her *Earthsea* trilogy for children, *A Wizard of Earthsea* (1968), *The Tombs of Atuan* (1971) and *The Farthest Shore* (1972), has become a modern classic.

Lehmann, Rosamond [Nina] (1901–90) English novelist. Her best-known novels are *A Note in Music* (1930), which caused controversy in its open treatment of homosexuality, *The Weather in the Streets* (1936), more frank sex plus an abortion, and *The Ballad and the Source* (1944), a study of adult sexuality seen through the eyes of an innocent child, which is generally regarded as her masterpiece.

Lem, Stanislaw (1921–) Polish novelist, critic and scientist. Lem's critically acclaimed science fiction novels include *Cyberiad*

(1967) and *Solaris* (1961). The latter novel, in which the crew of a space station circling a planet covered by a sentient ocean experience what they take to be hallucinations caused by the ocean, was made into a remarkable film by the Russian director Andrei Tarkovsky in 1972. The image of the ocean, and the crew's difficulties in communicating with it, serve as an extended metaphor for communication between man and God, a theme central to many Slav writers' fiction.

Lennox, Charlotte (1720–1804) American-born English novelist and dramatist. Her best-known work is the novel *The Female Quixote* (1752), a comedy modelled on CERVANTES' great novel, that was very popular in its day. Her work was praised by both FIELDING and her friend Dr JOHNSON, the latter crowning her with laurel at a BLUESTOCKING party to celebrate the publication of her first novel, *Harriot Stuart* (1751).

Lermontov, Mikhail Yurievich (1814–41) Russian novelist and poet. His works include a verse play, *Masquerade* (1842), and several very fine poems, e.g. 'The Novice', 'The Demon' and 'A Wish', the last reflecting his interest in things Scottish (he was of Scottish, 'Learmont', descent). He was exiled to the Caucasus after writing a poem on PUSHKIN's death in 1837; allowed to return to St Petersburg, he was then re-exiled after fighting a duel. His masterpiece is his novel *A Hero of our Time* (1840), a brilliant study of a disaffected, Byronic young aristocrat (like many Russians of the time, Lermontov was fascinated by BYRON's life and work). Like Pushkin, his life ended prematurely in a duel.

Lessing, Doris [May] (1919–) English novelist and short-story writer. Her novels include the *Children of Violence* quintet, beginning with *Martha Quest* (1952) and ending with *The Five-Gated City* (1969). Her most famous work is the seminal feminist novel, *The Golden Notebook* (1962). She has also written science fiction novels, e.g. *Briefing for a Descent into Hell*

(1971). *The Good Terrorist* (1985), a stunning account of the self-deception involved in political fanaticism, marked a new and intriguing departure in her work.

Lessing, Gotthold Ephraim (1729–81) German dramatist and critic. His plays include three important tragedies, *Miss Sara Sampson* (1755), an adaptation of LILLO's *The London Merchant*; *Emilia Galotti* (1772), a study of sexual obsession and oppression; and *Nathan the Wise* (1779), a remarkable plea for religious tolerance (the central character is modelled on Lessing's friend, the Jewish philosopher Moses Mendelssohn, grandfather of Felix Mendelssohn). Lessing's critical work is of great significance in the development of German ROMANTICISM, particularly his defence of SHAKESPEARE against the NEOCLASSICAL theorists of France. Lessing remains one of the most interesting and attractive personalities of German literature.

Levi, Primo (1919–87) Italian novelist, short-story writer and poet. His most famous work is his autobiographical trilogy, *If This is a Man* (1947), *The Truce* (1958) and *The Periodic Table* (1975). Levi was a survivor of Auschwitz, and his deeply moving writings on the subject, e.g. the first volume of his autobiography, are among the key texts of the 20th century. His *The Drowned and the Saved* was published posthumously in 1988 following Levi's suicide.

Levi-Strauss, Claude *see* **Structuralism**.

Lewis, C[live] S[taples] (1898–1963) English novelist and critic. His works include *The Allegory of Love* (1936), an important study of medieval literature; works of (conservative) Christian apologetics, e.g. *The Problem of Pain* (1940); and three science fiction novels, e.g. *Out of the Silent Planet* (1938). He is best remembered for his enchanting *Narnia* stories for children, e.g. *The Lion, the Witch and the Wardrobe* (1950), and for a 'spiritual' autobiography, *Surprised by Joy* (1955), both of which have been successfully dramatized for television, theatre and the cinema.

Lewis, Norman (1914–) English novelist and travel writer. His travel books include two modern classics of the genre, *A Dragon Apparent* (1952), on Vietnam, and his book on Burma, *Golden Earth* (1952). His novels include *A Small War Made to Order* (1966), a chilling study of the Bay of Pigs invasion of Cuba, and *The Sicilian Specialist* (1975), a thinly fictionalized account of President Kennedy's assassination, which was reputedly withdrawn from sale in several American cities following a Mafia ban on the book. Lewis regards as his main achievement the exposure of the genocidal campaign that has been waged against Brazilian Indians ('Genocide in Brazil' in *A View of the World*, 1986). He is one of our finest living writers.

Lewis, Sinclair (1885–1951) American novelist. His work is particularly noted for its satirical view of the self-righteous Philistinism of small-town American life. His best-known novels are *Main Street* (1920), a study of the monotonous life within a mid-West town appropriately called Gopher Prairie, *Babbitt* (1922), a searching and disturbing depiction of an average man's rebellion and consequent submission to conformity (the name 'Babbitt' has come to denote the average, conformist, 'don't make waves' man), and *Elmer Gantry* (1927), a still unsurpassed exposé of the dark, hypocritical side of American evangelism. Other notable novels include *Dodsworth* (1929) and *It Can't Happen Here* (1935). Lewis became the first American to win the NOBEL PRIZE for literature in 1930.

Lewis, [Percy] Wyndham (1882–1957) English painter, novelist and critic. He was a leader of the short-lived Vorticist movement and major contributor and editor of the two issues of its magazine, *Blast* (1914), in which he advocated a departure from traditional Victorian values. His use of violent colour and severe angularity in his paintings is reminiscent of Italian FUTURISM. Later works include some outstanding portraits, notably that of T.S. ELIOT (1938). His best-known fictional work is the novel *Apes of God* (1930), a withering satire on his intellectual contemporaries. Lewis was very much a singular figure described by AUDEN as 'that lonely old volcano of the right'.

Lillo, George (1693–1739) English dramatist. He wrote seven plays, the most important of which is *The London Merchant*, or *The History of George Barnwell* (1731), a DOMESTIC TRAGEDY which had great influence throughout Europe, most notably on Gotthold LESSING, whose adaptation had great success in Germany (DIDEROT was also much influenced by the work).

Li Shizheng *see* **Duoduo**.

literary ballad *see* **ballad**.

Llosa, Mario Vargas *see* **Vargas Llosa, Mario**.

Lodge, David (1935–) English novelist and critic. His best-known novels are the highly entertaining satires on academic life, *Changing Places* (1975) and *Small World* (1984). His novel *Nice Work* (1988) is a remarkable hybrid of the academic novel with the 19th-century 'condition of England' tradition, and contains many shrewd (and very funny) observations on modern British life.

London, Jack (1876–1916) American novelist and short-story writer. Born in San Francisco, he led an adventurous early life as a sailor, tramp and goldminer, before becoming a writer. His best-known works are the bloodily Darwinian dog stories *The Call of the Wild* (1903) and *White Fang* (1906); a documentary account of life in the London slums, *The People of the Abyss* (1903); and *The Iron Heel* (1908), a prophetic novel about future totalitarianism. London described himself as a socialist, but his 'blond beast' heroes and their ideals have more in common with Nazi thinking than with modern democratic socialism. His rarely read novel *The Mutiny of the 'Elsinore'* (1914), for example, is an unsavoury fable about white racial supremacy.

Longfellow, Henry Wadsworth (1807–82) American poet. Several of his poems, e.g. 'The Wreck of the Hesperus', 'The Village Blacksmith' and 'Excelsior!' were among the most popular poems of the 19th century. His narrative poems on American legends and folk tales, e.g. *Evangeline* (1849) and *The Song of Hiawatha* (1858), were also extremely popular. Hiawatha, thanks to its hypnotic unrhymed rhythms, 'By the shore of Gitche Gumme,/ By the shining Big-Sea-Water', became one of the most parodied poems of all time (e.g. by CARROLL). Several of Longfellow's phrases, e.g. 'Ships that pass in the night' (*Tales of a Wayside Inn*, 1874), have become firmly embedded in the English language.

Lorca, Federigo Garcia (1899–1936) Spanish poet and dramatist. His dramatic masterpiece is his trilogy of tragedies on the frustrated and oppressed life of Spanish women, *Blood Wedding* (1939), *Yerma* (1934) and *The House of Bernarda Alba* (1936). His poetry was heavily influenced by SURREALISM, e.g. in *Poet in New York* (1940). His gypsy songs, especially *Romancero Gitano* ('Gipsy Ballads', 1928, 1935) are still highly popular in Spain. Lorca was killed by Fascist forces near the beginning of the Spanish Civil War. *See also* BOWLES.

Lovelace, Richard *see* **Cavalier Poets**.

Lowell, Amy (1874–1925) American poet and critic. She became an enthusiastic member of the IMAGIST school of poetry after visiting England in 1913, where she met and befriended Ezra POUND who was to coin the term 'Amy-gism' ('When I get through with that girl she'll think she was born in free verse'). She described her verse as 'unrhymed cadence' and became a very popular figure on the American lecture circuit. Her volumes of poetry include *Sword Blades and Poppy Seed* (1914) and *Men, Women* *and Ghosts* (1916). Her critical works include *Tendencies in Modern American Poetry* (1917).

Lowell, James Russell (1819–91) American poet, essayist and diplomat. His best-known work, inspired by his fervent abolitionism, is contained in *The Biglow Papers* (1848, 1867). His verse is written in 'Yankee' dialect, and includes crushing satires against the pro-slavery lobby: 'It's wal enough agin a king/To dror resolves an' triggers,/But libbaty's a kind o' thing/Thet don't agree with niggers.'

Lowell, Robert [Traill Spence] (1917–77) American poet. Lowell's verse is intensely personal, with an occasionally impenetrable private symbolism. Notable volumes include his first, *Land of Unlikeness* (1944), and *Life Studies* (1959) and *Near the Ocean* (1967). He was a conscientious objector during World War II, and played an active role in opposing the Vietnam war.

Lowry, [Clarence] Malcolm (1909–57) English novelist and poet. Lowry's novels, e.g. *Ultramarine* (1933) and *Under the Volcano* (1947), often feature thinly veiled accounts of incidents from his own adventurous life. Alcoholism is a major theme in his much revised work. His *Selected Poems* appeared in 1962.

Lurie, Alison (1926–) American novelist, noted for her witty, ironic satires centred on the middle-class liberal way of life. Typical examples are *Love and Friendship* (1962), *Imaginary Friends* (1967) and *The War Between the Tates* (1974).

Lyly, John (*c.*1554–1606) English dramatist and prose romance writer. His romances, *Euphues, the Anatomy of Wit* (1579) and *Euphues and his England* (1580), are for the most part now unreadable, but were highly popular in Elizabethan times and had some influence on the development of the English novel. They consist mainly of conversations and observations on love, in language that came to be described as 'Euphusitic', a style characterized by an exaggerated use of antithesis and alliteration.

M

Macaulay, [Dame] Rose (1881–1958) English novelist, essayist and travel writer. Her post-World War I novels, e.g. *Dangerous Ages* (1921), are witty social satires that were very popular in their day. She underwent a spiritual conversion to Higher Anglicanism in the late 1940s, an experience reflected in what is held to be her best novel, *The Towers of Trebizond* (1956).

Macaulay, Thomas Babington (1800–1859) English essayist and historian. Macaulay's writings were very popular with the 'middlebrow' reading public of Victorian times, reflecting as they do, e.g. in *Essays Critical and Historical* (1834), a view of human society as a steady movement from barbarism to the triumph of the enlightened 19th-century middle classes. This view steadily lost ground from the 1880s onwards, when Macaulay's tone came to be seen as insufferably smug. He was created Baron Macaulay in 1857.

McCarthy, Mary (1912–89) American novelist, short-story writer and critic. Her most famous novel is *The Group* (1963), the narrative of which deals with the lives and careers of a group of upper-middle-class female university students, and which created a mild stir in its open, matter-of-fact account of female sexuality. *See also* Edmund WILSON.

McCullers, Carson (1917–67) American novelist and short-story writer. Her works include *The Heart is a Lonely Hunter* (1940), *Reflections in a Golden Eye* (1941), and the short-story collection *The Ballad of the Sad Café* (1951). Her central characters are usually loners and misfits, living in what she called 'spiritual isolation'.

MacDiarmid, Hugh [pseud. of Christopher Murray Grieve] (1892–1978) Scottish poet and critic. He was expelled from the

Scottish Nationalist Party in the 1930s for Communist sympathies, and shortly afterwards from the Communist Party for Nationalist sympathies. His masterpiece is *A Drunk Man Looks at the Thistle* (1926), a triumphant allegory of awakening Scottish consciousness that inspired many Scottish writers of the 1920s and 1930s. More broadly influential was his *First Hymn to Lenin* (1931), the first great leftist poem of the decade. His scathing epigram on the dilettante revolutionism of AUDEN, etc, 'Epitaph on British Leftish Poetry, 1930–40', remains one of the best short political poems of the 1930s.

Macdonald, George (1824–1905) Scottish novelist and poet, remembered chiefly for his children's stories, *At the Back of the North Wind* (1871) and *The Princess and the Goblin* (1872), and for two adult fantasy novels, *Phantastes* (1858) and *Lilith* (1895). His work has had a marked influence on many 20th-century fantasy writers, notably C.S. LEWIS, who regarded him as an important allegorical writer.

MacGonagall, William (*c*.1830–*c*.1902) Scottish poet, renowned for his memorably awful doggerel verse. His poems are uniformly bad: the lines do not scan, and the subject matter, frequently a disaster of some kind, is loaded with bathos. A typical example of his work is 'The Tay Bridge Disaster', which commemorates the collapse of the railway bridge over the River Tay in 1879: 'Beautiful railway bridge of the silv'ry Tay/Alas, I am very sorry to say . . .' His poems were published posthumously in *Poetic Gems* (1934) and *More Poetic Gems* (1963). A curious feature of his verse is that it is virtually impossible to produce convincing imitations of it.

Machen, Arthur [Llewellyn] (1863–1947) Welsh writer of supernatural and horror stories. Representative collections include *The Great God Pan* (1894) and the nasty *The Three Imposters* (1895).

Machiavelli, Niccolò (1469–1527) Italian statesman and political theorist. His treatise on the art of ruling, *The Prince* (1513), takes a somewhat dim view of human nature, seeing humanity as essentially corrupt and therefore best ruled by whatever method ensures the stability of the state, even if the method is merciless cruelty. Machiavelli's treatise caused outrage, especially in its suggestion that the ruler should maintain a reputation for being virtuous while indulging in treachery and brutality, and his name came to be virtually synonymous in Elizabethan drama with that of the devil (he appears in the prologue to Marlowe's *Jew of Malta*, 1592). Machiavelli's comedy *Mandragola* (*The Mandrake*, *c*.1518), is a notably licentious piece.

Mackenzie, Sir [Edward Montague] Compton (1883–1972) English novelist. His best-known novels are *Sinister Street* (1914), a semi-autobiographical account of a privileged young man's life at Oxford University and in London's slums, and his series of very popular comic novels set in the Scottish Western Isles, e.g. *Whisky Galore* (1947) and *Rockets Galore* (1957). He also wrote two memorable novels on homosexual relationships, *Extraordinary Women* (1928) and *Thin Ice* (1956), and his Scottish nationalist sympathies surface in his six-volume *Four Winds of Love* (1937–45).

Mackenzie, Henry (1745–1831) Scottish lawyer and novelist. His most famous work is the extraordinarily weepy novel *The Man of Feeling* (1771), the hero of which is a sort of 18th-century 'new man' who bursts into tears at every onslaught on his emotions. An edition published by Henry Morley in London in 1886 gives a useful index of the different varieties of tears in the book. Mackenzie also wrote *The Man of the World* (1773) and the EPIS-TOLARY *Julia de Roubigné* (1777), and was on the committee that investigated MACPHERSON's 'Ossian' hoax.

Maclean, Sorley [Somhairle Macgill-Eain] (1911–96) Scottish

Gaelic poet, who is widely regarded as one of the leading Scottish poets of the 20th century. Influenced by English poetry and by Celtic literature, he has reinstated Gaelic as a poetic language, and his own translations into English, e.g. *Spring Tide and Neap Tide* (1977) from his Gaelic *Reothairt is Contraigh*, have brought his work to a wider readership.

Macleish, Archibald (1892–1982) American poet and dramatist. He was one of the 'lost generation' (*see* HEMINGWAY) of American poets in 1920s Paris, and the fashionable disillusionment of the period is reflected in *The Pot of Earth* (1925). Subsequent volumes of poetry include *Conquistador* (1932), *Frescoes for Mr Rockefeller's City* (1933) and *New Found Land* (1930), all of which follow the left-wing trend of the 1930s.

Macleod, Fiona [pseud. of William Sharp] (1855–1905) Scottish writer of Celtic fantasy tales set in the Scottish Western Isles. An operatic version of his eerie 'faery' play, *The Immortal Hour* (1900), set to music by the socialist composer, Rutland Boughton, enjoyed great popularity in the 1920s. The identity of 'Fiona Macleod' was kept secret during Sharp's lifetime (Sharp would wear a dress while writing in the Fiona persona).

McLuhan, Marshall *see* **Structuralism**.

MacNeice, [Frederick] Louis (1907–63) Irish poet and classical scholar. He was one of the leading 'AUDEN generation' poets. Representative 1930s collections include *Letters From Iceland* (1937 written in collaboration with Auden) and *Autumn Journal* (1938). His later poems, e.g. *Solstices* (1961), are suffused with a less optimistic view of life. His translations of the *Agamemnon* (1936) from AESCHYLUS' *Oresteia* and of GOETHE'S *Faust* (1951) are still highly regarded.

Macpherson, James (1736–96) Scottish poet. His supposed translations of early Scottish Gaelic verse, *Fragments of Ancient Poetry* (1760), *Fingal* (1762) and *Temora* (1763), the latter two allegedly by an ancient bard called **Ossian**, achieved extraordinary popularity. GOETHE quoted from them in *The Sorrows of Young Werther*, and Napoleon slept with the poems under his pillow. Macpherson certainly used some ancient Gaelic poetry as the basis for the poems, but they are unquestionably largely his own creation. AUDEN claimed that Macpherson's Ossianic verse is the forerunner of advertising prose.

magic realism a term often applied with particular reference to the work of certain South American novelists, notably Mario VARGAS LLOSA and Gabriel Garcia MARQUEZ, whose work combines deadpan description of the everyday world with (often equally deadpan) excursions into fantasy. Some European novelists have been characterized as 'magic realists', e.g. CALVINO and RUSHDIE. The techniques of magic realism have a long ancestry; CHESTERTON's novel *The Man Who Was Thursday* is a notable early 20th-century example, and there are clear links with the GOTHIC NOVEL. By 1991, there were signs that the form was losing its avant-garde appeal. The cult TV series of 1990, *Twin Peaks*, provided a useful example of the degeneration of the form in its knowingly dissonant double act between the wacky FBI agent (surreal) and the hick sheriff (soap character).

Mahfouz, Naguib (*c*.1911–) Egyptian novelist and short-story writer. Now long established as the most important modern Arab novelist, his novels include the controversial and allegorical *Awlad Haritna* (1959), which was initially banned in Egypt for its treatment of Islam, and *Miramar* (1967), the action of which is set against a daring exposé of the sordid reality of Nasserite socialism. He was awarded the NOBEL PRIZE for literature in 1988.

Mailer, Norman (1923–) American novelist and essayist. His first novel, *The Naked and the Dead* (1948), based on his experiences in World War II, was highly successful. Subsequent novels include *The Deer Park* (1955), the semi-autobiographical *An*

American Dream (1966) and *Ancient Evenings* (1983), an enormous work set in Ancient Egypt. His nonfiction works include *The Executioner's Song* (1977), a gruesome CAPOTE-style 'factional' study of the murderer Gary Gilmore and his execution.

Malamud, Bernard (1914–86) American novelist and short-story writer. His best-known work is *The Fixer* (1967), a tragic tale of anti-Semitism in Czarist Russia. Other works include the novels *The Natural* (1952), *The Assistant* (1957), *Dublin's Lives* (1979) and the short-story collection *The Magic Barrel* (1958).

Mallarmé, Stéphane (1842–98) French SYMBOLIST poet. His impressionistic FREE-VERSE works include *Afternoon of a Faun* (1876), which was set to suitably sensuous music by Claude Debussy. His literary theorizing, e.g. in *Verse and Prose* (1893), had a strong influence on the development of the SYMBOLISM movement.

Malory, Sir Thomas (*fl.* 15th century) translator, largely from French sources, of *Le Morte d'Arthur* (printed by CAXTON, 1485), a collection of Arthurian legends (*see* ARTHUR). The work includes several episodes, e.g. the quest for the Holy Grail, that have been recycled by generations of authors, e.g. TENNYSON and T.H. WHITE. The author has been traditionally identified with a rather violently inclined Warwickshire knight of that name, but the attribution is doubtful.

Mamet, David (1947–) American dramatist. Mamet's plays, e.g. *American Buffalo* (1977) and *House of Games* (1985), are engrossing and highly ingenious studies of bluff and double-cross among American low-life characters. *House of Games* was filmed in 1987 and directed by Mamet. He is regarded by many critics as one of the most talented modern American dramatists.

Mandelstam, Osip (1891–1938) Russian poet, associated with AKHMATOVA in the **Acmeist group**. The collections published in his lifetime are *Stone* (1913), *Tristia* (1925) and *Poems* (1928).

In 1934 he read a satirical poem about Stalin to a group of friends, and within a few days was sent into exile with his wife, Nadezhda. He died in Siberia, probably of typhoid. Nadezhda's two books describing her husband's life and work, *Hope Against Hope* (1971) and *Hope Abandoned* (1974), contain much fascinating detail about the Acmeist poets, and are among the great books of the century, affirming as they do the resilience of the human spirit.

Mandeville, Sir John (*c.*14th century) Supposed English author of *The Travels of Sir John Mandeville*, an eventful and thoroughly mendacious travel book that has charmed countless readers since its first appearance in the 14th century. The work is ostensibly an account of the author's travels in the Holy Land, but is actually a gathering together of various unlikely travellers' tales from Africa to India, e.g. of a race of people with no heads but eyes on their shoulders. The influence of the book was widespread (there are references to it in SHAKESPEARE's work, for example).

Mann, Thomas (1875–1955) German novelist, critic and essayist. His chief preoccupation was the role of the artist and the purpose of artistic creation in modern society. Representative works include the novella *Death in Venice* (1912), and the novels *The Magic Mountain* (1930), a parable of European cultural disintegration set in a sanatorium; *Mario and the Magician* (1930), an anti-Fascist allegory; *Lotte in Weimar* (1939), based on an incident in the life of his hero, GOETHE; and *The Confessions of the Confidence Trickster Felix Krull* (1954), a masterly PICARESQUE comedy. He was awarded the NOBEL PRIZE for literature in 1929 and fled Nazi Germany in 1933. He is now universally recognized as one of the great novelists.

Mansfield, Katherine [pseud. of Kathleen Mansfield Beauchamp] (1888–1923) New Zealand-born English short-story writer. She is widely recognized as one of the masters of the short-story form, and is frequently compared with CHEKHOV. The story collections are *In a German Pension* (1911), *Bliss* (1920), *The Garden Party* (1922), *The Dove's Nest* (1923) and *Something Childish* (1924). She married Middleton Murry in 1918; they had a rather strained friendship with D. H. LAWRENCE and his wife.

Marinetti, Filipo *see* **Futurism**.

Marlowe, Christopher (1564–93) English dramatist and poet. He was one of the first English dramatists to use BLANK VERSE to great dramatic and poetic effect in his plays, the most famous of which are *Tamburlaine the Great* (1590) and his masterpiece, *Doctor Faustus* (1604). He also wrote some very fine classically inspired poetry, e.g. *Hero and Leander*, published posthumously in 1598, and the superb lyric 'Come Live with me, and Be My Love'. He was probably an atheist (*see* KYD), and was also probably a secret agent in the employ of the Elizabethan government at one stage. He was killed in a tavern brawl. SHAKESPEARE paid him a fine tribute in *As You Like It*: 'Dead Shepherd, now I find thy saw of might: / "Who ever lov'd that lov'd not at first sight?"'

Marquez, Gabriel Garcia (1928–) Colombian novelist. His masterpiece is *One Hundred Years of Solitude* (1967), a vivid narrative of the lives of a family in a decaying, provincial village. Marquez is generally regarded as the greatest practitioner of MAGIC REALISM. His novel *The General in his Labyrinth* (1990), a fictionalized biography of Simon Bolivar, the hero of Latin American independence, seemed to many critics to mark a new departure in his work in its sombre, realistic approach to its subject. He was awarded the NOBEL PRIZE for literature in 1982.

Marquis, Don[ald Robert Perry] (1878–1937) American newspaper columnist, author of several books, e.g. *archys life of mehita-*

bel [sic] (1934), narrated by a cockroach, Archy, often featuring an alley cat called Mehitabel, and with a minor cast drawn from all parts of the animal kingdom. The poems (written in lower case as Archy cannot use the shift keys) display a rare combination of sharp wit and knockabout humour, with flashes of remarkable lyricism. Marquis remains one of the most underrated American poets.

Marvell, Andrew (1621–78) English poet. A (passive) supporter of Parliament during the English Civil War, Marvell became member of parliament for Hull in 1659, a position he held until his death. His verse satires were much enjoyed by the wits of the day, even by those whose vices were attacked. His 'Last Instructions to a Painter', for example, a coldly brilliant assault on the moral and political corruption of the court, was particularly liked by Charles II. His strange, METAPHYSICAL poems, e.g. 'The Garden' and 'Upon Appleton House', display an enormous talent for symbolism and metaphor, and are now very highly regarded. His poem of 1650 celebrating Cromwell's suppression of the Irish Rebellion, 'An Horatian Ode upon Cromwell's Return from Ireland', remains one of the great political poems of all time, in its cool, restrained appreciation of Cromwell's stature.

Marx, Karl (1818–83) German philosopher. His theories on class struggle dominated 20th-century political thought from the Bolshevik Revolution of 1917 to the collapse of the Communist regimes in Eastern Europe in 1989–90. *Das Kapital*, his study of the economics of capitalism, appeared in 1867; subsequent volumes, edited by **Friedrich Engels** (1820–95), appeared in 1885 and 1895. *Das Kapital* is the most unread and unreadable influential book of all time. Marx himself seems to have been bored stiff by it. His literary criticism, however, which is scattered throughout his writing, is often intensely interesting and provocative, his favourite writers being AESCHYLUS, SHAKESPEARE and

GOETHE. HEINE was a friend, and he very much admired BALZAC. Marxist Literary Criticism is the application of Marx and Engels's theories to literature, a process that reached its lowest depths in the 1930s doctrine of 'socialist realism', and its accompanying feeble theorizing. The preference of Marx and Engels for Balzac over ZOLA, and Engels's advice to the English novelist Margaret Harkness that propaganda novels don't work, raise issues that socialist realism simply ignored.

Masefield, John [Edward] (1878–1967) English poet. His *Salt-Water Ballads* (1902) includes his best-known poem, 'I must go down to the sea again'. Many of his later poems, e.g. *The Everlasting Mercy* (1911), caused much scandal with their frank treatment of such themes as rural brutality and incest. His poetic reputation, once very large, shrank rapidly after his appointment as POET LAUREATE in 1930.

Matsuo Basho *see* **Basho**.

Maugham, W[illiam] Somerset (1874–1965) English novelist, dramatist and short-story writer. His first novel was *Liza of Lambeth* (1897), based on his experiences as a doctor working in the London slums. His best-known novels are *Of Human Bondage* (1915), which is another semi-autobiographical work, *The Moon and Sixpence* (1919), based on the life of the painter Paul Gauguin, and the satirical comedy *Cakes and Ale* (1930). Several of his plays, e.g. *The Circle* (1921) and *The Constant Wife* (1926), both of which examine the typical Maugham themes of hypocrisy and infidelity, were very successful. His masterpiece is often said to be the short story 'Rain', in *The Trembling of a Leaf* (1921), which describes the love of a sexually repressed missionary for a prostitute. Maugham was a British secret agent during World War I, and his experiences form the basis of his enthralling spy novel *Ashenden* (1928).

Mayakovsky, Vladimir *see* **Futurism**.

melodrama a form of drama, so named from the Greek word for 'song' plus the word 'drama', that seems to have arisen in 18th-century France and that contained elements of music, spectacle, sensational incidents and sentimentalism (*see* SENTIMENTAL COMEDY). The form reached its peak in the popular theatre of 19th-century England, when quite spectacular stage effects often accompanied the action, and villains became blacker than black in their persecution of pure heroes and heroines. A typical example of the form is *The Miller and his Men* (1813) by **Isaac Pocock** (1782–1835), a Gothic melodrama with splendid bandits, virtuous and faithful young lovers, battles, a wild ravine, and an exploding bridge at the climax. *See also* DOMESTIC TRAGEDY.

Melville, Herman (1819–91) American novelist, short-story writer and poet. His early experiences as a sailor, including service on a whaler, imprisonment for mutiny, and captivity among cannibals, are reflected in his early novels, e.g. *Typee* (1846) and *Omoo* (1847). His masterpiece, and one of the greatest of all novels, is *Moby Dick* (1851), a complex and symbolic narrative in which Captain Ahab leads his whaling crew in a doomed quest for the white whale that bit off his leg. Other notable works include the satirical romance *Pierre, or the Ambiguities* (1852), the magnificent story 'Bartleby the Scrivener' (about a clerk who lives and eventually dies by the phrase 'I would prefer not to') and his great short novel *Billy Budd, Foretopman*, published posthumously in 1924. This last work, a tale of innocence destroyed by evil, was turned into a popular opera by Benjamin Britten in 1951. Melville died poor and neglected, but is now regarded as a great writer.

Menander (*c*.342–*c*.292 BC) Greek dramatist, whose 'new comedies' (*see* COMEDY) were known only from small fragments and through adaptations by the Roman dramatists TERENCE and PLAUTUS until the 20th century. A complete play, *The Misanthropist*, was discovered in Egypt in 1957.

Meredith, George (1828–1909) English novelist and poet. His novels, e.g. *The Ordeal of Richard Feverel* (1859) and *The Egoist* (1879), are complex studies of human relationships in which the woman's perspective is often the most sympathetically represented. Meredith's strange, intricate dialogue and narration is quite unique. His sonnet sequence, *Modern Love* (1862), virtually a novel in verse form, is an intriguing and innovative study of the dissolution of a marriage.

Metaphysical poetry a poetry movement of the 17th century, noted for intense feeling, extended metaphor and striking, elaborate imagery, often with a mystical element. DONNE is regarded as the first important Metaphysical poet. Other notable poets described as metaphysical include CRASHAW, COWLEY, HERBERT, TRAHERNE and VAUGHAN.

method acting *see* **Stanislavsky, Konstantin**.

Meyerhold, Vsevolod (1874–1940) Russian theatrical producer and director. By the time the Bolsheviks came to power in 1917, he was recognized as the most prominent exponent of avant-garde ideas and productions on the Russian stage. Among the plays he produced at his Meyerhold Theatre were those of Mayakovsky (*see* FUTURISM). His productions (which were strongly influential on BRECHT) cheerfully abandoned traditional conventions, such as the sanctity of the proscenium arch, and broke plays up into episodic segments. Stage sets were determinedly Constructivist, i.e. they used technological artefacts derived from industrial processes to emphasize the kinetic, active nature of the stage (in large part, this was a development from Russian FUTURISM). Actors were encouraged to think of themselves as 'biomechanisms', and to study circus acrobatics and the conventions of COMMEDIA DELL'ARTE. Meyerhold's ideas inevitably proved intolerable to the Soviet cultural commissars of SOCIALIST REALISM and he was executed in 1940. *See also* STANISLAVSKY.

Meynell, Alice *see* **Thompson, Francis**.

Middleton, Thomas (*c.*1570–1627) English dramatist. His two powerful tragedies, *The Changeling* (1622) and *Women Beware Women* (1627), are now highly regarded. His other works include the satirical comedy *A Trick to Catch the Old One* (1608) and a political satire, *A Game at Chesse* (1624). The latter play almost resulted in himself and the actors being imprisoned. He collaborated with many other dramatists, e.g. DEKKER.

Millay, Edna St Vincent (1892–1950) American poet. Her early collections, e.g. *Renascence and Other Poems* (1917) and *A Few Figs from Thistles* (1920), established her reputation as a daring, Bohemian-style New Woman, a real-life example of the fictional 'liberated' females who were appearing in the novels and drama of the period.

Miller, Arthur (1915–) American dramatist. His well-constructed tragedies include three classics of the American stage: *Death of a Salesman* (1949), which describes the destruction of a travelling salesman by the false values of everyday society, *The Crucible* (1952), in which the Salem witchcraft trials are used to comment on Cold-War McCarthyism, and *A View from the Bridge* (1955), a curious yet successful combination of naturalism with the conventions of Greek drama. He married Marilyn Monroe in 1955 (they divorced in 1961), and wrote the screenplay for her last film *The Misfits* (1961).

Miller, Henry (1891–1980) American novelist, notorious for his graphic descriptions of his numerous sexual experiences in such works as *Tropic of Cancer* (1931) and *Tropic of Capricorn* (1939). He was a strong influence on the BEAT GENERATION and on other writers (*see* DURRELL). The best examination of his work is in ORWELL's essay 'Inside the Whale'.

Milne, A[lan] A[lexander] (1882–1956) English writer and dramatist. His children's books, e.g. *When We Were Very Young*

(1924), *Winnie-the-Pooh* (1926) and *The House at Pooh Corner* (1928), are much loved classics of children's literature.

Milton, John (1608–74) English poet. One of the most formidably learned of all English poets, Milton had a European-wide reputation by his late twenties. His early poems, e.g. the magnificent elegy *Lycidas* (1637), are steeped in the humanist tradition which looked to classical literature for ethical principles and modes of expression, and to Scripture and the Christian tradition for faith. He supported Parliament during the Civil War and wrote tracts attacking royalty and episcopacy. His most famous prose work is the tract *Areopagitica* (1644), a rousing defence of the liberty of free speech. His masterpiece is the great epic poem on the Fall of Man, *Paradise Lost* (1667–74). Other notable works include the verse drama *Samson Agonistes* (1671), i.e. 'Samson at the Games', in which the blind hero is clearly to be identified with Milton himself (he was completely blind by 1651). Some of his sonnets, e.g. 'On His Blindness', are among the greatest ever written. Robert GRAVES's novel *Wife to Mr Milton* (1942), is an intriguing study of one obsessive genius by another.

Mishima, Yukio (1925–70) Japanese novelist and short-story writer. His work, e.g. the novel *The Temple of the Golden Pavilion* (1956), is dominated by the themes of homosexuality, beauty and death. The opening words of the epigraph to his *Confessions of a Mask* (1949), from DOSTOYEVSKY's *The Brothers Karamazov*, sum up his central concern: 'Beauty is a terrible and awful thing!' (WILDE was another European influence on him). He committed suicide in public while exhorting his followers to perform a military coup. A good introduction to the man and his work is Paul Schrader's film of 1985, *Mishima*.

Mitchell, James Leslie *see* **Gibbon, Lewis Grassic**.

Molière [pseud. of Jean-Baptiste Poquelin] (1622–73) French dramatist. Molière's great comedies are as popular now as when they were first performed; only SHAKESPEARE's plays have been performed more widely. Some examples of the plays are: *Tartuffe* (1664), a crushing satire on religious hypocrisy; *The Misanthrope* (1666), a study of a cynic in love; and *The Imaginary Invalid* (1673), a hilarious depiction of hypochondria and quack medicine.

Montagu, Mrs Elizabeth (1720–1800) English author and BLUE-STOCKING, whose *Essay on the Writings and Genius of Shakespeare* (1769), a reply to VOLTAIRE's daft criticisms of SHAKESPEARE's work, was highly acclaimed by her contemporaries (her friend Dr JOHNSON, however, was not impressed, declaring that Voltaire's arguments were not worth responding to).

Montaigne, Michel Eyquem de (1553–92) French essayist. His essays first appeared in 1580. His achievement was to establish the essay as a literary form; his fascinating self-examination of his reflections on incidents in his life and on his favourite (usually Stoic) authors, has had a wide and lasting influence. His motto was 'What do I Know?', with tolerance and anti-dogmatic scepticism being the dominant theme in his work. The essays were translated into English by John FLORIO in 1603, and SHAKESPEARE used this translation as one of the sources for *The Tempest* (1611).

Moore, Brian (1921–99) Irish-born Canadian novelist. Moore's highly praised novels place him in the first rank of modern writers. The novels range in setting from a Jesuit mission in 17th-century Canada in *Black Robe* (1985), to 1980s Eastern Europe in *The Colour of Blood* (1987), and, as in these two and *Catholics* (1972), frequently involve Roman Catholic doctrine and practice. *The Lonely Passion of Judith Hearne* (1955) and *I am Mary Dunne* (1968) have been hailed as being among the most penetrating analyses of the female psyche by any author. Moore also had a quite extraordinary gift for blending supernatural events with the commonplace patterns of everyday life, as in the astonishing novel *Cold Heaven* (1983), in which a woman is haunted by visions of the Virgin Mary.

Moore, George [Augustus] (1852–1933) Irish novelist. His novels, e.g. *Esther Waters* (1894) and *The Brook Kerith* (1916), were heavily influenced by BALZAC and ZOLA and other French NATURALIST and REALIST novelists. His first novel, *A Modern Lover* (1883), is a fairly typical example of his risqué novels of modern life. He was a friend of YEATS, and played a leading role in the founding of the ABBEY THEATRE.

Moore, Marianne [Craig] (1887–1972) American poet, noted for sophisticated and witty verse. T.S. ELIOT wrote the introduction to her *Selected Poems* (1935). Her description of poetry, in the poem 'Poetry', as 'imaginary gardens with real toads in them', is the best known of her teasing, oblique observations.

Moore, Thomas (1779–1852) Irish poet. His *Irish Melodies* (1807–34), songs of his own composition set to traditional Irish airs, achieved great popularity and are still loved and sung. Some of the best known are 'Believe me, if all those Endearing Young Charms', 'The Harp that once through Tara's Halls', and 'The Last Rose of Summer'. His *Lalla Rookh* (1817), a series of oriental tales in verse, also enjoyed great popularity. He was a friend of BYRON, who praised him extravagantly. Byron gave Moore his unpublished *Memoirs*, which were subsequently bought and burned by their publisher John MURRAY, because of their sexually explicit content.

More, Hannah (1745–1833) English writer, who became one of the most prominent and popular members of the BLUESTOCKING circle gravitating around Dr JOHNSON, a world captured in her good-natured poem *Bas Bleu* (1786). Her works include tragedies, one of which, *Percy* (1777), was produced by her friend

David GARRICK (earning her over £750), and many poems. The greater part of her output, however, consisted of 'improving' works directed at reforming the morals and domestic economy of the poor, e.g. the monthly tracts published in 1795–98 under the title of *The Cheap Repository*, and the didactic novel *Coelebs in Search of a Wife* (1809). (Ten editions of the latter were sold in one year.) She was also concerned with reforming the morals of the upper classes, e.g. *Thoughts on the Importance of the Manners of the Great to General Society* (1788), a work which, after the French Revolution, was much pondered upon by writers and policy formers of all parties in Britain. More was in fact a sharply witty and tough-minded writer. She made a lot of money from her writing, gave generously to charity, and died leaving £30,000 to various causes.

More, Henry (1614–87) English philosopher, who became the leading light of a small group of Anglican divines known as the **Cambridge Platonists** (*see* PLATO, NEOPLATONISM). The writings and teachings of all the Cambridge Platonists can be cloudy and contradictory, but may be summarized as: (a) a rejection of dogmatism, e.g. of Calvin's strictures on man's sinful nature, and of materialism, especially that of HOBBES; (b) the compatibility of reason with Christianity in an essentially harmonious universe; (c) the fundamental unity of truth and goodness; (d) the necessity for combining reason, Christian faith and the writings of great pagan philosophers such as Plato, in the quest to explain the true, orderly nature of God's creation. The Cambridge Platonists were much influenced by Humanist thinkers such as ERASMUS, and by the tolerant, learned writings of the great Anglican divine HOOKER. More's works include *Psychozoia Platonica* (1642) and *Divine Dialogues* (1668). Other notable members of the group were **Benjamin Whichcote** (1609–83) and **Ralph Cudworth** (1617–88).

More, Sir Thomas (1478–1535) English statesman and Roman Catholic saint. He was Henry VIII's Lord Chancellor, and his refusal to recognize the annulment of Henry's marriage to Catherine of Aragon and declaration of supremacy over the Church of England led to his execution for treason. More was widely recognized as an honourable man, and his execution repelled moderate Catholic and Protestant opinion throughout Europe. More's greatest work is his fantasy of a supposedly ideally organized state, *Utopia* (1516). More's close friend, the great humanist ERASMUS, supervised the printing of *Utopia* (the word means 'no place'). The work spawned a host of imitations throughout the centuries but the impact of 20th-century totalitarianism has lessened enthusiasm for the form. Aldous HUXLEY's *Island* (1962) is a modern example of a Utopian novel; the same author's *Brave New World* (1932) is an example of its opposite, a 'dystopia' or 'bad place'. More was canonized in 1935, and has always been admired for his firm principles and love of justice. His involvement in heresy trials, however, and his dispute with Tyndale (*see* AUTHORIZED VERSION) show a less attractive side of his character.

Morgan, Edwin George (1920–) Scottish poet and translator, best known for his witty, experimental verse, e.g. the much anthologized 'The First Men on Mercury', and for his poems on Scottish life, e.g. *Glasgow Sonnets* (1972).

Morris, William (1834–96) English designer, poet, writer, artist and craftsman. Morris was a social reformer who believed that people would be enabled to do better work if they had beautiful surroundings, and to this end he was instrumental in founding the Arts and Crafts Movement. He drew his inspiration from the medieval guild systems of the Middle Ages, convinced that utility and art were inseparable. He formed a manufacturing and decorating company producing wallpapers, fabrics and artefacts, and also started the Kelmscott Press to produce a better quality of books in a range of typefaces.

Morris's best-known prose romance, *News from Nowhere* (1891), is a Utopian (*see* Thomas MORE) fantasy about a future socialist commonwealth of England. His other prose fictional works are mostly sagas of ancient northern Europe, e.g. *The House of the Wolfings* (1889), and are a curious blend of gore and sentiment. His best-known poem, *The Earthly Paradise* (1868–70), is a long, Norse-inspired saga in which a group of stranded Vikings recount stories at tedious length.

Morrison, Toni [Chloe Anthony Wofford Morrison] (1931–) American novelist whose novels, e.g. *Sula* (1974), *Beloved* (1987), *Jazz* (1992) and *Paradise* (1998), strongly reflect Afro-American community life. A Pulitzer prize-winner in 1988, she was also awarded the NOBEL PRIZE for literature in 1993.

Mosley, [Sir] Nicholas [3rd Baron Ravensdale] (1923–) English novelist. His early novels, e.g. *Accident* (1964, filmed by Joseph Losey in 1967) and *Impossible Object* (1968), were highly acclaimed in their day, but interest in Mosley's work declined due to a growing critical distaste for anyone labelled, as he was, an 'experimental' English writer. His novel *Hopeful Monsters* (1990), however, a wide-ranging study of the dilemmas of modern life, reinstated his reputation as a highly distinctive and gifted author. Mosley's father was the British fascist leader Sir Oswald Mosley, of whom he wrote a damning two-volume biography, *Rules of the Game* (1982) and *Beyond the Pale* (1983).

Muggeridge, Malcolm [Thomas] (1903–90) English journalist. He was Moscow correspondent for The *Manchester Guardian* (1930–33), an experience which resulted in complete disillusion with Communism. He published a semi-autobiographical novel about his experiences in the USSR, *Winter in Moscow* (1934), a remarkably clear-eyed view of the horror of the Soviet Union, which is spoiled for modern readers by some unpleasant anti-Semitic passages. By 1940, when he published his creepily entertaining review of the decade, *The Thirties*, he had become a noted cynic, disliked by both left and right. His friend ORWELL's review of *The Thirties*, 'brilliant but depressing', pointed out that the trouble with Muggeridge was not that he was wrong in seeing the 20th century as a 'cesspool full of barbed wire', but that he seemed to enjoy it. Muggeridge served in World War II as a spy, most notably in Africa, where his nearest colleague was Graham GREENE, and in Paris at the end, where he did his best to help P. G. WODEHOUSE, whom most British people then regarded as a traitor. Muggeridge eventually became a non-denominational Christian, then, under the influence of Mother Teresa, a Roman Catholic. He produced two superb volumes of autobiography, *The Green Stick* (1972) and *The Infernal Grove* (1973), collectively titled *Chronicles of Wasted Time*.

Muir, Edwin (1887–1959) Scottish poet, translator and critic. He and his wife **Willa** (1890–1970) produced what are still the standard English translations of KAFKA's novels in the 1930s. His volumes of poetry include *The Labyrinth* (1949) and *One Foot in Eden* (1956). His best poems, e.g. 'A Child Dying', are powerfully elegiac in tone. His essays, collected in *Essays in Literature and Society* (1949), are still highly regarded.

Munro, Alice (1931–) Canadian novelist and short-story writer. Her stories, e.g. *Dance of the Happy Shades* (1968) and *Something I've Been Meaning to Tell You* (1974), are set in the fictional town of Jubilee, Ontario. The typical Munro story features a sensitive young girl's reactions to the petty struggles of small-town life.

Munro, Hector Hugh *see* **Saki**.

Murdoch, Dame Iris (1919–99) Irish-born English novelist. Her novels are often described as intellectual sex comedies, with complex symbolism and a strong dash of the macabre. The novels include *A Severed Head* (1961), *The Sea, the Sea* (1978) and *The Book and the Brotherhood* (1987).

Murray, John (1778–1843) English publisher whose authors included Jane AUSTEN, Thomas MOORE, BYRON, CRABBE and COLERIDGE. Despite Byron's alleged misquotation of the Bible, 'Now Barabbas was a publisher', to Murray, he was renowned for his hospitality and generous assistance to authors, and his premises became a common meeting ground for many of the literary figures of the day. Murray was also a shrewd businessman; the basis for his prosperity was the burgeoning middle-class market for books in the Regency period. His edition of Byron's *The Corsair* (1814) sold over 10,000 copies on the first day of publication; he paid Byron around £20,000 for his works (and burned his *Memoirs*; *see* Thomas MOORE).

Musil, Robert [Elder von] (1880–1942) Austrian novelist and dramatist. His masterpiece is his huge unfinished novel, published in English as *The Man Without Qualities* (1953–60), a psychological study, in the EXISTENTIALIST manner, of a purposeless drifter in pre–1914 Vienna. Musil was a qualified engineer and also studied philosophy and psychology, and adopted an 'empirical, scientific' approach to his characters and their decaying milieu. *The Man Without Qualities* is widely regarded as required reading for anyone interested in early 20th-century German and Central European intellectual currents.

N

Nabokov, Vladimir (1899–1977) Russian-born American novelist and short-story writer. Nabokov and his family left Russia in 1919, following the 1917 Bolshevik Revolution. After studying in England, Nabokov lived in Berlin and Paris, writing several novels in Russian, including *Despair* (1926). After settling in the US in 1940, he wrote and published in English. His most famous novel is one of his slightest, *Lolita* (1955), in which a middle-aged lecturer falls obsessively in love with a nymphet. Novels such as *Bend Sinister* (1947) and *Pale Fire* (1962) are better examples of his marvellous gift for narrative and sharp, ironic wit.

Naipaul, V[idiadhar] S[urajprasad] (1932–) Trinidad-born English novelist and travel writer. His family were of Indian (Brahmin) ancestry. He settled in England in the mid–1950s, and began writing novels set in Trinidad. His fourth novel, *A House for Mr Biswas* (1961), a humanely ironic semi-autobiographical study of Trinidad, established him as an important writer. His travel writing is also of the highest quality. He is a sharp observer of the various modes of oppression and exploitation, whether native or colonial, and (as with Norman LEWIS) his experiences can result in a novel, e.g. *A Bend in the River* (1979), a disturbing portrait of post-colonial Africa, or a travel book, e.g. *An Area of Darkness* (1964), a deeply pessimistic study of India. His brother, **Shiva Naipaul** (1932–85), was also a noted travel writer.

Narayan, R[asipuram] K[rishnaswami] (1906–) Indian novelist who writes in English. Most of his gentle, witty fiction, e.g. *The World of Nagaraj* (1990), is set in a fictional Indian town called Malgudi (based on Mysore, where he lives), yet his appeal is worldwide. Graham GREENE recommended his first novel, *Swami and Friends* (1935), for publication.

Nash, Ogden [Frederick] (1902–71) an American humorous poet. His fiendishly clever and unique irregular verse, as in *You Can't Get There from Here* (1957), was originally published in *The New Yorker* magazine (for which he worked) and has achieved lasting popularity.

Nashe, Thomas (1567–1601) English writer of pamphlets and tracts on various subjects, which were usually satirical and often contain barbs directed at his many literary and religious enemies. He was particularly virulent against the Puritans, and was heavily involved in the so-called 'Martin Marprelate' pamphlet war. He also wrote poems, plays, and a striking PICARESQUE NOVEL, *The Unfortunate Traveller* (1594).

naturalism a late 19th-century French literary movement denoting fiction characterized by close observation and documentation of everyday life, with a strong emphasis on the influence of the material world on individual behaviour. Naturalistic novels therefore tended to adopt a very deterministic approach to life and fiction, and most practitioners of the form would have described themselves as socialists or social Darwinists. The leading exponent of the school was ZOLA. (Some followers of Zola were reputed to have written novels in which the dialogue was a scrupulous reproduction of everyday speech heard on the street; few of their works seem to have survived.) The influence of the school on writers in English was patchy; there are strong elements of naturalism in George MOORE and Arnold BENNETT. (Virginia WOOLF's rather severe strictures on Bennett, in *The Common Reader* (1925), encapsulate the standard English highbrow response to the school. Many American writers, however, e.g. DREISER, were strongly influenced by the naturalist doctrines. *See also* MARX; *compare* REALISM.

neoclassicism a term denoting any movement in the Arts emphasizing the virtues of imitating the style and precepts of the great classical writers and artists (neoclassicist principles in literature derive mostly from the writings of ARISTOTLE—principally the *Poetics*—and some observations by the Augustan Roman poets, VIRGIL and HORACE). The hallmarks of neoclassicism are traditionally defined as balance, moderation, attention to formal rules—such as the dramatic Unities, in which time and space is strictly ordered around a sequential plot with a beginning, middle and end—avoidance of emotional display and distrust of enthusiasm, and the assumption that human nature has changed little, if at all, since classical times. Neoclassicism is frequently contrasted with ROMANTICISM, and, interestingly, the strongest period of neoclassicism in art and architecture is contemporary with the peak period of romanticism, the late 18th and early 19th centuries (*see* GOETHE). (A less savoury aspect of neoclassicism was identified by the art historian Kenneth Clark, when he observed that although not all neoclassical art was totalitarian, much if not all of totalitarian art was neoclassical.

In literature, neoclassicism is generally held to have begun with PETRARCH in the mid–14th century. The greatest neoclassical English poets are DRYDEN and POPE; the greatest neoclassical English critic is sometimes said to be Dr JOHNSON, but Johnson's espousal of neoclassical virtues was heavily qualified, particularly in response to French criticism of SHAKESPEARE as virtually a 'literary savage'. Neoclassicism had been a powerful influence on French literature of the 17th century, particularly in drama (*see* CORNEILLE, RACINE), but has never won wide acceptance among writers in English, not even in the 18th century.

Neoplatonism a synthesis of Platonic (*see* PLATO) and mystical concepts that originated in the Greek-speaking Mediterranean world of the 3rd century. **Plotinus** (*c*.205–*c*.270) was the main figure behind the synthesis. His ideas, such as the notion of a world soul and the perception of the poet as an inspired prophet who sees the real world behind the shadowy illusions of the material world, have been influential on many English writers, notably SHELLEY (*see also* Henry MORE). The metaphysical thrillers of Charles WILLIAMS are modern examples of the Christian Neoplatonist tradition in fiction.

Neruda, Jan (1834–91) Czech writer. His plays and prose, e.g. *Tales of the Little Quarter* (1878), are highly regarded, as are his lyrical poems, e.g. *Ballads and Romances* (1883). He has been described as a late ROMANTIC writer, an early REALIST, and as a Classicist. However labelled, he is one of the great Czech writers.

Neruda, Pablo [pseud. of Ricardo Neftali Reyes] (1904–73) Chilean poet and diplomat, noted both for his highly political (socialist) verse and for highly personal, cryptic lyrics. He was awarded the NOBEL PRIZE for literature in 1971.

Nerval, Gerard de (1808–55) French writer, whose life and work, in roughly equal proportions, influenced both the SYMBOLISM and SURREALISM movements. His fantastic short stories, e.g. *Tales and Drolleries* (1852), were particularly influential, and his poem 'El Desdichado' is quoted by T. S. ELIOT in *The Waste Land*. His eccentricities, such as taking his pet lobster for a walk on a lead, were developed to the point of mannerism.

Nesbit, E[dith] (1858–1924) English writer of children's books such as *The Treasure Seekers* (1899), which went against the patronizingly moralistic tradition in children's literature of the time. Her books are still very popular, and several, e.g. *The Railway Children* (1906), have been filmed.

Newbery, John (1713–67) English publisher, who became the first publisher to specialize in selling books written for children, usually 'improving' works such as *Goody Two Shoes* (1766), which was written partly by him and possibly with GOLDSMITH. He was a friend of many writers, and Goldsmith based the character of the bookseller in *The Vicar of Wakefield* on him.

Newbolt, Sir Henry [John] (1862–1938) English poet, whose patriotic naval poems, e.g. 'Drake's Drum', were extremely popular at the turn of the century and still crop up in anthologies.

new comedy *see* **comedy**.

Newman, Cardinal John Henry (1801–90) English theologian, whose spirited defence of his faith, *Apologia pro vita sua* (1864), created a deep impression on believers and nonbelievers alike.

Nibelungenlied an anonymous medieval German epic recounting the hero Siegfried's capture of a hoard of gold belonging to a race of dwarfs (the Nibelungs). The epic forms the basis for Wagner's great opera cycle, *The Ring of the Nibelungs*, and was influential on TOLKIEN's *Lord of the Rings*.

Nicolson, Sir Harold [George] (1886–1968) English diplomat, essayist and literary critic. He married Vita SACKVILLE-WEST in 1913. His *Diaries and Letters 1930–1962*, published in three volumes in 1966, 1967 and 1968, are a fascinating record of the political, social and literary world of his day. The comic/sinister figure of Sir Ralph Brompton in Evelyn WAUGH's *Sword of Honour* trilogy is modelled partly on Harold Nicolson.

Nietzsche, Friedrich Wilhelm (1844–1900) German philosopher and poet, whose works, e.g. *Thus Spake Zarathustra* (1866) and *Beyond Good and Evil* (1886), were highly critical of traditional morality and Christianity ('slave morality') and proclaimed the advent of the superman, the 'splendid blond beast'. He has been very influential on many 20th-century writers, e.g. D.H. LAWRENCE, MANN, SARTRE and SHAW. He was claimed by the Nazis to be one of their spiritual fathers, but Nietzsche, who despised anti-Semitism, would probably have rejected this paternity claim.

nihilism a philosophical movement originating in mid–19th century Russia that rejected all established authority and values. The revolutionary Bazarov in TURGENEV's *Fathers and Sons* is the first significant fictional portrait of a nihilist. Much of DOSTOYEVSKY's work, e.g. *The Possessed*, is concerned with exposing the essential shallowness and banality of nihilism. Nihilist characters crop up frequently in English fiction of the late 19th and early 20th century, e.g. in Joseph CONRAD's *The Secret Agent*.

Nin, Anais (1903–77) French-born American novelist and essayist. She is best known for her seven volumes of diaries (1966–80) depicting life among the literary coteries of Paris and New York from the 1930s.

No *see* **Noh**.

Nobel Prize any of the annual awards endowed by the Swedish chemist **Alfred Nobel** (1833–96) (apparently in penance for his invention of dynamite) for significant contributions in the fields of chemistry, physics, literature, medicine or physiology, and peace, with economics added later. Winners of the Nobel prize for literature include KIPLING (1907), YEATS (1923), SHAW (1925), T.S. ELIOT (1948), PASTERNAK (1958), HEMINGWAY (1954) and BECKETT (1969). For many years, British reaction to the annual announcement of the award mostly consisted of parochial irritation that Graham GREENE had once again not been awarded it, but some unreadable foreigner has. Most recipients of the literature prize have in fact been distinguished writers. The standard reference work (in three volumes covering the years 1901–26, 1927–61, 1962–87) on the Nobel prizewinners is *The Nobel Prize Winners: Literature* (1990), published by the Salem Press. The devaluation of the Nobel peace prize in the 1980s, however, with its award to the likes of Henry Kissinger, has contributed to a parallel lowering of the esteem of its award in literature.

Noguchi, Yone [Jiro] (1875–1947] Japanese poet and essayist who wrote in both Japanese and English, e.g. *Selected Poems* (1921). His works are regarded as forming an important bridge between Japanese and Western culture.

Noh or No a form of highly stylized drama originating in 14th-century Japan. The typical Noh play is short, slow-paced, draws heavily on classical Japanese symbolism, and usually involves song, dance, mime and intricately detailed costume.

Norris, [Benjamin] Frank[lin] (1870–1902) American novelist, heavily influenced by ZOLA. He became one of the chief American NATURALISTIC novelists in works such as *McTeague* (1899), and his unfinished trilogy attacking American capitalism, the first two of which, *The Octopus* (1901) and *The Pit* (1903), are polemical assaults on the railroad and wheat industries.

North, Sir Thomas (*c*.1535–*c*.1601) English author. His translations of works such as PLUTARCH'S *Lives* (1579) exerted a strong influence on Elizabethan writers, notably SHAKESPEARE, who seems to have largely derived his knowledge of ancient history from North's works.

Nostradamus [Michel de Notredame] (1503–66) French astrologer and physician. He published two books of cryptic prophecies in rhymed quatrains, called *Centuries* (1555–58), which enjoyed a huge vogue throughout Europe and were first published in English in 1672. His work has no literary merit.

Novalis [pseud. of Friedrich Leopold von Hardenberg] (1772–1801) German poet and novelist, who was called the 'Prophet of ROMANTICISM' in Germany. He wrote two novels, both unfinished, the best known of which is *Heinrich von Ofterdingen* (1802), which involves a symbolic quest for a 'blue flower'. He also wrote mystical and love poetry, e.g. *Hymns to the Night* (1800), a series of laments on the death of his fianceée. He died of consumption.

novel a sustained fictional prose narrative. Although most of the essential characteristics of the form can be found in ancient texts, such as the Greek Romances of the 3rd century, and in the works of writers of the Roman world, such as APULIEUS and PETRONIUS, the novel as the term is generally understood, with complex characterization and multilayered strands of plot and character development, is essentially a creation of 18th-century writers in English, particularly DEFOE, RICHARDSON and FIELDING.

Like all generalizations about the novel, however, the foregoing is at best only a grouping of partial truths; Petronius's *Satyricon* is a fine novel by any standards, and CERVANTES' *Don Quixote* is one of the very finest.

In the early years of the 19th century, the dual tradition of the novel—adventure in the great world outside, and exploration of personality—reached striking new levels in the novels of Sir Walter SCOTT and Jane AUSTEN respectively, with the latter setting standards of characterization that have rarely been matched. In the course of the 19th century, writers throughout Europe and America, e.g. DICKENS, STENDHAL, George ELIOT, TOLSTOY, DOSTOEVSKY, BALZAC, MELVILLE and Henry JAMES, developed the novel into a highly sophisticated vehicle for exploring human consciousness. The 20th century has seen many adaptations of the traditional form of the novel, from the use of the stream-of-consciousness (*see* William JAMES) technique by JOYCE and WOOLF, to the MAGIC REALISM of South American writers such as MARQUEZ, with such oddities as the so-called 'antinovels' of writers such as ROBBE-GRILLET occurring along the way. Finally, it is worth noting Gore VIDAL's observation that the fact that a modern novelist can work with greater freedom of expression, and in a wider variety of forms, than earlier novelists, does not necessarily mean that the modern novelist has anything more profound to say.

Some quotes: a novel is 'some work in which the most thorough knowledge of human nature, the happiest delineation of its varieties, the liveliest effusions of wit and humour are conveyed to the world in the best chosen language' (Jane AUSTEN); 'A good novels tells us the truth about its hero; but a bad novel tells us the truth about its author' (CHESTERTON); 'Yes—oh dear, yes—the novel tells us a story' (FORSTER); 'A novel is a mirror walking down a main road' (STENDHAL). *See also* MARX, NASHE, NOVELLA, PICARESQUE NOVEL, GOTHIC NOVEL, CAMPUS NOVEL.

novella a short version of the NOVEL; a tale usually leading up to some point, and often, in early versions of the form such as the tales in BOCCACCIO's *Decameron*, of a satirical or scabrous nature.

Noyes, Alfred (1880–1958) English poet. His work, e.g. the epic poem *Drake* (1908), is representative of the once common, bluff, hearty, out-of-doors and patriotic tradition within English verse. Like NEWBOLT and AUSTIN, he was happiest when writing manly verses about sailors.

nursery rhyme a (usually traditional) short verse or song for children. Many nursery rhymes, e.g. 'Ring a Ring o' Roses' (which refers to the Great Plague) have their roots in ancient and occasionally unsavoury events.

O

Oates, Joyce Carol (1938–) American novelist and poet. Her novels are naturalistic in form with strong elements of symbolism (as in ZOLA), linking the American way of life with violence and destructive emotions. Her novels include *A Garden of Earthly Delights* (1967), the title taken from a painting by Hieronymus Bosch, with whom she has much in common, and *A Bloodsmoor Romance* (1982).

O'Brien, Edna (1932–) Irish novelist and short-story writer. Her first three novels, describing the lives of provincial Irish girls in Dublin and London, form a trilogy that is still regarded as her best work: these are *The Country Girls* (1960), *The Lonely Girl* (1962) and *Girls in their Married Bliss* (1963). Subsequent novels include *A Pagan Place* (1971) and *Night* (1972), as well as several screenplays.

O'Brien, Flann [pseud. of Brian O'Nolan *or* O Nuallain] (1911–66) Irish novelist and journalist. His regular column in the *Irish Times*, 'Cruiskeen Lawn', written under the name Myles na Gopaleen, established him as one of the major Irish satirists, ridiculing the clichés of Irish life. A collection of the articles was published in 1968 as *The Best of Myles*. His reputation outside Ireland has risen sharply since his death, and he is now regarded as a comic writer of genius. His novels include *The Dalkey Archive* (1964), in which James JOYCE (who admired O'Brien's work) is discovered to be alive and a writer of pious tracts.

O'Casey, Sean (1880–1964) Irish dramatist. His three early plays, *The Shadow of a Gunman* (1923), *Juno and the Paycock* (1924) and *The Plough and the Stars* (1926), caused great controversy in Ireland by focusing, not altogether approvingly, on the outburst of patriotism which followed the 1916 Easter Rising (the first production of *The Plough and the Stars* was disrupted by outraged Irish nationalists). His later plays, e.g. *The Silver Tassie* (1928), belong more to the world of experimental Expressionist drama and were less controversial (and less popular).

O'Connor, Frank [pseud. of Michael Francis O'Donovan] (1903–66) Irish short-story writer and critic. He is best known for his affectionate but sharply observed portraits of Irish life in such short-story collections as *Bones of Contention* (1936) and *Domestic Relations* (1957).

O'Connor, [Mary] Flannery (1925–64) American novelist and short-story writer. Her main theme is religious fanaticism in the Southern US States, where life is portrayed as veering grotesquely from tragedy to comedy. Her masterpiece is *Wise Blood* (1952), a novel about a young religious fanatic and his misconceptions, which was made into an equally fine film by John Huston.

ode in Ancient Greece, originally a poem intended to be sung, a lyric poem written in an elaborate form and usually dignified in subject and style. The word is now loosely applied to any elaborate lyric poem.

Odets, Clifford (1906–63) American dramatist. A committed socialist, his masterpiece is *Waiting for Lefty* (1935), a play about a taxi-drivers' strike which ends in a mass meeting (in which the audience is invited to participate) calling for a strike.

O'Faolain, Sean (1900–1991) Irish novelist and short-story writer. Like Frank O'Connor, his stories focus on the constricting patterns of provincial Irish life, but from a more edgily critical perspective. His *Collected Stories* were published in 1981. His vigorous campaign against censorship and narrow-mindedness is a prominent theme in his autobiography, *Vive-Moi!* (1964).

O'Flaherty, Liam (1897–1984) Irish novelist and short-story writer. His novels include *The Informer* (1925), and collections of short stories, e.g. *Spring Sowing* (1948).

O'Hara, John [Henry] (1905–70) American novelist and short-story writer. His tough, satirical works on 'sophisticated' American life, e.g. the novels *Butterfield 8* (1935) and *Pal Joey* (1940), were very popular in the 1930s and 1940s.

old comedy *see* **comedy**.

Oliphant, Margaret [née Wilson] (1828–97) Scottish novelist. Her novel *Passages in the Life of Mrs Margaret Maitland* (1849) was the first of almost 100 novels to be published. The five novels of *The Chronicles of Carlingford*, e.g. *Salem Chapel* and *Phoebe Junior*, published between 1863 and 1876, are her best-known works. She also wrote biographies, e.g. of CERVANTES and SHERIDAN, and other non-fiction works.

O'Neill, Eugene [Gladstone] (1885–1923) American dramatist. His plays of the early 1920s, e.g. *Beyond the Horizon* (1920), *The Emperor Jones* (1921) and *Desire Under the Elms* (1924), established him as one of America's finest dramatists. His greatest plays are *Mourning Becomes Electra* (1931), a tragedy based on AESCHYLUS's *Oresteia* trilogy transposed to the American South in the aftermath of the Civil War, *The Iceman Cometh* (1946), a tragicomedy set in the Bowery, and the semi-autobiographical *Long Day's Journey into Night* (1940–41), a gloomy study of family breakdown which is often regarded as his masterpiece. He was awarded the NOBEL PRIZE for literature in 1936.

Orton, Joe [John] (1933–67) English dramatist. His first play, *Entertaining Mr Sloane* (1964), a black comedy in which a businessman and his sister compete for the favours of a young villain, was a surprise hit on the London stage. His two other best-known works, *Loot* (1966) and the posthumously performed *What the Butler Saw* (1969), are, like the first, cleverly constructed dramas focusing on sexual depravity and social corruption. Orton was murdered by his lover, Kenneth Halliwell, who also killed himself.

Orwell, George [pseud. of Eric Arthur Blair] (1903–50) Indian-born English novelist and essayist. Brought up in the upper-middle class and educated at Eton, Orwell became a socialist in the 1920s. His first published work was a documentary work, *Down and Out in Paris and London* (1933), which describes his often gruesome experiences as a tramp. His other two great nonfiction works are *The Road to Wigan Pier* (1937), a passionate, coldly angry study of poverty in the North of England, and *Homage to Catalonia* (1939), an account of experiences fighting for the Republican Government in the Spanish Civil War. The latter book caused great offence to many of Orwell's socialist friends for its strong condemnation of Communist treachery and brutality. His first published novel, *Burmese Days* (1934), was based on his experiences as a colonial police officer in Burma. His two greatest novels have become classics of world literature: *Animal*

Farm (1945), a grim allegory of the history of the Soviet Union in which farm animals create a revolutionary state that goes horribly wrong; and *Nineteen Eighty-Four* (1949), an even more grim picture of a future totalitarian world. He is also recognized as one of the greatest English essayists; his *Collected Essays, Journalism and Letters* were published in four volumes in 1968.

Osborne, John [James] (1929–94) English dramatist. His first play, *Look Back in Anger* (1956), the hero of which is an irascible and frustrated young working-class man, was an immediate and influential success on the British stage. No one was quite sure what the hero was angry about (*see* ANGRY YOUNG MEN), but whatever it was, it was felt to be significant. The best known of his later plays are *The Entertainer* (1957), in which a seedy music-hall comedian long past his best (played by Laurence Olivier) represents the decadent spirit of post-imperial Britain, and *Luther* (1961), an intriguing psychological study of Martin Luther. Like his friend AMIS, Osborne moved sharply to the right politically in the 1960s, and became increasingly notorious for his bad-tempered invective against anything that smacked of permissiveness or the loosening of society's ties.

Ossian *see* **Macpherson, James**.

Otway, Thomas (1652–85) English dramatist, remembered chiefly for one work, the great tragedy *Venice Preserved* (1682), a penetrating study of treason and loyalty.

Ovid [Publius Ovidius Naso] (43 BC–*c*.AD 17) Roman poet. His sensual, witty love poems have always been admired, but his long narrative poem *Metamorphoses*, which describes myths in which characters change their forms, is of much greater significance. It was used as a source book for Greek and Roman mythology by many Renaissance writers, e.g. MARLOWE and SHAKESPEARE.

Oz, Amos (1939–) Israeli novelist, essayist and short-story writer. Regarded as one of the most important Israeli writers, his novels include *My Michael* (1968), *To Know a Woman* (1990) and *The Third Condition* (1991). Oz's work shows a deep and humane concern for what Israel's struggle for existence is doing to the soul of the Israeli nation.

P

Paine, Thomas (1737–1809) English-born American political theorist and pamphleteer. He travelled to America in 1774, where he wrote the highly influential pamphlet *Common Sense* (1776), which argued for American independence. The pamphlet's lucid, expertly argued prose was recognized by George Washington as being a sigificant contribution to the Revolution. Paine returned to England in 1787 and published a defence of democratic principles, *The Rights of Man* (1791–92), in reply to Edmund BURKE's *Reflections on the Revolution in France*. In danger of arrest (he was apparently warned to escape by BLAKE), he moved to France where he was welcomed as a revolutionary hero and was elected to the National Convention. He sided with the moderates, was imprisoned by Robespierre's faction and released after 11 months, having narrowly escaped execution. He returned to America in 1802, where he alienated most of his old allies by publishing the deist work, *The Age of Reason* (1793), a no-holds-barred attack on Christian revelation. BYRON was one of the many former allies who now detested Paine; he wrote a vitriolic epigram of COBBETT's return from America with Paine's bones.

Parker, Dorothy [Rothschild] (1893–1960) American journalist, poet and short-story writer, noted especially for her dry wit and sharply ironic epigrams and satires, many of which were first published in *The New Yorker* magazine.

Pasternak, Boris (1890–1960) Russian poet, novelist and translator. His third poetry collection, *My Sister, Life* (1922), established him as a highly original and passionate lyric poet. He published a 'political' poem in 1927, *The Year 1905*, but his heart
was clearly not in it. Like his friends AKHMATOVA and MANDEL-
STAM, his position became increasingly dangerous under a regime that demanded safe verse praising its achievements. Pasternak turned to translation as a safe and honourable way of earning
a living, and his translation of SHAKESPEARE's works is still
highly valued. His great novel *Dr Zhivago* was first published in
Italy in 1958. He was awarded the NOBEL PRIZE for literature in
that year, but was forced to decline acceptance by the Soviet authorities, who subjected him to a hate campaign until his death.
All his works are now freely published in the USSR, where he is
ranked as one of Russia's greatest writers.

pastoral any piece of literature celebrating the country way of
life. The first pastoral poems of any significance are those of
Theocritus (*c.*310–*c.*250 BC), a Greek poet whose work established the standard frame of the form: shepherds and shepherd-
esses (none of whom seems to do any actual work) singing to
one another of their loves in a world of peace and plenty, in
which the sun always shines. Death, however, is occasionally
present in the form of a shepherd lamenting the death of a friend
(SHAKESPEARE's 'Dead shepherd' couplet—*see* MARLOWE—is a
moving, later example of this convention being used as a tribute). Theocritus's form was used by VIRGIL in his *Eclogues*, so
establishing a tradition that lasted for centuries. Later practitioners of the form include PETRARCH, MILTON and SHELLEY. William
EMPSOM's *Some Versions of Pastoral* (1935) is a notable (and
highly entertaining) study of the form and its variations.

Pater, Walter [Horatio] (1839–84) English essayist and critic,
noted especially for his flowery, ornate prose style, described by

Oscar WILDE as 'the holy writ of beauty'. His essay on Leonardo da Vinci in *Studies in the History of the Renaissance* (1873) includes his famous description of the Mona Lisa, 'older than the rocks among whom she sits'. Pater was a strong influence on the AESTHETIC MOVEMENT: Max BEERBOHM, however, described his prose as lifeless, laid out like 'a corpse for inspection'.

Paton, Alan [Stewart] (1903–88) South African novelist. His best-known work is *Cry, the Beloved Country* (1965), a moving study of the hideous consequences of South Africa's race laws.

Paz, Octavio (1914–98) Mexican poet and critic. His collections of poems include *The Violent Season* (1958) and *Configurations* (1971). His other works include two important reflections on Mexican cultural identity and society, *The Labyrinth of Solitude* (1950), and *Eagle or Sun* (1990). Like ORWELL, Paz became a strong opponent of the totalitarian ideologies of both left and right while in Spain during the Civil War, and has been a fearless champion of the rights of the individual against what Orwell called the 'smelly little orthodoxies'. His poem 'Nocturne of San Idelfonso' describes poetry as the bridge between history and truth. He was awarded the NOBEL PRIZE for literature in 1990.

Peacock, Thomas Love (1785–1866) English novelist, essayist and poet. His highly entertaining satirical novels consist mostly of ingeniously witty dialogue between characters modelled on Peacock's friends and contemporaries, e.g. BYRON, COLERIDGE and SHELLEY. The novels include *Headlong Hall* (1816), *Nightmare Abbey* (1818), *Crotchet Castle* (1831) and *Gryll Grange* (1860–61).

Peake, Mervyn [Laurence] (1911–68) English artist, novelist and poet. His best-known literary work is the *Gormenghast* trilogy, which is widely held to constitute one of the great fantasy worlds in modern fiction. The novels are *Titus Groan* (1946), *Gormenghast* (1950) and *Titus Alone* (1959). Peake was an official war artist during World War II, and his visit to Belsen concentration camp in 1945 profoundly affected him.

Pepys, Samuel (1633–1703) English diarist and Admiralty official. His diary (written in code) was first published in 1825. The full uncensored version was published in 11 volumes, 1970–83, and contains much fascinating detail of life in 17th-century London. *See also* EVELYN.

Percy, Thomas *see* **ballad**.

Perelman, S[idney] J[oseph] (1904–79) American humorist. He wrote the sceenplays for some of the Marx Brothers' films, and published several collections of articles under such Marxist titles as *The Road to Milltown; or, Under the Spreading Atrophy* (1957).

Petrarch [Francesco Petrarca] (1304–74) Italian lyric poet and humanist. His love poems are sonnets, madrigals and songs in praise of a woman he called 'Laura' (whose true identity is unknown), and were strongly influential on Tudor and Elizabethan writers and poets, notably WYATT. His work popularized the sonnet form, subsequently used to great effect by people as diverse as Michelangelo and SHAKESPEARE. Petrarch is regarded as the first major poet of the Renaissance.

Petronius [Gaius Petronius Arbiter] (d. AD *c*.66) Roman courtier and satirist. His great satirical novel, *Satyricon*, gives a unique and vivid portrait of the seamy side of Roman life; salacious, funny, and occasionally deeply moving, the work is an important landmark in Western literature. The 'Trimalchio's banquet' scene in the book gave T.S. ELIOT the epigraph for *The Waste Land*. Petronius was ordered to commit suicide by Emperor Nero.

Philips, Ambrose (1671–1749) English poet. As a Whig politician, he obtained various lucrative posts from the House of Hanover, but as a poet he was ridiculed by SWIFT and POPE, re-

ceiving the nickname 'Namby Pamby'. He also wrote three tragedies: *The Distrest Mother* (1712), taken from RACINE; *The
Briton* (1722); and *Humphrey, Duke of Gloucester* (1723).

Philips, John (1676–1708) English poet. His works include *The
Splendid Shilling* (1701), a burlesque poem in Miltonic blank
verse. He subsequently wrote *Blenheim* (1705), a poem in celebration of the Duke of Marlborough's victory, and *Cyder*
(1708), a work in imitation of VIRGIL's *Georgics*.

Philips, Katherine (1631–64) English poet. Her work was much
admired by her contemporaries, e.g. COWLEY and DRYDEN,
among whom she was known as the 'Matchless Orinda'. The
name 'Orinda' seems to have been chosen by herself in a social
and literary group of 'Antenors', 'Rosanias', etc, which seems to
have been a precursor of the 18th-century BLUESTOCKINGS, but
not much is known about the group. Her collected poems were
issued posthumously in 1667.

Piaget, Jean *see* **Structuralism**.

picaresque novel a type of NOVEL in which the hero (very rarely,
the heroine—Defoe's *Molly Flanders* is the best-known example
in English) undergoes an episodic series of adventures. The term
derives from the Spanish *picaro*, a rogue or trickster. Many examples appear in 16th-century Spanish literature, when the genre
first established itself, but picaresque novels have been appearing since the very earliest days of the novel; both Petronius's
Satyricon and Apulieus's *Golden Ass* may be classed as picaresque novels. The first major English example is Thomas
NASHE's lurid *The Unfortunate Traveller*, which appeared in the
1590s along with other, lesser examples. Several great novels of
the 18th and 19th centuries, e.g. Smollett's *Roderick Random*,
Fielding's *Tom Jones* and Dickens's *Pickwick Papers*, have picaresque elements, but inhabit an entirely different emotional and
moral world from that of the earlier examples of the genre. Thus,

Tom Jones will have a characteristically picaresque sexual escapade with Molly Seagrim, but will not abandon her to the mob, as his scabrous fictional predecessors would cheerfully have done.

Pindar (*c*.522–*c*.443 BC) Greek lyric poet, noted for his odes (based on the choral odes of Greek drama) celebrating victories in the Greek games, e.g. at Olympia. His carefully constructed and elaborate poems became influential in late 17th-century England (through COWLEY's works), where he was (mistakenly) seen as a much freer, less restrained poet than HORACE. KIPLING's marvellous spoof Horatian ode 'A Translation' (in *A Diversity of Creatures*, 1917) has Horace saying: 'Me, in whose breast no flame hath burned/Lifelong, save that by Pindar lit . . .'

Pinter, Harold (1930–) English dramatist. The adjective 'Pinteresque' to describe dialogue derives from his use of halting, menacing dialogue punctuated by sinister pauses. *The Birthday Party* (1958), *The Caretaker* (1960) and *No Man's Land* (1975) are the most performed of Pinter's plays, which are usually characterized as belonging to the tradition of the Theatre of the ABSURD. He has also written several screenplays, notably that for John FOWLES's novel *The French Lieutenant's Woman*.

Pirandello, Luigi (1867–1936) Italian dramatist, short-story writer and novelist. His two best-known plays are *Six Characters in Search of an Author* (1921) and *Henry IV* (1922), both of which are very influential experimental plays with fragmented action and characterization, and feature relentless questioning of theatrical conventions, such as the barrier between performers and audience. He was awarded the NOBEL PRIZE for literature in 1934.

Plath, Sylvia (1932–63) American poet and novelist. She married Ted HUGHES in 1956, and settled in England in 1959. She published only two books in her lifetime: a volume of poems, *Colos-

sus (1960), and a semi-autobiographical novel, *The Bell Jar* (1963). She died by her own hand. Her posthumous collection of poems, *Ariel* (1965), which has many fine lyrics describing her personal problems, has been much admired. Following her sad end, Plath became the subject of a rather creepy elevation to cult status.

Plato (*c*.427–*c*.347 BC) Greek philosopher, who is regarded as the main founder of Western philosophy. Taught by SOCRATES, Plato was in turn ARISTOTLE's tutor. His *Theory of Forms*, in which the objects as we perceive them are distinguished from the idea of the objects, has had a strong influence on many writers, e.g. DONNE, WORDSWORTH, and, most of all, SHELLEY (*see also* NEOPLATONISM). The term 'Platonic love' has been derived from Plato's works to denote a selfless non-physical love for another, although Plato's interest in young men was certainly not non-physical. Plato's speculations are contained in dialogue form in several works, notably the *Symposium* and *Phaedo*, and in *The Republic*, the last being an examination of the principles of good government.

Plautus, Titus Maccius (*c*.254–*c*.184 BC) Roman dramatist. His COMEDIES were adaptations of lost Greek originals (*see* MENANDER). He wrote about 130 plays, of which 20 are extant, featuring such stock characters as the wise servant who knows more than his master (WODEHOUSE's Jeeves is a distant descendant). It was through the plays of Plautus and TERENCE that succeeding dramatists inherited the classical comic tradition, and many of his plots, adaptations themselves, have been adapted by others (SHAKESPEARE's *Comedy of Errors* is a version of a Plautus play).

Plotinus *see* **Neoplatonism**.

Pocock, Isaac *see* **melodrama**.

Poe, Edgar Allan (1809–49) American short-story writer, poet and critic. His macabre, highly Gothic horror stories, e.g. *Tales of the Grotesque and Arabesque* (1839), are studies in pathological obsession with a strong element of sadism, and feature themes such as premature burial and necrophilia. The best of the stories, e.g. 'The Masque of the Red Death', have retained their power, as have the best of his poems, e.g. 'The Raven'. His detective stories, e.g. 'The Murders in the Rue Morgue', are very good (and influential) early examples of the form.

poet laureate a poet appointed to a court or other formal institution. In Britain, the post is held for life and the poet laureate is expected, although not forced, to write a poem to commemorate important events. Ben JONSON held the post unofficially, being succeeded by DAVENANT. The first official poet laureate was DRYDEN, who was also the first to lose the post before his death, in the upheaval surrounding the 'Glorious Revolution'. Dryden's successor in 1689 was SHADWELL. TATE held the office from 1692 until 1715, and Nicholas ROWE from 1715 until 1718. **Laurence Eusden** (1688–1730) succeeded in 1718, more for political reasons than for poetic ones. He is better known for being mentioned in POPE's *Dunciad* for his drinking habits than for any skill as a poet. His successor in 1730, the actor and dramatist **Colley Cibber** (1671–1757), also became a target of the *The Dunciad*, Pope personifying him as 'Dullness' in the final edition. The appointment in 1757 of the dramatist **William Whitehead** (1715–85) also attracted satirical comment, in the face of which he remained calm, a course he recommended in *A Charge to the Poets* (1762). WARTON held the post from 1785 to 1790, and **Henry James Pye** (1745–1813) from 1790 to 1813. The reputation of the post revived a little with the appointment of SOUTHEY in 1813 and considerably with WORDSWORTH (1843–50) and TENNYSON (1850–92) but suffered a setback with the appointment of AUSTIN in 1896. The 20th-century holders of the post were BRIDGES (1913–30), MASEFIELD (1930–67), DAY-LEWIS (1968–72), BETJEMAN (1972–84), and Ted HUGHES (1984–98).

Pope, Alexander (1688–1744) English poet. His poetry is generally divided into three (rather arbitrary) periods; an early period in which he made his name as a poet with, especially, the *Essay on Criticism* (1711), a poetic manifesto of NEOCLASSICAL principles, the nature poems such as *Windsor Forest* (1713), a mock-heroic love poem, *The Rape of the Lock* (1714), designed to reunite two feuding upper-class Roman Catholic families (Pope was himself a Catholic); a middle period in which his translations of HOMER's *Iliad* (1720) and *Odyssey* (1725–26) and his edition of SHAKESPEARE (1725) made him rich; a third period spent at Twickenham (outside London) where he completed his great satire on his contemporaries, *The Dunciad* (1728), and philosophical poems such as *An Essay on Man* (1733–34). Pope's reputation suffered a partial eclipse during the 19th century (although BYRON vigorously defended his verse). However, his mastery of the rhymed couplet, his deadly satirical powers and gift for sustaining a metaphor, place him as one of the most important English poets. *See also* ADDISON.

Poststructuralism *see* **Structuralism**.

Pound, Ezra [Weston Loomis] (1885–1972) American poet, editor, translator and critic. Notable poetry volumes include *Quia Pauper Amavi* (1919), *Hugh Selwyn Mauberley* (1920) and the unfinished sequence of poems entitled *Cantos* (1925–70). Pound gave generous support to T.S. ELIOT, JOYCE, ROSENBERG and HEMINGWAY, and many others. He lived in Italy from 1925, where he became a supporter of Italian Fascism and broadcast propaganda against the Allies during World War II. He was committed to a US mental asylum after the war until 1958, when he returned to Italy. *See* IMAGISM.

Powell, Anthony [Dymoke] (1905–) English novelist, noted particularly for his sequence of 12 novels entitled *A Dance to the Music of Time*, beginning with *A Question of Upbringing* (1951) and ending with *Hearing Secret Harmonies* (1975). The sequence is a large canvas (the title is from a Poussin painting) of British cultural, social and political life from the 1930s to the 1970s.

Powys, J[ohn] C[owper] (1872–1963) English novelist, essayist and poet. His novels include *Wolf Solent* (1929), *Weymouth Sands* (1934) and his masterpiece, *A Glastonbury Romance* (1932), in which the ancient spiritual world of the town of Glastonbury (a centre of Arthurian, Christian and pagan legend) is entwined with the everyday lives of the novel's characters. His brother **T[heodore] F[rancis] Powys** (1875–1953) also wrote novels and stories in the same West Country setting, the most notable of which is the remarkable fantasy novel *Mr Weston's Good Wine* (1927), in which God descends upon an English village in the form of a vintner selling the wines of love and death (the title taken from Jane AUSTEN's *Emma*). Another brother, **Llewellyn Powys** (1884–1939), was a journalist and essayist, whose *Skin for Skin* (1925) is an account of his fight against tuberculosis and contains periods of West Country idyll when the disease abated.

Priestley, J[ohn] B[oynton] (1891–1984) English novelist and dramatist. His huge output includes the novels *The Good Companions* (1929) and *Angel Pavement* (1930), the plays *Time and the Conways* (1937) and the much staged mystery *An Inspector Calls* (1947). His uplifting radio broadcasts during World War II made him one of the best-known literary figures in the 1940s.

Prior, Matthew (1664–1721) English poet, diplomat and spy. His first important work, *The Hind and Panther Transvers'd* (1687), was a satire on DRYDEN's defence of Roman Catholicism. Much of Prior's subsequent life was spent immersed in the murky waters of political intrigue and espionage, and earned him a year in jail. The best of his poems are light, mock-serious lyrics such as 'Jinny the Just' and 'Henry and Emma'. Addison described him as a master of the 'easy way of writing', i.e. of epigrammatic, everyday expression.

Pritchett, Sir V[ictor] S[awdon] (1900–97) English short-story writer, novelist, essayist and critic. He is best known for his excellent short stories, a collected edition of which was published in 1983. His critical works, e.g. *The Living Novel* (1946), have been highly praised for their shrewd insights into the creative process.

Proust, Marcel (1871–1922) French novelist, essayist and critic, known principally for his long semi-autobiographical novel in seven sections, *À la recherche du temps perdu* (1913–27). It was first translated into English as *Remembrance of Things Past* (1922–31) by **Charles Scott-Moncrieff** (1889–1930) and consists of *Swann's Way*, *Within a Budding Grove*, *The Guermantes' Way*, *Cities of the Plain*, *The Captive*, *The Sweet Cheat Gone*, and *Time Regained*. The novel provides a fascinating picture of the narrator Marcel's often convoluted relationships and artistic vocation in upper-class French society. By subjecting a mass of detail to an analytical eye and by using a circular form for the novel, Proust broke new ground in conveying the complexity of life and time and the importance of memory, and had a great influence on 20th-century novelists, e.g. Virginia WOOLF.

Pryce-Jones, David (1936–) English novelist, biographer and travel writer. His work includes the novel *Owls and Satyrs* (1960); his nonfiction work includes *Paris in the Third Reich* (1981) and a controversial and pessimistic study of Arab culture, *The Closed Circle* (1989).

Psalmanazar, George (*c.*1679–1763) French-born English literary hoaxer. Little is known for certain of his origins; he arrived in London in 1703, claiming to be a 'Formosan', for which country he invented a language and to which he published a travel guide. After years as a hack writer, he eventually (in 1728) renounced his imposture and became, strangely enough, a much respected literary figure. Dr JOHNSON called him 'the best man he ever knew'.

Pushkin, Alexander (1799–1837) Russian poet, novelist and dramatist. Widely regarded as Russia's greatest poet, the best known of his works are the historical tragedy *Boris Godunov* (1825), the verse novel *Eugene Onegin* (1823–31) and the macabre short story 'The Queen of Spades'. His life was brought to a premature end in a duel.

Pye, Henry James *see* **poet laureate**.

Pym, Barbara (1913–80) English novelist, whose works are gently satirical, occasionally melancholic, comedies of middle-class life, with clergymen and/or university dons frequently involved in a foreground dominated by an ironically observant (unmarried) lady. Representative examples are *Excellent Women* (1952), *Less than Angels* (1955), *A Glass of Blessings* (1958) and *Quartet in Autumn* (1977). She was a friend of Philip LARKIN, who admired her work greatly.

Pynchon, Thomas (1937–) American novelist, whose huge and complex books employ black humour to portray his vision of humanity's struggle against technology. His best-known novels are *V* (1963) and *Gravity's Rainbow* (1973).

Q

Q *see* **Quiller-Couch, Sir Arthur Thomas**.

Quarles, Francis (1592–1644) English poet. Educated at Christ's College, Cambridge, he entered Lincoln's Inn, and in 1613 was appointed cup-bearer to Princess Elizabeth, daughter of James I, on her marriage to Frederick V, short-lived king of Bohemia. After a spell in Dublin as secretary to Archbishop Ussher, he was appointed chronologer to the City of London in 1639. His most popular work was *Emblems* (1635), a set of devotional poems illustrated by engravings. His other poems include *Divine Poems* (1630), *Divine Fancies* (1632), and *Argalus and Parthenia* (1629). His prose works include *Enchiridion* (1640), a collection of brief essays and aphorisms in vigorous and occasionally eloquent language. On the outbreak of the Civil War he joined Charles I at Oxford and wrote pamphlets, e.g. *The Loyal Convert*, in the royalist cause, which offended Parliament and led to the sequestration of his property and the destruction of his manuscripts, possibly hastening his death.

Quiller-Couch, Sir Arthur Thomas (1863–1944) British author and critic. Born in Cornwall and educated at Trinity College, Oxford, he taught classics there for a year after graduating before turning to writing. His career began with *Dead Man's Rock* (1887), an improbable but thrilling story which became very popular. He followed this success with a great number of books, including a series of novels set in Cornwall, written under the pseudonym 'Q' and exhibiting a keen sense of humour. He edited some well-chosen anthologies, e.g. *The Oxford Book of English Verse* (1900), *The Oxford Book of Ballads* (1910) and *The Oxford Book of Victorian Verse* (1912). He was knighted in 1910, and in 1912 was appointed professor of English literature at Cambridge. As a critic, he was a sworn foe of pedantry and often entertaining. His critical works include *On the Art of Writing* (1916), *Shakespeare's Workmanship* (1918), and *On the Art of Reading* (1920).

Quintilian [Marcus Fabius Quintilianus] (*c.*35–*c.* AD 100) Roman rhetorician and critic, born in Spain. His fame rests on his major work *De Institutione Oratoria* (*c.* AD 93), a manual for the training of orators, beginning with his views on what constitutes the best education from the cradle upwards. Having observed that the reading of good authors is indispensable for the acqusition of a good style, he proceeds to give a brief sketch of the most notable Greek and Latin authors, and their merits. This part of the work is the best-known piece of literary criticism that has survived from antiquity. Extant in a mutilated version, the complete text was discovered in 1413 and influenced writers such as JONSON and POPE.

R

Rabelais, François (*c*.1494–*c*.1553) French physician and satirist, noted for his huge, rambling prose fantasy *Gargantua and Pantagruel* (1553–62), which includes many fascinating insights into the intellectual currents of the age. The adjective 'Rabelaisian' is used to denote language that is healthily and robustly bawdy; however, as ORWELL pointed out, there is little that is healthy about the grossly anti-female content of *Gargantua and Pantagruel*, even by late medieval standards.

Racine, Jean (1639–99) French dramatist, regarded as the finest of the French tragedians. Several of his plays, e.g. *Andromaque* (1667) and *Phèdre* (1677), have been performed in English translations from the late 17th century onwards, but the only productions that have achieved any real popularity on the British and American stage are those that have parted quite radically from Racine's strict NEOCLASSICAL principles. The full impact of Racine's powerfully restrained language can only be appreciated in the original French.

Radcliffe, Mrs Ann (1764–1823) English novelist, whose GOTHIC NOVELS, e.g. *A Sicilian Romance* (1790) and *The Mysteries of*

Udolpho (1794), were very popular in their day, but are now largely remembered as part-sources for Jane AUSTEN's wonderful satire on the Gothic novel, *Northanger Abbey*.

Raine, Kathleen [Jessel] (1908–) Anglo-Scottish poet and critic, whose work reflects her life-long mystical vision of the world (Blake and Neoplatonism are the major concerns of her critical work). Her works include *Collected Poems* (1981), and three autobiographical volumes, *Farewell Happy Fields* (1973), *The Land Unknown* (1975) and *The Lion's Mouth* (1977).

Ransome, Arthur (1884–1967) English novelist and journalist. Ransome's first popular success was as a popularizer of Russian folk tales, with his *Old Peter's Russian Tales* (1916), and he subsequently became an authority on (and propagandist for) the Bolshevik Revolution, and one of British journalism's best-known foreign correspondents (he married Trotsky's ex-secretary in 1924). He is best remembered, however, for his classic children's adventure novels, the first three of which were *Swallows and Amazons* (1930), *Swallowdale* (1931) and *Peter Duck* (1932). Nine more children's bestsellers were to follow. (His publisher only reluctantly accepted *Swallows and Amazons*, being much more interested in his fishing essays, *Rod and Line*, 1929).

Ransom, John Crowe (1888–1974) American poet and critic. His poetic output, e.g. *Poems about God* (1919) and *Two Gentlemen in Bonds* (1926), was small but is highly regarded, as are his literary studies, *God without Thunder* (1930) and *The New Criticism* (1941).

Rattigan, Sir Terence [Mervyn] (1911–77) English dramatist. Many of his plays, e.g. the comedy *French Without Tears* (1936), and the melodramas of middle-class hypocrisy and crisis, *The Browning Version* (1948) and *The Deep Blue Sea* (1952), having become firm repertory favourites. Another notable play is *Ross*

(1960), a psychological study of T. E. LAWRENCE during his life in semi-hiding as an RAF aircraftsman. The new wave of dramatists of the 1950s and 1960s (primarily the ANGRY YOUNG MEN), tended to denigrate Rattigan's plays, describing them as middleclass and trivial. More recent critical opinion regards Rattigan as a sensitive explorer of regions of spiritual aridity.

Realism in literature, a true and faithful representation of reality in fiction. Once defined, discussion of the term usually breaks down into personal prejudices of various kinds. The process of distinguishing the term from NATURALISM is particularly fraught; any artist must select from the chaos of life in order to create, and in the process of choosing must impose some personal, even if banal, vision on the world, and in the process either convince the reader that the world portrayed is a real one, or fail. In the last analysis, there is only good writing and bad writing. Sometimes the process of conviction occurs despite the author's intervention; thus George ELIOT, often described as the first great realist of English fiction, begins a chapter of *Middlemarch* with the words 'Destiny stands by sarcastic, our fate in her hands'. The action of the novel in fact contradicts this snooty deterministic pronouncement rather well. BALZAC is regarded as the founding father of literary realism in the novel (*see* MARX).

The genre of *socialist realism*, which GORKY helped to create (*see also* DEUS EX MACHINA, NEOCLASSICISM), bears no relation to realism; the term usually denotes any form of fiction, within a socialist dictatorship, that is written to serve the interests of the ruling clique of that state by lauding the achievements of 'the socialist paradise where there is no more pain or suffering, where happy people under the guidance of wise leaders construct a new life and harshly chastise their enemies'. (Igor Golomstock, *Totalitarian Art* 1990). *See also* FUTURISM, MAGIC REALISM.

Redskins and Palefaces a distinction between authors who write about outdoor, manly topics such as men at war (Red-skins), and those who write about the problems and relationships of indoors, 'cultivated' people. The distinction was formulated by an American academic, Leslie Fielder, and works easily in terms of much American literature, e.g. HEMINGWAY is as obviously a Redskin as Henry JAMES is a Paleface. The distinction is less helpful elsewhere.

Renaissance in literature, the revival that occurred in Europe in the 14th–16th centuries, as a result of the rediscovery of the writing of the great classical writers, notably the works of PLATO and ARISTOTLE. In the case of the latter, the 'rediscovery' occurred in terms of reinterpretation; instead of taking the texts of Aristotle as literal, unchallengable authority, as medieval scholars had tended to do, the new thinkers, such as Francis BACON (the father of modern scientific method) approached written authority with a new, sceptical eye. The Renaissance period in England is usually given as 1500–1660, i.e. from the visit of ERASMUS (*see also* Thomas MORE) in 1599 to the RESTORATION.

Restoration (1) the re-establishment of the British monarchy in 1660, following the return to England of Charles II in that year. (2) the period of Charles II's reign (1660–85). The characteristics of Restoration literature are wit, salaciousness, and religious and philosophical questioning. Some typical Restoration literary figures include ROCHESTER, DRYDEN, ETHEREGE, CONGREVE, WYCHERLEY, PEPYS, BUNYAN, HOBBES, MARVELL, FARQUHAR (*see also* WESLEY, MILTON).

Restoration comedy *see* **comedy of manners**.

revenge tragedy a form of TRAGEDY that appeared in the late Elizabethan period, heavily influenced by the bloodthirsty language and plots of SENECA's plays, in which revenge, often for the death of a son or father, is the prime motive. Thomas KYD's *The Spanish Tragedy* (1588–89) is the earliest example, *Hamlet*

(1602) the greatest. MARLOWE's *The Jew of Malta* (1592) and TOURNEUR's *The Revenger's Tragedy* (1607) are two other notable examples (*see* JACOBEAN TRAGEDY).

Reyes, Ricardo Neftalí *see* **Neruda, Pablo**.

Richardson, Dorothy [Miller] (1873–1957) English novelist, noted for her 'stream-of-consciousness' (*see* William JAMES) narrative technique or 'interior monologue', as she called it, which anticipated JOYCE's use of the technique in *Ulysses* (the device was not really new; similar effects can be found in, e.g. DICKENS). Her work enjoyed a considerable revival in the 1970s. Her best-known work is the semi-autobiographical *Pilgrimage* sequence of novels, e.g. *Pointed Roofs* (1915) and (posthumously) *March Moonlight* (1967).

Richardson, Samuel (1689–1761) English novelist. All his novels were written in EPISTOLARY form, and all were highly popular. The first was *Pamela; or Virtue Rewarded* (1740), in which a servant girl achieves an upwardly mobile marriage by resisting seduction (the work was savagely attacked by FIELDING in *Shamela* for its dubious morality). Richardson subsequently published *Clarissa Harlowe* (1747–48) and *Sir Charles Grandison* (1753–54). Fielding was not the only contemporary to feel unease at the moral ambiguity of Richardson's work, or the tendentious verbosity of much of the prose. However, Fielding's sister Sarah (also a novelist) and Dr JOHNSON were convinced of Richardson's superiority to all novelists for his insight into human (especially female) character, and for his portrayal of the darker aspects of human behaviour.

Riding, Laura Jackson *see* **Graves, Robert**.

Rilke, Rainer Maria (1875–1926) German poet. His lyrical, mystical poems, in such volumes as *Duino Elegies* (1922) and *Sonnets to Orpheus* (1923), are regarded as being amongst the finest religious verse published this century.

Rimbaud, Arthur (1854–91) French poet. An early SYMBOLIST, he stopped writing poetry at the age of 19 after a torrid affair with VERLAINE, described in *Une Saison en enfer* (*A Season in Hell*) (1873). Some of the pieces in his collection of hallucinatory, vivid prose poems, *Les Illuminations* (1884), were set to music by Benjamin Britten.

Robbe-Grillet, Alain (1922–) French novelist, whose works, e.g. *Topology of a Phantom City* (1975), and the screenplay *Last Year in Marienbad* (filmed 1961), are regarded as 'new novels' or 'antinovels', or, more simply, as unreadable novels. His work has not achieved a great deal of popularity, not even in France.

Robinson, Edwin Arlington (1869–1935) American poet. His early poems are mostly concerned with New England small-town characters, e.g. *The Children of the Night* (1897). His later verse includes a trilogy on the Arthurian legend (*see* ARTHUR), *Merlin* (1917), *Lancelot* (1920) and *Tristram* (1927).

Rochester, John Wilmot, 2nd Earl of (1647–80) English poet. Renowned (and feared) for his savage wit and supposedly limitless depths of depravity, his verse is among the most sexually explicit in English (or any language). A representative (and very fine) poem is his 'Satyr Against Mankind' (1675), with its memorable image of man as, in death, 'a reasoning engine' huddled in dirt. Graham GREENE's *Lord Rochester's Monkey* (1974) is the best introduction to the man and his work.

Rolle, Richard *see* **Julian of Norwich, Dame**.

Romanticism a term denoting any movement in the arts which emphasizes feeling and content as opposed to form and order. The Romantic movement can be roughly dated from the late 18th century to the early 19th century, although the contrast between the need to express emotion and the desirability of following artistic rules dates back as far as the great Athenian dramatists (e.g. the contrast between AESCHYLUS and SOPHOCLES). Other distinctive features of the Romantic movement are: the supremacy of individual over collective judgment; a 'progressive' faith in the reformability and essential goodness of humanity; the supremacy of 'natural' and 'organic' virtues over society's artifical construction. The extent and meaning of Romanticism in 18th-century English literature is still a matter of hot debate. It is certainly true that elements of what we call Romanticism can be found in poets such as COWPER and SMART, and even in Dr JOHNSON's writings, but the first great works of Romantic literature are BLAKE's works of the 1790s and WORDSWORTH and COLERIDGE's *Lyrical Ballads* (1798). Debate on the merits or demerits of Romanticism tends to be conducted in aphoristic terms, e.g. GOETHE's dictum (in rejection of his early Romantic principles) that 'Classicism is health, Romanticism disease.' Other prominent Romantic poets are BYRON, SHELLEY, KEATS, HEINE and SCOTT. *Compare* NEOCLASSICISM.

Rosenberg, Isaac (1890–1918) English poet and artist. His family were emigré Romanian Jews who settled in London's East End. By 1914 he had established a reputation as a promising poet; his first collection, *Night and Day* (1912), was praised by POUND. He enlisted in the British Army in 1914, and was killed in action in 1916. His war poems have a more objective tone than those of contemporaries such as OWEN and SASSOON, although they are no less grim (e.g. 'Dead Man's Dump'). His *Collected Poems* were published in 1937.

Rosenstock, Samuel *see* **Tzara, Tristan**.

Rossetti, Christina Georgina (1830–94) English poet, noted for her reflective, occasionally melancholic religious poems. She also wrote verses for children, and the remarkable verse fairy story *Goblin Market* (1882). Her brother, **Dante Gabriel Rossetti** (1828–82), was both a poet and an artist. With the painters Millais and Holman Hunt, he founded the Pre-Raphaelite Brotherhood school of painting. His most famous poems are 'The Blessed Damozel' (1850) and the fine sonnet sequence 'The House of Life', the complete version of which is in *Ballads and Sonnets* (1881).

Rostand, Edmond (1868–1918) French dramatist and poet. His best-known work is his verse drama *Cyrano de Bergerac* (1897). *See* CYRANO DE BERGERAC.

Roth, Philip (1933–) American novelist and short-story writer. Much of his fiction is concerned with the problems (often sexual) of Jewish family life, e.g. the novella *Goodbye Columbus* (1959) and his hymn to masturbation, *Portnoy's Complaint* (1969). His novel *Deception* (1990) is an intriguing semi-autobiographical work.

Rousseau, Jean-Jacques (1712–78) French philosopher. His most notable fictional works are the novels *Julie, or the New Héloïse* (1761) and *Émile* (1762), the former describing a highly improbably virtuous *menage à trois*, the latter being a didactic work on how to educate children (whom he saw as naturally good). These works and others, notably the political tract *The Social Contract* (1762), which begins with the famous statement 'Man is born free, and is everywhere in chains', were profoundly influential on the intellectual ferment which resulted in the French Revolution (*see also* VOLTAIRE). His very frank 12 volumes of autobiography, *Confessions*, were published posthumously in 1781–88 and set a fashion for this style of reminiscence.

Rowe Nicholas (1674–1718) English dramatist and poet, his best-known plays being *Tamerlane* (1702) and *Jane Shore* (1714), the latter written for the actress Sarah Siddons. His translation of the Roman poet Lucan's *Pharalia* (1718) was much admired by Dr JOHNSON, and he also produced an important edition of SHAKESPEARE. He was POET LAUREATE from 1715 until his death.

Runyon, [Alfred] Damon (1884–1946) American short-story

writer, noted for his humorous, racy short stories about New York low life and the seamier side of Broadway, e.g. *Guys and Dolls* (1931).

Rushdie, Salman (1947–) Indian-born British novelist. Regarded as one of the leading young British novelists, his first major success was *Midnight's Children* (1981), a fantasy on post-independence India seen through the eyes of children born at midnight on Independence Day, 1947. After the publication of his *The Satanic Verses* (1988), in 1989 Ayatollah Khomeini of Iran pronounced a *fatwa* (death sentence) for blasphemy on the author. The offence caused by the book was (and is) primarily the assertion that parts of the Koran are of Satanic origin and led to a worldwide debate on free speech and censorship. In 1998 the Iranian government withdrew its support of the fatwa, thus ameliorating the situation.

Ruskin, John (1819–1900) English writer, artist and influential art critic. He came to prominence with his book *Modern Painters* (1843) in which he championed the works of Turner. This and subsequent writings eventually totalled 39 volumes through which he virtually dictated Victorian taste in art for over half a century. His works include *Modern Painters* (1843–60), *The Seven Lamps of Architecture* (1849), *The Stones of Venice* (1851–53), *Unto this Last* (1860) and *Sesame and Lilies* (1865, 1871). Ruskin was an enthusiast for Gothic art, and supported the Pre-Raphaelite Brotherhood, of which he was a member, being himself a prolific and talented artist. Like his friend CARLYLE, he was a strong critic of the values and ugliness of industrial England. His personal life was not happy. He was educated by tutors before entering Oxford University; his marriage was annulled, and his wife married his friend, the painter John Millais. During the 1870s he began to lose his reason, and he lost a notorious libel case against Whistler in 1878. His writings and philosophies had a profound influence on the Arts and Crafts Movement.

Russian Futurism *see* **futurism**.

S

Sackville-West, Vita [Hon. Victoria Mary] (1892–1962) English poet and novelist, best known for her novels *The Edwardians* (1930) and *All Passion Spent* (1931), and her long pastoral poem *The Land* (1926). Her *Collected Poems* were published in 1933, and she also wrote books on her travels with her husband, the diplomat Sir Harold NICOLSON, and on gardening. Her many female lovers included Virginia WOOLF, who used her as the model for the reincarnated hero/heroine Orlando in the novel of the same name. Her unconventional marriage was described by her son, Nigel Nicolson, in *Portrait of a Marriage* (1973).

Sade, Marquis de (1740–1814) French soldier and novelist. He was condemned to death in 1772 for acts of extreme depravity, escaped, was recaptured and spent most of the rest of his life in prison. His highly licentious works include several novels, of which the least difficult to read is *Justine* (1791). The term 'sadism' derives from the dominant theme in his life and work, the desire to inflict pain in the pursuit of (usually sexual) pleasure. He was released from prison during the French Revolution and was appointed a judge, but was soon back in prison for being too lenient in sentencing. (His main contribution to the Revolution was a memorably evil speech in praise of Marat's blood lust.) He died insane.

Saki [pseud. of Hector Hugh Munro] (1870–1916) Burmese-born Scottish short-story writer, noted for his satirical short stories, e.g. *The Chronicles of Clovis* (1911) and *Beasts and Super-*

Beasts (1914). The stories are wickedly funny, often have a macabre or supernatural slant, and are studded with aphorisms, e.g. 'It's the Early Christian that gets the fattest lion.' His finest story is 'Sredni Vashtar', in which a young boy's ferret, which he worships as a god, answers his prayers by killing his cruel aunt. Saki was killed in the trenches during World War I, shot by a sniper. His last words were 'Put out that light.'

Salinger, J[erome] D[avid] (1919–) American novelist and short-story writer, best known for his highly successful novel of adolescence, *The Catcher in the Rye* (1951). The close Wertherlike (*see* GOETHE) identification of many readers with the young narrator's distrust of the adult world has been widely commented upon. A curious feature of the book's appeal is its strong influence on many disturbed young males, such as John Lennon's killer. An equally curious feature of the author is his extreme reluctance to give interviews, which has given rise on occasions to rumours of his death.

Sandburg, Carl August (1878–1967) American poet. His WHITMAN-influenced poems, e.g. *Chicago Poems* (1916) and *Smoke and Steel* (1920), celebrate the lives of ordinary people. He also wrote a six-volume life of Abraham Lincoln (1926–39).

Sappho (b. *c*.650 BC) Greek poet. The Greeks regarded her as one of the greatest of all lyric poets, but only tantalizingly short fragments of her poetry have survived, e.g. her magical little hymn to the Evening Star.

Sartre, Jean-Paul (1905–80) French philosopher, novelist and dramatist. His attempts at combining EXISTENTIALIST philosophy, which places humanity in a largely meaningless universe in which human actions count for little, with Marxist political philosophy, which sees humanity as progressing to an ever brighter future, are now only of interest as period pieces. His novels, however, particularly *Nausea* (1938) and the *Roads to Freedom* trilogy (1945–49) are highly readable. Several of his plays, e.g. *The Flies* (1943) and *Huis Clos* (1944, in English *No Exit*), which features the famous line, 'Hell is other people', are frequently performed. In 1964 he was awarded the NOBEL PRIZE for literature, but declined to accept it. *See* BEAUVOIR

Sassoon, Siegfried [Lorraine] (1886–1967) English poet and novelist, whose grimly realistic poems have established him as one of the two major poets, with OWEN, of World War I. He was awarded the Military Cross during the war, and achieved notoriety by organizing a public protest against the war and throwing his medal away. Two notable collections of the poems are *Counter-Attack* (1918) and *Satirical Poems* (1926). His semi-autobiographical trilogy of novels, *Memoirs of a Fox-Hunting Man* (1928), *Memoirs of an Infantry Officer* (1930) and *Sherston's Progress* (1936), describes the progress of a young man from sports-loving boyhood through the horrors of trench warfare.

Saussure, Ferdinand de *see* **Structuralism**.

Schreiner, Olive (1855–1920) South African novelist, remembered chiefly for one work (published under the pseudonym of 'Ralph Iron'), *The Story of an African Farm* (1883). The work, which has a lovingly described background based on Schreiner's own childhood on a South African farm, has a 'New Woman' heroine who defies convention by refusing to marry the lover by whom she has a baby.

Sciascia, Leonardo (1921–1989) Italian novelist, short-story writer and essayist. Sciascia's work, whether fictional or nonfictional, is concerned with the endemic public corruption at the heart of Italian society. Sciascia was born and raised in Sicily, where he developed a strong sense of injustice at the immorality of any political system working to oppress the poor and preserve social injustice. He was no ordinary polemicist, but a highly gifted and original writer, with a rare talent for exposing self-delusion and hypocrisy. Notable examples of his work include *Sicilian Uncles* (1958), *Candido* (1977) and *The Moro Affair* (1978).

Scott, Sir Walter (1771–1832) Scottish novelist and poet. His early, highly romantic narrative poems, set in the Scottish past, e.g. *Marmion* (1808), *The Lady of the Lake* (1810) and *The Lord of the Isles* (1815), established his popularity with both the reading public and the literary world, BYRON being particularly generous in his praise. His historical novels (a genre he refined and made into an art form), particularly *Waverley* (1814), *The Heart of Midlothian* (1818) and *Ivanhoe* (1819), were enormously popular and influential, and spawned a host of imitators, e.g. Fenimore COOPER. Scott's re-creation (or invention) of Scottish Highland culture, e.g. making the kilt respectable and glorifying the Highland virtues of courage and loyalty, was also of enormous influence, and inspired similar undertakings throughout all Europe. Mark TWAIN claimed that Scott's novels were an indirect cause of the American Civil War by creating the myth of the noble, warlike gentleman, an ideal that many Southern men aspired to.

Sedley, Sir Charles (1639–1701) English poet and dramatist. He was a friend of both DRYDEN and ROCHESTER, and, like the latter, was involved in many sordid incidents; he was once fined for indecent exposure, but reformed to some extent when the roof fell in on him during a tennis match (with ETHEREGE). His three plays are the tragedy *Antony and Cleopatra* (1677) and two comedies, *The Mulberry Garden* (1668) and *Bellamira* (1687). His lyrics include the magical 'Love still has something of the sea' and several other very fine poems, collected in the posthumously issued *Miscellaneous Works* (1702).

Semiotics *see* **Structuralism**.

Seneca [Lucius Anneus Seneca] (*c*.4 BC–AD 65) Roman dramatist and Stoic philosopher. The violent rhetoric of his verse tragedies (which often have a supernatural content) was very influential on Elizabethan dramatists such as SHAKESPEARE, although the plays were probably meant for private readings rather than public performance. T.S. ELIOT's essays 'Shakespeare and the Stoicism of Seneca' and 'Seneca in Elizabethan Translation', in *Elizabethan Essays* (1934), provide valuable insights into Seneca's philosophy and influence. Like PETRONIUS, he was ordered to commit suicide by Emperor Nero.

sentimental comedy a form of English COMEDY that arose in the early 18th century, focusing on the problems of middle-class characters. The plays always end happily and feature strongly contrasting good and bad characters and high emotional peaks. The form was developed by Richard STEELE in a conscious reaction to the excesses of Restoration comedy (*see* COMEDY OF MANNERS). Examples include Steele's *The Tender Husband* (1705) and, notably, *The Conscious Lovers* (1722). The form led on to MELODRAMA (*see also* DOMESTIC TRAGEDY).

Shadwell, Thomas (*c*.1642–92) English dramatist and poet. In the best of his 17 plays, the comedies, he gives a lively and often satirical account of contemporary life, e.g. *The Virtuoso* (1676). In 1682 he quarrelled with DRYDEN, his political opponent (Shadwell was a 'true-blue' Whig), and from then until after the 'Glorious Revolution' of 1688 his plays were not produced on the London stage. He replaced Dryden as POET LAUREATE in 1689.

Shakespeare, William (1564–1616) English dramatist and poet. He was born and brought up in Stratford-upon-Avon, where he attended the local grammar school. He married Anne Hathaway in 1582, and they had three children by 1585 (his last surviving descendant, a granddaughter, died in 1670). Nothing is known for certain of the circumstances of his move to London and entry into the theatrical world, but in 1592 there appeared a reference to him in a pamphlet by Robert GREENE. Shakespeare's plays are

generally divided into three groups. The first group (late 1580s–
c.1594) consists of histories, e.g. the *Henry VI* trilogy, early
comedies such as *The Two Gentlemen of Verona*, *The Comedy of
Errors* and *Love's Labour's Lost*, and the tragedy *Romeo and
Juliet*. The second group (c.1595–c.1599) includes histories such
as *King John*, *Henry IV* Parts I and II, and *Henry V*, the comedies
A Midsummer Night's Dream, *Much Ado About Nothing* and *As
You Like It*, and the tragedy *Julius Caesar*. The third group
(c.1600–c.1612) includes the great tragedies *Hamlet*, *Othello*,
King Lear, *Macbeth*, *Antony and Cleopatra*, *Coriolanus* and
Timon of Athens, the so-called 'dark comedies', *Troilus and
Cressida*, *All's Well That Ends Well*, and *Measure for Measure*,
and tragicomedies such as *The Winter's Tale* and *The Tempest*.
(The plays are unquestionably by Shakespeare and not, as some
argue, by BACON.) Shakespeare's other major works are the narrative poems *Venus and Adonis* (1593) and *The Rape of Lucrece*
(1594), and the magnificent *Sonnets*, which are known to have
been in private circulation in London in 1598 before being published, possibly not with his approval, in 1609. The sonnets feature a romantic triangle between the poet (Shakespeare), a dark
lady (identity unknown) and a beautiful young nobleman (possibly the Earl of Southampton). Speculation about the background
to the sonnets has been intense, and occasionally manic (AUDEN
doubted the sanity of anyone who had a theory concerning
them). Shakespeare's status as the greatest of all dramatists and
poets has only rarely been challenged in modern times. The
works have been translated into every major language, and are
among the greatest products of Western culture. *See also*
FLETCHER.

Sharp, William *see* **Macleod, Fiona**.

Shaw, George Bernard (1856–1950) Anglo-Irish dramatist and
critic. He began his literary career as a drama, literary and music

critic in the 1880s, and after a false start in novel-writing (he wrote five) began writing plays in the 1890s. His treatise *The Quintessence of Ibsenism* (1891) sets out his belief in the new 'IBSENite' drama of social realism (and also in socialism). The plays, e.g. *Man and Superman* (1903), *Major Barbara* (1905), *Pygmalion* (1913, which later became the musical *My Fair Lady*) and *Back to Methuselah*, bear the hallmarks of a failed novelist, with fussily detailed stage directions about the characters' motivations, colour of eyes, etc, but have proved very successful, thanks largely to Shaw's mastery of bright, witty dialogue, and ability to persuade the watcher or reader of the plays that he or she is ranged with the author against the boors and bores. Shaw seems to have genuinely believed that he was a greater dramatist than SHAKESPEARE. He adopted the role of 'intellectual maverick', delighting all sections of society with his wit, and became something of a national institution in Britain. Like many intellectuals, he longed for a 'great man' to put his 'rational, commonsense' ideas into practice, and wrote admiringly of both Hitler and Stalin (like Hitler, he was a vegetarian who hated cruelty to animals, yet was capable of monstrous intellectual callousness; his praise of Stalin's prison camps has to be read to be believed). YEATS described him as an atheist, 'haunted by the mystery he flouts'. He was awarded the NOBEL PRIZE for literature in 1925.

Shelley, Mary Wollstonecraft (1797–1851) English novelist. The daughter of two prominent social reformers, William Godwin and Mary Wollstonecraft, she eloped with SHELLEY in 1814 and married him in 1816 after his wife died. Her masterpiece is *Frankenstein, or the Modern Prometheus* (1818), a GOTHIC fantasy that has been hailed as the first science fiction novel. There have been innumerable (usually very loose) stage and film adaptations of the novel, which arose out of an agreement between Shelley, BYRON and herself to write supernatural tales.

Shelley, Percy Bysshe (1792–1822) English poet. His extraordinary talent for creating public scandal got off to a flying start at Oxford University, where he was expelled for co-writing a tract called *The Necessity of Atheism* (1811), in which year he married Harriet Westwood. Two years later, his poem *Queen Mab* was published, which celebrated a future republican millennium of free love and vegetarianism. In 1814, he eloped with Mary Godwin (*see* Mary Wollstonecraft SHELLEY) and her fifteen-year-old step-sister. Harriet committed suicide in 1816, in which year he married Mary. Shelley and his entourage moved to Italy in 1818, where he drowned in 1822. His poems are among the greatest of English ROMANTIC poetry. The highlights are: *The Revolt of Islam* (1817); *Prometheus Unbound* (1820); *Adonais* (1821), his elegy on the death of KEATS; and several of the finest poems in the language, notably 'Ode to the West Wind' and 'To a Skylark' (both 1820). His essay *A Defence of Poetry* (1821, published 1840) finishes with the defiant assertion that 'poets are the unacknowledged legislators of the world.' His last great (unfinished) poem, *The Triumph of Life* (1824), is a very bleak work (the title is profoundly ironic). *See also* SOCRATES, BYRON.

Sheridan, Richard Brinsley (1751–1816) Irish dramatist and politician, noted for his superb comedies of manners, *The Rivals* (1775) and *School for Scandal* (1777), both of which are firm repertory favourites. His other major play is *The Critic* (1779), an extremely funny burlesque which mercilessly satirizes the conventions of tragedy and the (seemingly eternal) sleazy aspects of theatrical production.

Shizheng, Li *see* **Duoduo**.

Sholokhov, Mikhail [Alexandrovich] (1905–84) Russian novelist. Sholokhov's *And Quiet Flows the Don* (issued in 4 volumes,

1928–40), which presents a panorama of Don Cossack life before and during the Bolshevik Revolution, has been hailed as a masterpiece by many critics. There have been persistent rumours, however, that the work is not entirely his own (it has been suggested that Sholokhov stole the basis of the book from a manuscript by a dead White Army officer). He was awarded the NOBEL PRIZE for literature in 1965.

Sidney, Sir Philip (1554–86) English poet, soldier and courtier. His works include *Arcadia* (1590), the first major English pastoral poem; the sonnet sequence *Astrophel and Stella* (1591), which inspired a host of imitations; and *A Defence of Poetry* (1595), a spirited defence of English as a medium for writing great poetry. His death in action against the Spaniards in the Netherlands was followed by a host of tributes from his many admirers throughout Europe. *See* BALLAD.

Simon, [Marvin] Neil (1927–) American dramatist. His very popular (New-York based) comedies of manners include *Barefoot in the Park* (1963) and *The Odd Couple* (1965). More recent works, e.g. *Brighton Beach Memoirs*, have an autobiographical element while retaining their wit and humour.

Sinclair, Upton [Beall] (1878–1968) American novelist. The best-known works of his huge fictional output are *The Jungle* (1906), which features a no-holds-barred account of the Chicago meat trade and resulted in legislation against the horrors described in the book, and the 'Lanny Budd' sequence of political novels, e.g. *World's End* (1940) and *The Return of Lanny Budd* (1953).

Singer, Isaac Bashevis (1904–91) Polish-born American Yiddish short-story writer and novelist. He emigrated from Poland to the US in 1935. Much of his fiction deals with the now vanished world of Polish Judaism, e.g. *The Magician of Lublin* (1960). He was awarded the NOBEL PRIZE for literature in 1978.

Sitwell, Dame Edith Louisa (1887–1964) English poet and critic. She and her brothers, **Sir Osbert Sitwell** (1892–1969) and **Sacheverell Sitwell** (1897–1988), were ardent proponents of modernism in the arts, and worked quite hard at attracting controversy. Edith Sitwell's works include *Facade*, an 'entertainment' consisting of jazz-influenced abstract verses, which was first performed in 1923 with music by William Walton, and several fine elegiac poems, e.g. 'Still Falls the Rain' (on the 'total war' of World War II). The essential work on the Sitwells is Sir Osbert's six-volume autobiography, from *Left Hand, Right Hand* (1945) to *Tales my Father Taught Me* (1962), which also provides a remarkable portrait of upper-class English life in the 20th century.

Smart, Christopher (1722–71) English poet. His best-known works are his great, highly idiosyncratic religious poems *A Song to David* (1763) and *Jubilate Agno* (unpublished until 1939), a wonderfully original celebration of God's creation written while Smart was confined in a lunatic asylum (1759–63). The most quoted lines from the poem are those describing his cat Jeoffrey. Dr JOHNSON (another cat lover) was an admirer of Smart's piety if not his poetry, and his strange, beguiling verse has only gained full recognition in this century.

Smart, Elizabeth (1913–86) Canadian author of two short novels, *By Grand Central Station I sat Down and Wept* (1945) and *The Assumption of the Rogues and Rascals* (1978). The first book, a lush, rhapsodic study of desire, was inspired by Smart's love for the poet George BARKER. She fell in love with him through reading his poetry, pursued him ('I must marry a poet') and had four children by him (Barker remained married to someone else). Her journal for 1933–40 was published in 1991 under the title *Necessary Secrets*.

Smith, Stevie [Florence Margaret] (1902–71) English poet and novelist. Her graceful, melancholic, and occasionally fiercely funny verse has been much admired, especially the superb collection *Not Waving but Drowning* (1957). She also wrote three novels, *Novel on Yellow Paper* (1936), *Over the Frontier* (1938) and *The Holiday* (1949), in a style likened by some to that of Gertrude STEIN.

Smollett, Tobias [George] (1721–71) Scottish novelist. He served in the Royal Navy as a ship's surgeon and took part in an attack upon a Spanish port in the West Indies. In the early 1740s, he set up a surgical practice in London. His PICARESQUE NOVELS, of which the most important are *The Adventures of Roderick Random* (1748), *The Adventures of Peregrine Pickle* (1751), and his masterpiece, *The Expedition of Humphrey Clinker* (1771), are cleverly plotted satirical works rich in characterization, which achieved lasting popularity. His works have had a strong influence on many other authors, notably DICKENS.

socialist realism *see* **realism**.

social realism a form of realism, in which an artist's political viewpoint (usually on the left) affects the content of his work. It is not the same as socialist realism (*see* REALISM), the name given to official art in the Soviet Union, which was intended to glorify the achievements of the Communist Party.

Socrates (469–399 BC) Greek philosopher, the tutor of PLATO. The sources of Socrates' teachings are many and widely varied, but it is Plato's Socrates, a somewhat maddening genius with a gift for answering questions with another question, who has come down to posterity in Plato's 'Socratic dialogues', e.g. *Protagoras*. The central theme in Socrates's thinking is a quest for truth through rigorous self-examination: 'the unexamined life is not worth living' (Plato, *Apology*). Shelley paid him a very high compliment in *The Triumph of Life*, describing Socrates and Jesus as the only two humans to break free from the murderous wheel of life. Soc-

rates was forced to commit suicide by the Athenians for supposedly corrupting youths through teaching them 'impiety'.

Solzhenitsyn, Alexander [Isayevich] (1918–) Russian novelist
and historian. His novella *One Day in the Life of Ivan
Denisovich* (1962), based on his experiences in a Soviet labour
camp, created a sensation when published in the USSR during a
brief thaw in cultural restrictions. His subsequent novels, *The
First Circle* and *Cancer Ward*, were too critical of Soviet life for
the authorities' liking, and were published abroad in 1968, as
was his study of the history and organization of the labour camp
system, *The Gulag Archipelago* (1973–75). He was awarded the
NOBEL PRIZE for literature in 1970, was deported from the USSR
in 1974 and settled in Vermont. In a remarkable development in
September 1990, the Soviet Communist Youth League newspaper published a long article by Solzhenitsyn entitled 'How We
are to Rebuild Russia', calling for a return to pre-Bolshevik,
Christian Slavic values. His Soviet citizenship was restored, and
he returned to Russia in 1994.

Sophocles (*c.*496–406 BC) Greek dramatist. Seven of his *c.*120
plays are extant. He was the most popular of the three great
Athenian tragedians (the others being AESCHYLUS and EURIPIDES).
The reasons for his popularity still hold good for audiences: his
characters are plausible, have recognizable human failings, and
their tragic situations have a strong element of pathos. His plays
have been very influential on many writers, e.g. on MILTON,
SHELLEY and ARNOLD (who mentions him in 'Dover Beach').
Oedipus Rex and *Oedipus at Colonus* have had a powerful influence on modern thought through the theories of FREUD. *Antigone*,
in which Oedipus's daughter Antigone decides to obey divine
law in burying her brother rather than the law of the state which
forbids his burial, has acquired strong resonances in the context
of 20th-century totalitarianism. *See also* ANOUILH.

Southey, Robert (1774–1843) English poet. He was closely associated with WORDSWORTH and COLERIDGE, but only a few of his large output of poems are still regarded as having much merit. He was POET LAUREATE from 1813, and was heavily satirized by BYRON (particularly in *Don Juan*), for his abandonment of revolutionary principles.

Soyinka, Wole (1934–) Nigerian poet, novelist, dramatist and critic. He worked in London in the late 1950s, where three of his plays, *The Swamp Dwellers*, *The Lion and the Jewel* and *The Invention*, were produced in 1958–59. He supported the Biafran side in the Nigerian Civil War, and was imprisoned by the Nigerian Government for nine months; *The Man Died: Prison Memoirs* (1972) describes his experiences in prison. His early works, e.g. the novel *The Interpreters* (1965), are more optimistic about the future of post-colonial Africa than his later novels and poems. He was awarded the NOBEL PRIZE for literature in 1986.

Spark, Muriel [Sarah] (1918–) Scottish novelist. She became a Roman Catholic in 1954, and her conversion forms the basis of her first novel, *The Comforters* (1957). Graham GREENE had given her £20 a month to give up publishing hack work—described with brutal accuracy in *A Far Cry from Kensington* (1988)—to concentrate on writing novels; she wrote six in four years. Her novels are usually comic and satirical, with a strong element of the fantastic or supernatural, as in *Memento Mori* (1958) and *The Ballad of Peckham Rye* (1960). Her novel *Symposium* (1990) begins with an epigraph from PLATO stating that 'the genius of comedy is the same with that of tragedy', and this is a key to much of her work. She sees evil as a form of moral blindness, a self-destructive self-love. The problem of the nature of God and his tormented creation also appears in her novels, e.g. *The Only Problem* (1984). Her best-known novel is *The Prime of Miss Jean Brodie* (1961), a tragicomedy in which an eccentric teacher is gradually brought to face the consequences of her self-deluding domination over 'her' schoolgirls.

Spender, Sir Stephen [Harold] (1909–95) English poet and critic. He was a close associate of AUDEN, and one of the most prominent of the left-wing 'Auden generation' poets of the 1930s. His poem 'The Pylons' in *Poems* (1933) resulted in the derisive label of 'Pylon poets' being applied to Spender and other left-wing poets who celebrated the industrial era and the coming triumph of the industrial working class. His critical work, *The Destructive Element* (1935), is a useful guide to the thought processes of the politically committed writers of the 1930s. He abandoned communism in the 1950s. A few of his poems, e.g. 'I think continually of those who are truly great', have become anthology standards.

Spenser, Edmund (*c.*1552–99) English poet, noted particularly for his huge allegorical poem *The Faerie Queene* (1590–96), which describes the adventures of 12 knights (who represent 12 virtues). Many of the adventures begin at the court of Gloriana, the Faerie Queene (an idealized version of Elizabeth I; she does not appear in the poem, however). Despite determined efforts by many critics to persuade the general public of the work's readability, it remains one of the Great Unread among English classics. Many poets have been influenced by it, notably MILTON and KEATS. Others share LANDOR's view, in 'To Wordsworth', that 'Thee gentle Spenser fondly led,/But me he mostly sent to bed.'

Stanislavsky, Konstantin (1863–1938) Russian director and actor, who was co-founder of the Moscow Art Theatre in 1897. Stanislavsky made his name as a director of CHEKHOV's plays, although the latter was not always convinced by Stanislavsky's emotion-saturated, highly detailed approach to production, which often involved a fanatically NATURALISTIC attention to stage sets and sound effects. Chekhov's main objection was that the subtlety and delicate ambiguity of his plays tended to get lost along the way.

Stanislavsky's influence on the training of actors through his theory of acting has been immense. The actor is to immerse himself in the 'inner life' of the character he is playing, and, using the insights gained in this study, convey to the audience the hidden reality behind the words. His theory is contained in such works as *An Actor Prepares* (1929) and *Building a Character* (1950). His theories were adopted and adapted by the American director **Lee Strasberg** (1901–82), whose method style of acting achieved world fame (or notoriety) through pupils such as James Dean and Marlon Brando. *See also* MEYERHOLD.

Steele, Sir Richard (1672–1729) Anglo-Irish essayist and dramatist. He was a close associate of ADDISON, with whom he was chief contributor to *The Tatler* (1709–11) and *The Spectator* (1711–12). His plays, which were determinedly moral, Christian responses to the excesses of Restoration dramatists such as WYCHERLEY and ETHEREGE, were, apart from *The Conscious Lovers* (1722), not terribly successful on the stage, but had lasting influence on the course of 18th-century SENTIMENTAL drama. He was a good man, and was much liked by his contemporaries.

Stein, Gertrude (1874–1946) American author. She settled in Paris, 1902, where her home became a focal point for 'modernist' writers and artists. HEMINGWAY and Sherwood ANDERSON were among the many writers she encouraged. Her phrase 'a lost generation' to describe the post-World War I generation of American poets and artists, was used by Hemingway as the epigraph to *The Sun Also Rises* (1926). Her own best-known work is her autobiography, which she eccentrically presented as the work of her life-long companion Alice B. Toklas, *The Autobiography of Alice B.Toklas* (1933). Stein's highly distinctive narrative technique, with its disregard for standard punctuation, makes her prose instantly recognizable. Her works on literary theory include *Composition as Exploration* (1926).

Steinbeck, John [Ernst] (1902–68) American novelist, who achieved great success with his novels about America's rural poor, e.g. *Of Mice and Men* (1937) and *Grapes of Wrath* (1939). Like quite a few other American novelists of his generation, Steinbeck took a rather deterministic, 'biological' view of human nature, and his literary reputation is not as high as it once was. He was awarded the NOBEL PRIZE for literature in 1962.

Stendhal [pseud. of Henri Beyle] (1788–1842) French novelist and critic, noted for his great mastery of character analysis in such historical novels as *The Red and the Black* (1830) and *The Charterhouse of Parma* (1839). He was a firm supporter of SHAKESPEARE and the ROMANTIC view of life and culture generally, as his *Racine* and *Shakespeare* pamphlets of 1823 and 1835 demonstrate.

Sterne, Laurence (1713–68) Irish-born English novelist. He was ordained as an Anglican clergyman in 1738, and his learned, witty and offbeat sermons at York became very popular. His wildly eccentric 'novel', *The Life and Opinions of Tristram Shandy* (1759–67), created a sensation in the 1760s. The work, with its deliberately disordered narrative (the Preface appears in Volume III), lack of plot, practical jokes on the reader and mordant sense of humour, remains one of the most unclassifiable works of fiction ever published. Sterne also published *A Sentimental Journey through France and Italy* (1768), another odd 'novel' recounting the adventures of Parson Yorick on holiday (he gets as far as Lyon). Interest in Sterne's two peculiar books seems to have declined rapidly after his death. By 1776, Dr JOHNSON was observing: 'Nothing odd will do long. Tristram Shandy did not last', but they are now established as engagingly idiosyncratic classics of English prose.

Stevens, Wallace (1878–1955) American poet, whose elegant, enigmatic poems have gained increasing recognition since his death. Collections include *Harmonium* (1923), *The Man with the Blue Guitar* (1937) and *Collected Poems* (1954). He also published a book of essays, *The Necessary Angel* (1951). Further poems, essays and plays were published posthumously, *Opus Posthumous* (1957).

Stevenson, Robert Louis (1850–94) Scottish novelist, poet and essayist. He trained in Edinburgh as an advocate but had decided by his early twenties that his true vocation was to be a writer. He was encouraged by HENLEY, with whom he co-wrote a number of plays, notably *Deacon Brodie* (1880). By the time his first important fictional work, the classic tale of piracy and adventure, *Treasure Island* (1883), had been published, he had established himself as an author of note with his essays, poems and two travel books, *Travels with a Donkey in the Cevennes* (1879) and *The Silverado Squatters* (1883). His masterpiece is a work that has become part of world myth, *The Strange Case of Dr Jekyll and Mr Hyde* (1886), a strange, disturbing story of dual personality and the clash between good and evil. His other works include his Scottish romances, e.g. *Kidnapped* (1886) and *The Master of Ballantrae* (1889), and his great, sombre unfinished work, *Weir of Hermiston* (1896). He settled in Samoa, where he died. The Samoan nickname for him was 'Tusitala', i.e. 'The Storyteller'.

Stewart, J[ohn] I[nnes] M[ackintosh] (1906–) Scottish novelist and critic. Under the pseudonym of Michael Innes, he has published around 30 detective novels starring Inspector John Appleby, a cultured, erudite individual whose sometimes fiendishly complex but always enjoyable adventures include *Death at the President's Lodging* (1936), *Hamlet's Revenge* (1937) and *Lament for a Maker* (1938). Under his own name, he has published several notable works of criticism, most notably *Eight*

Modern Writers (1963), a superb and entertaining study of HARDY, Henry JAMES, SHAW, CONRAD, KIPLING, YEATS, JOYCE and D.H. LAWRENCE.

Stewart, [Lady] Mary [Florence Elinor] (1916–) English novelist. She has written several popular thrillers, e.g. *Madam, Will You Walk* (1955) and *Thunder on the Right* (1957). Her masterpiece, however, is her excellent retelling of the Arthurian legend, a trilogy consisting of *The Crystal Cave* (1970), *The Hollow Hills* (1973) and *The Last Enchantment* (1979). She has also written several children's adventure stories, e.g. *The Little Broomstick* (1971) and *A Walk in Wolf Wood* (1980).

Stoker, Bram [Abraham] (1847–1912) Irish novelist and short-story writer who is noted primarily for one work, the novel *Dracula* (1897), which has been filmed many times and remains one of the classic horror stories of all times.

Stoppard, Tom (1937–) Czech-born British dramatist. His plays have been very successful on the stage because of their sharp, witty wordplay and dialogue, and fast, cleverly plotted action. Examples include *Rosencrantz and Guildenstern are Dead* (1966), *The Real Inspector Hound* (1968), *Jumpers* (1972), *Every Good Boy Deserves Favour* (1977) and *The Real Thing* (1982). Stoppard's willingness to engage with complex intellectual and political issues, and to challenge totalitarianism of the left as well as that of the right, combined with his undoubted talents as a writer, have given him a special status in modern drama. *See also* TZARA.

Stowe, Mrs Harriet Elizabeth Beecher (1811–96) American novelist. She wrote several novels, but the one she is remembered for is the anti-slavery novel, *Uncle Tom's Cabin, or, Life Among the Lowly* (1852). The novel, and its succeeding dramatization, created a sensation in the US and Europe, and has been described as one of the significant events leading up to the Civil

War. The novel has been criticized for being oversentimental and melodramatic, and patronizing to black people ('Uncle Toms'), but it was written for a particular purpose, to expose the horrors of slavery, and this it did remarkably well. It remains a compelling and readable work.

Strasberg, Lee *see* **Stanislavsky, Konstantin**.

stream of consciousness *see* **James, William**.

Strindberg, Johan August (1849–1912) Swedish dramatist and novelist. His unremittingly bleak plays, in which the strongest element is a pathological fear and hatred of women, are powerful, highly innovative works that have had a strong influence on many 20th-century dramatists, notably O'NEILL. The plays include *Miss Julie* (1888), *The Dance of Death* (1901), *A Dream Play* (1902) and *The Ghost Sonata* (1907).

Structuralism (in literary criticism) a critical approach to literature in which the text being studied is viewed as a 'cultural product' that cannot be 'read' in isolation, and in which the text is held to absorb its meaning from the interconnected web of linguistic codes and symbols of which it is but a part. The process of studying the codes, etc, and their relation to each other, is called *Semiotics*. A Structuralist approach to the novels of Fennimore COOPER, for example, would include recognition of the linguistic and cultural conventions underlying the author's use of language, with particular reference to the significance of both the 'Noble Savage' myth in Western culture and the emerging frontier myth in American culture. The heroic persona of the Deerslayer, and his portrayal as a transient figure between the mythic world of primitive America and the swelling wave of modern civilization, results in a creative tension ripe for hours of happy exploration and parallel (e.g. with John Ford's film *The Man Who Shot Liberty Valance*).

Figures associated with the development of Structuralist theory are the Canadian critic **Marshall McLuhan** (1911–80), whose studies of mass culture and communication include *The Gutenberg Galaxy* (1962) and *The Medium is the Message* (1967); the linguist **Ferdinand de Saussure** (1857–1913); the anthropologist **Claude Levi-Strauss** (1908–); the critic **Roland Barthes** (1915–80); and the psychoanalyst **Jacques Lacan** (1901–81). Structuralism is thus an approach drawing on a wide range of disciplines, with some critics, e.g. followers of Lacan, focusing on the play between unconscious and conscious concepts, while others, e.g. followers of Saussure, will focus on the linguistic relativism that emerges between the signifier (the spoken word) and the signified (the mind's concept of the word). *Deconstruction*, a concept developed by the French philosopher **Jacques Derrida** (1930–), is a term for the process or 'strategy' of examining the elements (signs) of language in isolation from other elements, thus exposing the contradictions inherent within language. This approach is also called *Poststructuralism*.

The psychologist **Jean Piaget** (1896–1980) usefully defines structure as composed of wholeness, transformation and self-regulation (*Structuralism*, 1971). Thus, HOMER's *Iliad*, for example, (a) is a work with a unity of structure conforming to the conventions of epic poetic form; (b) includes recognizable 'types' of characters who appear in other such works, e.g. warriors, who may also behave in ways outside the expected form, as when the young Achilles hides himself amongst women dressed as a girl; (c) can alter its meaning according to external factors, e.g. the reader's understanding of the characters' behaviour can vary at diffeent times, as fresh experiences alter the reader's perception.

The Structuralist approach can, perhaps surprisingly, be rewarding and even fun for the general reader, and some of its aspects are hardly new; it has long been recognized, for example, that reading a great novel such as TOLSTOY's *Anna Karenina* can be an entirely different experience at different stages of one's life. It is sometimes asserted by critics hostile to Structuralism and its progeny that the approach is essentially a spiritually barren one, an enmeshment in 'ways of reading' that gets in the way of understanding rather than being an aid to appreciation. This is certainly true of some Structuralists, but is also true of some non-Structuralists. (For a sane discussion of Structuralist theory, and such issues as the 'lucidity' debate, i.e. the weird and elitist argument that literary theory should not be accessible to the general reader, *see* Frank Kermode's collection of essays, *The Uses of Error*, 1991.)

Suckling, Sir John (1609–41) English poet and dramatist. Suckling is classed as one of the finest of the CAVALIER POETS. The best known of his lyrics is the charming 'Ballad upon a Wedding', which often appears in a discreetly bowdlerized version (the 'Dick' addressed in the poem is Richard Lovelace). Most of his works are included in the posthumous collection, *Fragmenta Aura* (1646). He was reputed to be the best card-player and bowler in England, and may have invented the game of cribbage.

surrealism an avant-garde art movement of the 1920s and 1930s in France, which was inspired by the dream theories of Sigmund FREUD and by the literature and poetry of RIMBAUD and BAUDELAIRE. Surrealism took from Dadaism a love for the juxtaposition of incongruous images, the purpose of which in the surrealist view was to express the workings of the unconscious mind. The term 'surrealism' had been coined by the poet Guillauime APOLLINAIRE, but the movement really got going with the publication of the poet **André Breton**'s (1896–1966) first *Surrealist Manifesto* in 1924. According to Breton (who was much influenced by FREUD), the 'higher reality' could only be achieved in art by freeing the mind from the lower world of superficial rationality. *See also* ARTAUD.

Surrey, Earl of [Henry Howard] (*c*.1517–47) English poet, soldier and courtier. His translations of parts of VIRGIL's *Aeneid*, printed posthumously in a miscellaneous collection, *Tottel's Miscellany* (1557), are notable for being the first (printed) BLANK VERSE in English. He was also among the first English poets to use the sonnet form (and was strongly influenced by PETRARCH). WYATT's version of the form, the so-called 'English sonnet', is the form used by Shakespeare in his sonnets. Surrey's brave, unruly life ended in his execution for treason.

Surtees, Robert Smith (1803–64) English sports journalist, creator of a remarkable series of novels mainly concerned with the sporting life of the foxhunting grocer, Mr Jorrocks, e.g. *Jorrock's Jaunts and Jollies* (1838) and *Handley Cross* (1843). His fictions are boisterous, rowdy celebrations of the hunting life: 'all time is lost wot is not spent in 'unting . . . it's the sport of kings, the image of war without its guilt' (*Handley Cross*), and are highly addictive. Surtees wrote eight novels in all; his complete oeuvre is being issued in a long-term project by the Surtees Society.

Swift, Jonathan (1667–1745) Anglo-Irish divine, poet and satirist. His first important satirical works, published in 1704, were *The Battle of the Books*, a defence of the merits of classical literature against the claims of the moderns, and *A Tale of a Tub* (which also includes digressions on the ancient/modern debate), a satire on religious extremism, with particular emphasis on the excesses of Roman Catholicism, with Calvinism coming a close second and Lutheranism (close to Swift's own position) getting off fairly lightly. In politics, Swift started out with Whiggish sympathies (he was friendly with two notable Whig propagandists, ADDISON and STEELE) but soon became a staunch Tory, closely associated with such Tory wits as POPE. He was appointed Dean of St Patrick's Cathedral in Dublin in 1713, and over the course of his life published several tracts defending the rights of the Irish poor against their overlords, the most notable being *A Modest Proposal* (1729), in which he argues with merciless wit that the children of the poor should be fattened to feed the rich. His masterpiece, and one of the greatest satires ever written, is *Gulliver's Travels* (1726), which culminates in Gulliver's voyage to the Houyhnhnms ('whin-ims'), intelligent horses whose nobility is contrasted with the degraded brutality of mankind. It is sometimes said that Swift's work was intended to satirize mankind but ended up being a harmless children's book. This view is only tenable if one regards heavily BOWDLERized versions of the book as valid. Swift died leaving money to found a hospital for imbeciles; he was much mourned by the Irish people. His own epitaph (in Latin) describes him as lying 'Where fierce (or savage) indignation can no longer tear his heart.'

Swinburne, Algernon [Charles] (1837–1909) English poet and critic, noted for his sensuous verse, accurately described by himself as having a 'tendency' to a 'dulcet and luscious form of verbosity'. His poems, e.g. *Poems and Ballads* (1866), created a public scandal not just for their sexuality, heavily tinged with undertones of depravity (he had read SADE), but for the author's clear dislike of Christianity ('Thou hast conquered, O Pale Galilean') and sympathy for paganism. In later years, he lived in respectable retirement with his friend, Theodore Watts-Dunton, at The Pines, Putney, where Max BEERBOHM visited them and later wrote a cruelly funny essay on the pair.

symbolism in literature, a French poetry movement of the late 19th century that rejected the dictates of both REALISM and NATURALISM by seeking to express a state of mind by a process of suggestion rather than by attempting to portray 'objective reality'. As MALLARMÉ put it, 'not the thing, but the effect produced'. Other prominent poets associated with symbolism include VERLAINE, RIMBAUD and VALÉRY. The movement has strong links with the world of Impressionist composers, such as Claude Debussy. Poets outside the French-speaking world who were influenced by symbolism include T.S. ELIOT, POUND, RILKE, and, notably, YEATS, whose superb epigram, 'Three Movements', serves as an epitaph both for the movement and for his own involvement with it. Several important plays of the late 19th century, e.g. CHEKHOV's *The Seagull* (1895) and IBSEN's *The Master Builder* (1896), also display the influence of symbolism.

Synge, [Edmund] John Millington (1871–1909) Irish dramatist, whose plays of Irish peasant life (written at YEATS's suggestion) were performed at the ABBEY THEATRE in Dublin. The first two (both one-acters) were *In the Shadow of the Glen* (1903), a dour 'comedy' about infidelity, and *Riders to the Sea* (1904), a superb little tragedy about a mother and the death of her last son. A comedy, *The Well of the Saints*, followed in 1905, and after that his masterpiece, the highly controversial comedy *The Playboy of the Western World* (1907). A riot broke out at the latter's premiere, when the word 'shifts', i.e. female undergarments, was used. (The play was claimed by its detractors to be a vicious slur on the virtuous Irish peasantry.) Synge's language is not really an authentic rendering of peasant speech, as he claimed; it is an artificial language, but no less charming for that in its occasionally haunting lyricism. Yeats described Synge as having a heart like his race, 'passionate and simple'.

T

Tarkington, [Newton] Booth (1869–1946) American novelist and dramatist, remembered chiefly for his novel of Midwest life, *The Magnificent Ambersons* (1918), which was made into a major film by Orson Welles in 1942.

Tate, [John Orley] Allen (1899–1979) American poet and critic. A 'regional patriot', he supported the concept of a local sense of identity against the corrupting abstract notion of 'America'. His *Collected Poems* was published in 1977.

Tate, Nahum (1652–1715) English poet and dramatist, whose notorious version of SHAKESPEARE's *King Lear* gave the play a happy ending (Cordelia and Edgar become lovers). Dr JOHNSON, who could not bear to reread the closing scenes of the play, gave qualified approval to Tate's version for the stage. Shakespeare's original ending was not restored until the early 19th century. Tate's other main claim to fame is his metrical version of the psalms, written with **Nicholas Brady** (1659–1726). Many of their versions of the psalms, e.g. 'While shepherds watched their flocks by night', remain popular standards. Tate became POET LAUREATE in 1692 and was one of the many poetasters satirized by POPE in *The Dunciad*.

Taylor, Jeremy (1613–67) English bishop and theologian. His prose has been highly praised by many critics, notably T.S. ELIOT and COLERIDGE, for its daring and colourful use of imagery and metaphor, combined with a talent for expressing complex issues in a simple way. He was also a believer in religious toleration, in the moderate high Anglican tradition (*see also* Lancelot ANDREWES). His works include *The Rule and Exercises of Holy Living* (1650) and *The Rule and Exercises of Holy Dying* (1651).

Tennyson, Alfred Lord [1st Baron Tennyson] (1809–92) English poet. He first came to public notice with *Poems, Chiefly Lyrical* (1830). Subsequent volumes, e.g. *Poems* (1833), established him as a highly skilled and popular poet. He was appointed POET LAUREATE in succession to WORDSWORTH in 1850, the year in which he published his great elegy for his dead friend A. H. HALLAM, *In Memoriam*. He became a much respected public figure; several of his poems, e.g. 'Locksley Hall' (1842) and 'Locksley Hall

Revisited' (1886) being regarded by many of his contemporaries as oracular statements on the Spirit of the Age. (He himself felt that he was a great poet with nothing much of consequence to say about anything.) His literary reputation sank somewhat in the late 19th century, but he is now universally regarded as a great poet.

Terence [Publius Terentius Afer] (*c*.190–159 BC) Roman dramatist. He wrote six plays, all of which are extant and, like those of PLAUTUS, are adaptations of Greek 'new comedy' originals (*see* MENANDER, COMEDY). Terence's works are less coarse than those of Plautus, and the characters have more depth.

Thackeray, William Makepeace (1811–63) Indian-born English novelist and essayist, noted particularly for the witty social satire of both his novels and his non-fiction works, e.g. *The Book of Snobs* (1846–47), a wickedly funny description of the different varieties of British snobbery. His masterpiece is *Vanity Fair* (1847–48), a decidedly non-moralistic tale of the opportunistic 'anti-heroine' Becky Sharp, set during the Napoleonic wars. His other main fictional works are the novels *Pendennis* (1850) and *Henry Esmond* (1852). His American lecture tours (1851–53, 1855–56) were very popular.

Theocritus *see* **pastoral**.

Thomas, Dylan [Marlais] (1914–53) Welsh poet. He worked as a journalist in Wales before moving to London in 1934, in which year his book of poems, *18 Poems*, appeared. He rapidly acquired a reputation as a hard drinking, boisterous pub poet, which, combined with his exuberant, florid and occasionally obscure verse, created a lived-up-to persona that ultimately led to his death (in New York). His own recordings of his work are superb. His first collected edition, *Collected Poems* (1952), sold over 30,000 copies in its first year. His best-known single work is *Under Milk Wood* (1954), a radio drama in poetic prose that is regarded as a milestone in broadcasting.

Thomas, [Philip] Edward (1878–1917) English poet. He began his literary career by writing books on rural Britain, e.g. *Beautiful Wales* (1905), and various journalistic pieces. He met Robert Frost in 1913, who encouraged him to write poetry. He enlisted in 1915 and was killed in action before the publication of his *Poems* (1917). His best-known poem is 'Adlestrop', which typifies the quietly reflective nature of much of his work.

Thomas, R[onald] S[tuart] (1913–) Welsh poet and Anglican priest, who is regarded by many critics as one of the foremost religious poets of modern times. His poems, e.g. *The Stones of the Field* (1946) and *An Acre of Land* (1952), display a Crabbe-like, deep concern for the bleak and often spiritually barren way of life of the poor of rural Wales.

Thompson, Flora [Jane] (1876–1947) English author, noted for her autobiographical trilogy *Lark Rise* (1939), *Over to Candleford* (1941) and *Candleford Green* (1943), issued in one volume as *Lark Rise to Candleford* (1943). The trilogy gives a valuable picture of the vanished pre-World War I life of the rural poor in England. A curious feature of modern editions of the work is that they are often packaged and publicized in such a way as to suggest that the world the book depicts is one of comfort, cosiness and stability, which is far from the case.

Thompson, Francis (1859–1907) English poet. Rescued from opium addiction by the poet and fellow Roman Catholic **Alice Meynell** (1847–1922), Thompson produced three volumes of poetry in the 1890s, *Poems* (1893), *Sister Songs* (1895) and *New Poems* (1897). The best known of his poems, e.g. 'The Hound of Heaven' and 'In No Strange Land', are intensely spiritual, with elaborate imagery.

Thompson, Jim (1906–76) American novelist. His grim crime novels are solidly in the tradition of seedy American determinism, and feature the usual stock characters of no-hopers, whores, psychotics and freaks (he has been dubbed 'the dime-store Dostoyevsky', not to be confused with 'the poor man's Dostoyevsky', Nelson ALGREN). Thompson's novels have a firm cult following (especially in France), and there have been many film adaptations, most notably of *The Getaway* (1959, filmed 1972) and *The Grifters* (1963, filmed 1990). Thompson wrote the screenplays for *Paths of Glory* (1957) and *The Killing* (1956), and made one screen appearance himself, in the 1975 version of CHANDLER's *Farewell, my Lovely.*

Thomson, James (1700–1748) Scottish poet and dramatist. His once very popular tragedies, e.g. *Sophonisba* (1730), are tediously rhetorical works that are no longer performed, or even read much. His most famous poems are *The Seasons* (1726–30) and *The Castle of Indolence* (1748). His work was admired by the ROMANTIC poets, e.g. WORDSWORTH, who saw him as a true nature poet struggling free from the fetters of 18th-century poetic diction.

Thomson, James (1834–82) Scottish poet, chiefly remembered for his poem 'City of Dreadful Night' (1874), a long, nightmarish vision of a decaying city, through which runs a River of Suicides. The city is presided over by a personification of melancholy, and is inhabited by wandering, suffering souls. Thomson died an alcoholic.

Thoreau, Henry David (1817–62) American philosopher (and friend of EMERSON), whose advocacy of self-sufficiency and passive resistance to tyrannical government has been very influential, Gandhi being his most notable admirer. The best known of his books is *Walden, or Life in the Woods* (1854), which describes his two-year retreat to live in a cabin in the woods. He was an aphorist of genius, e.g. 'The mass of men lead lives of quiet desperation.'

Thurber, James [Grover] (1894–1961) American humorist, cartoonist and essayist. As with Dorothy PARKER, much of his work first appeared in *The New Yorker*, including his most famous story, 'The Secret Life of Walter Mitty', in which a typical Thurber-style mousy little man, who is dominated by his wife, has fantasies in which he features in various heroic roles, e.g. as a fighter pilot. The Thurber world is one where such men stumble through minefields of everyday banality and absurdity, coming home at the end of the day to women even more fearful and incomprehensible than the objects outside. Representative works include *My Life and Hard Times* (1933) and *Thurber Country* (1953).

Tolkien, J[ohn] R[onald] R[euel] (1892–1973) South African-born British fantasy writer and scholar. Tolkien is probably the most influential (and best-selling) fantasy writer of all time. The success of his stories, and the cult that grew around them, seems to have somewhat bemused Tolkien, who trained as a philologist and had acquired a deep knowledge of myth and the structures of language by the mid–1930s, when he published his paper 'Beowulf: the Monsters and the Critics' (1936). The works on which his fame rests are *The Hobbit* (1937), and the remarkable three-volume quest romance, *The Lord of the Rings* (1954–55). He was a friend of C.S. LEWIS and Charles WILLIAMS, with whom he formed an informal little group of myth-makers called the 'Inklings'.

Tolstoy, Count Leo [Lev Nikolaevich Tolstoy] (1828–1910) Russian novelist, dramatist, short-story writer and philosopher. Born into the Russian aristocracy, Tolstoy lived the normal dissolute life of a young aristocrat, joined the army in the Caucasus, and commanded a battery at Sevastopol during the Crimean war. His autobiographical trilogy, *Childhood* (1852), *Boyhood* (1854) and *Youth* (1857), is one of the most remarkable autobiographies ever published by a young man. By the time he had settled at Yasnaya Polyana, he had established a reputation as a writer of

great talent, and had embarked upon the spiritual self-questioning that resulted in some of the greatest works of fiction ever
produced. Two of his novels, in particular, are frequently described as the greatest of all novels. The first of these, *War and
Peace* (1863–69), is a panoramic epic of the Napoleonic invasion of Russia, in which the muddled Pierre Bezuhov represents
the author's own spiritual and moral confusion. The second is
Anna Karenina (1875–77), a tragic tale of adulterous love which
raises profound questions about personal and social morality.
Tolstoy's remorseless examination of how a Christian should
live, and such principles as his belief that the 'normal' married
situation, in which an experienced man is wed to a 'pure' female,
is profoundly immoral, led to his excommunication in 1901. His
version of Christian pacificism (virtually an anarchist position)
came to be called 'Tolstoyanism', and influenced many modern
thinkers, notably Gandhi.

Tourneur, Cyril (*c*.1575–1626) English dramatist. He was the author of *The Atheist's Tragedy* (1628), and possibly also the author of one of the greatest examples of the REVENGE TRAGEDY
genre, *The Revenger's Tragedy* (1607), a highly bloodthirsty
piece with cold, brilliantly malevolent dialogue.

tragedy a form of drama in which a hero or heroine comes to a
bad end. The cause of the protagonist's failure can be either a
personal flaw or a circumstance beyond his or her control, or
both. (The origin of the term, which means 'goat song', is obscure, but possibly derives from the sacrifice of goats in
Dionysian fertility rituals.) The earliest tragedies known, those
by AESCHYLUS, SOPHOCLES and EURIPIDES, are still among the
greatest. The first critical study of the form is in ARISTOTLE's *Poetics*, where Aristotle defines tragedy as an imitation (*mimesis*)
of a serious, complete action on a grand scale, 'grand' meaning a
momentous action involving highly placed characters in society.

The protagonist will make an 'error of judgment'—the word for this, *hamartia*, has often been rendered, a bit misleadingly, as 'tragic flaw'—but the protagonist's main fault is as often the result of having to undertake a certain action at a certain time, as in any character defect; thus, in Sophocles's *Antigone*, the heroine is in the position of having to choose between divine and human law. The protagonist is usually a good person, but not perfect, and progresses from happiness to misery. Another important concept in the *Poetics* is that of catharsis, the 'purging' (or purification, cleansing) of the emotions of pity and fear aroused in the spectators by the play.

The great tradition of the Greek tragedians was filtered through the plays of SENECA to the dramatists of the RENAISSANCE, although Renaissance tragedies, such as those of SHAKESPEARE, differ significantly from those of the past. The interplay in Shakespeare's tragedies between the heroic and the ironic or comic commonplace worlds, e.g. the banter between the rustic clown and Cleopatra at the end of *Antony and Cleopatra*, is profoundly foreign to the world of the *Poetics*, just as the pagan, multideistic and fate-haunted world of the Greeks was ultimately alien to Renaissance dramatists brought up in the Christian tradition.

Several 20th-century dramatists, e.g. Arthur MILLER and Eugene O'NEILL, have tried, with debatable results, to adapt the form of Athenian tragedy to the modern stage. The most that can be said for such adaptations is that they may result in effects similar to those of the originals. Miller, for example, in *Death of a Salesman*, locates the cause of Willy Loman's fall in a social (capitalist) directive to compete for victory in the American Dream rather than in blind fate. However, the fact that such dramas invariably have as subtext the notion that this state of affairs is reformable, and the equally invariable ironic presentation of the protagonists such as Loman as 'losers of history', rather than as victims of forces as permanent as they are merciless, puts such plays as *Death of a Salesman* at a further remove from the Athenian drama than, say, *King Lear*, with its bleak vision of a fallen world in which bloody tyranny is an ever present threat.

See also DOMESTIC TRAGEDY, HEROIC TRAGEDY, JACOBEAN TRAGEDY, REVENGE TRAGEDY.

tragicomedy *see* **comedy**.

Traherne, Thomas (1637–74) English poet and author of religious meditations. He was ordained into the Anglican Church in 1660, and was renowned for living 'a devout life', according to the normally uncharitable antiquary, Anthony Wood. The manuscript of his *Centuries of Meditations*, which includes many beautiful mystical passages, was discovered on a London bookstall in 1896, and published in 1908.

Traven, B. [pseud. of Albert Otto Max Feige] (*c.*1882–1969) German-born American novelist. Traven's origins and career are shrouded in an artfully constructed obscurity. He was described by his biographer, Will Wyatt (in *The Man who was B. Traven*, 1980), as 'one of the most mysterious figures of the 20th century'. Traven wrote approximately 12 adventure novels, of which the best known are *The Death Ship* (1925) and *The Treasure of the Sierra Madre* (1934).

Trevor, William [William Trevor Cox] (1928–) Irish novelist and short-story writer. His highly regarded fiction, often set in rural Ireland or on the down-at-heel fringes of English middle-class life, includes the novels *The Old Boys* (1964) and *Fools of Fortune* (1983); short-story collections include *Angels at the Ritz* (1975) and *Beyond the Pale* (1981).

Trilling, Lionel (1905–75) American critic. His collection of essays, *The Liberal Imagination* (1950), was very influential in its concern for locating literary criticism as something central to Western, liberal culture. He was much influenced by FREUD in his later work, which includes close and highly perceptive analysis of the creative imagination. His short book *Sincerity and Authenticity* (1972) is one of the key postwar critical works.

Trollope, Anthony (1815–82) English novelist, whose more than 50 books have a wide and devoted following (a thriving Trollope Society exists). His mother, **Frances Trollope** (1780–1863), was herself a prolific author, whose most notable work is a bad-tempered (and very successful) study of American life, *Domestic Manners of the Americans* (1832). Trollope wrote two main novel sequences: the 'Barsetshire' novels ('Barsetshire' is an imaginary West Country county where the home life is very different from that of Thomas Hardy's 'Wessex'), which focus on the trials and tribulations of the provincial lives of the gentry, clergy and middle classes, e.g. *Barchester Towers* (1857) and *The Last Chronicle of Barset* (1867), and the 'Palliser' novels of political life, e.g. *Can You Forgive Her?* (1864) and *Phineas Finn* (1869). Each sequence includes characters who reappear in the action of succeeding novels, thus building up an evolving panorama of English life that has fascinated generations of readers. Trollope was also a highly industrious civil servant, with a formidable Victorian appetite for life and work. Nathaniel HAWTHORNE described him as 'just as English as beefsteak'.

Tupper, Martin Farquhar (1810–89) English poet, whose monotonous and rhythmically plodding versified maxims were immensely popular in both Britain and the US, particularly *Proverbial Philosophy* (1838–42). By the 1890s, he had become a standard target for parodists such as GILBERT, and editions of his work were issued with tongue-in-cheek commendations. (It should be pointed out that much of his work, although rambling and sententious, is wholly admirable in content, e.g. his attacks on cruelty to animals.) He also invented some rather strange devices which never quite caught on, e.g. safety horseshoes.

Turgenev, Ivan Sergeyevich (1818–83) Russian novelist, short-story writer and dramatist. His great novels, e.g. *A Nest of Gentlefolk* (1859), *On the Eve* (1860), and his masterpiece, *Fathers and Sons* (1862), explore such major issues of Russian life as serfdom and the question of revolutionary change through the lives, thoughts and actions of his characters, particularly those of the intelligentsia. Unlike his great contemporaries TOLSTOY and DOSTOEVSKY, Turgenev looked to Western culture for help in solving Russia's problems, and was friendly with many Western authors, e.g. DICKENS and George ELIOT. The greatest of his plays is *A Month in the Country* (1850).

Twain, Mark [pseud. of Samuel Langhorne Clemens] (1835–1910) American novelist, short-story writer and humorist. After training as a printer, he became a Mississippi river pilot, taking his pseudonym from the depth-sounding call meaning 'by the mark two fathoms'. His two most famous books, *The Adventures of Tom Sawyer* (1876) and (his masterpiece) *The Adventures of Huckleberry Finn* (1884), have become world classics of children's literature, despite the fact that the latter work includes much that is quite grim and indeed shocking, e.g. the brutal tarring and feathering of the two shysters, the King and the Duke. *Huckleberry Finn* is perhaps the greatest of all American novels; outwardly simple and entertaining, but with complex undercurrents (Huck's river journey down the Mississippi with Jim, the escaped slave, and Huck's innocent compassion, humour and growing consciousness, have haunted American literature since the book's publication). Twain's other works include a satirical travel book, *The Innocents Abroad* (1869); an autobiographical account of his experiences in Nevada, self-explanatorily titled *Roughing It* (1872); and several dark little misanthropic fables, e.g. *The Man that Corrupted Hadleyburg* (1900). *See also* SCOTT.

Tyndale, William *see* **Authorized Version**.

Tzara, Tristan [pseud. of Samuel Rosenstock] (1896–1963) Romanian-born French poet and essayist. He was one of the founders of Dada at the Cabaret Voltaire in Zurich, 1916 (*see* STOPPARD's play *Travesties*, 1974, for a brilliantly funny presentation of the birth of Dada; James JOYCE and Lenin also appear). The word 'Dada', from the French children's word for 'hobbyhorse', was apparently taken at random from a dictionary. The Dada movement rejected rationality, sense and order; its most notable principles were irreverence and incongruity, its impetus deriving from the mad background of World War I and the influence of NIHILISM. In the *Seven Dada Manifestoes*, Tzara argued for the reduction of poetry to meaningless jumbles of words, and, in Paris, staged some deliberately shambolic theatrical events. Dada waned in Paris in the early 1920s, becoming gradually supplanted by SURREALISM, which movement Tzara happily joined. Tzara's best-known volume of poetry is *Approximate Man* (1931).

U

Unities *see* **Neoclassicism**.

Updike, John (1932–) American novelist, short-story writer and poet. His best-known work is the 'Rabbit' sequence, i.e. *Rabbit, Run* (1960), *Rabbit Redux* (1971), *Rabbit is Rich* (1981), and *Rabbit at Rest* (1990), which describes the troubles and relationships of a middle American (Harry Angstrom, 'Rabbit') in his progress through the changing fabric of American society in the 1960s, 1970s and 1980s. Updike's other works include the novels *The Centaur* (1963) and *The Coup* (1979), and short-story collections, e.g. *Pigeon Feathers and Other Stories* (1979).

Utopian novel *see* **More, Sir Thomas**.

V

Valéry, Paul (1871–1945) French poet and critic associated with the SYMBOLIST MOVEMENT. Volumes of his poetry include *The Young Fate* (1917) and *Graveyard by the Sea* (1920). He published five collections of essays on literature and aesthetics, all called *Variety* (1922–44).

Vanbrugh, Sir John (1664–1726) English dramatist and architect, noted for his witty comedies, e.g. *The Relapse* (1696), *The Provok'd Wife* (1697), and *The Confederacy* (1705). He was also an architect of note, the most famous of his buildings being Blenheim Palace.

Van der Post, Sir Laurens (1906–96) South African novelist, travel writer and mystic. His works are strongly influenced by JUNG and display a strong sympathy for the 'primitive' peoples of the world, particularly the African Bushmen. His fiction includes the novels *The Seed and the Sower* (1963), *The Hunter and the Whale* (1967) and *A Story Like the Wind* (the first of these, based on his experiences as a prisoner of war of the Japanese, was filmed as *Merry Christmas, Mr Lawrence*). His travel books include two African classics, *Venture to the Interior* (1952) and *The Lost World of the Kalahari* (1958). In the mid–1980s he acquired a good deal of public notice as the Prince of Wales's reputed 'guru'.

Vargas Llosa, [Jorge] Mario [Pedro] (1936–) Peruvian novelist. His novels include *The Time of the Hero* (1966), a satire on Peruvian society centred on Llosa's former military academy (which burned the book publicly), the historical novel *The War of the End of the World* (1984), and *The Storyteller* (1990), a powerful fable on power and the rights of the Peruvian Indians. Vargas Llosa's fiction, with its often radical restructuring of time, space and even character identity within the narrative, has some affinities with MAGIC REALISM and the work of his friend MARQUEZ. His brave and passionate opposition to the murderous policies of the Maoist Sendero Luminoso party in Peru and espousal of democratic right-wing policies (he ran for President in 1990) has earned him many enemies on both the left and right. The themes of dictatorship and of Utopian terrorism are central to his work, and both of these themes are incarnated in Vargas Llosa's main enemy, the infamous Sendero leader, Professor Guzman, who, in a magically realist situation, may be alive or may have been dead for years.

Vaughan, Henry (1621–95) Welsh poet, best known for his collection of mystical religious verse, *Silex Scintillans* (1650, 1655). Several of his poems, like those of HERBERT, have startlingly vivid opening lines, e.g. 'They are all gone into the world of light', or 'I saw Eternity the other night'.

Vega Carpio, Lope de (1562–1635) Spanish poet and dramatist. His eventful life included service in the Spanish Armada in 1588, and, near the end of his life, in the Spanish Inquisition. He reputedly wrote around 1,500 plays, of which a few hundred survive.

Vergil *see* **Virgil**.

Verlaine, Paul (1844–96) French poet, regarded with his lover RIMBAUD as an early SYMBOLIST. The affair ended when Verlaine shot and wounded Rimbaud, spending two years in prison for the deed. Collections of Verlaine's verse include *Saturnian Poems* (1866), the religious poems of *Wisdom* (1881) and *Romances Without Words* (1874). His memoir, *Accursed Poets*, includes studies of contemporaries such as Rimbaud and MALLARMÉ.

Verne, Jules (1828–1905) French novelist, whose innovative fantasy novels, e.g. *Voyage to the Centre of the Earth* (1864) and *20,000 Leagues Under the Sea* (1869), are regarded as the earliest great science fiction novels of the modern era.

Vidal, Gore (1925–) American novelist, dramatist and critic. His American historical fiction constitutes an unofficial and waspishly entertaining alternative history of the US and its leaders and customs, e.g. *Burr* (1973) and *1876* (1976). His other work includes a comedy of sexual identity, *Myra Breckenridge* (1968), and several important essay collections, e.g. *The Second American Revolution* (1982) and *Armageddon* (1987).

Villiers, George [2nd Duke of Buckingham] (1606–67) English poet, dramatist and courtier. The son of one of James I's catamites, Villiers became one of the most notorious rakes and political intriguers of his day. He was satirized by DRYDEN in *Absalom and Achitophel* (1681), where he features as 'Zimri', and was the central figure of a loosely connected group of wits (including ROCHESTER, WYCHERLEY and Samuel BUTLER (1613–80). Villiers produced, in the manner of his time, several vicious and funny poems, but his main claim to literary fame is his superb send-up of the conventions of the HEROIC TRAGEDY genre, *The Rehearsal* (1672; written in collaboration with, among others, Butler), which mercilessly satirizes Dryden and other dramatists specializing in the genre. The play was updated by SHERIDAN as *The Critic* (1779). Villiers's sordid death in 'the worst inn's worst room' is described in POPE's *Moral Essays*.

Villon, François (*c.*1431–1463?) French poet. The little that is known of his life indicates a violent, unstable personality. He graduated from the University of Paris, became involved with a criminal gang and killed a priest, being eventually pardoned for the murder. He was banished from Paris in 1463, and nothing is known of him after this date. Two main collections of his work survive: *Le Lais* or *Little Testament*, and *Testament* or *Great Testament*. The latter includes the remarkable 'Ballad of Ladies of Long Ago', with its haunting refrain, 'Mais où sont les neiges d'antan?' ('But where are the snows of yesteryear?'). A curious feature of this poem (and of much of Villon's work) is the poet's ability to present the exalted (Joan of Arc) in conjunction with the common (Bertha of the Big Foot) without creating a bathetic or ridiculous effect.

Virgil *or* **Vergil** [Publius Vergilius Maro] (70–19 BC) Roman poet. His works include the *Eclogues* or *Bucolics*, ten pastoral poems; the *Georgics*, poems on agricultural subjects that also celebrate the rural way of life; and his masterpiece, the *Aeneid*, an epic poem in 12 books that charts the progress of the Trojan hero Aeneas from the fall of Troy to the founding of the Roman state. He was a friend of HORACE, and one of the most influential poets of all time.

Voltaire [pseud. of François Marie Arouet] (1694–1778) French philosopher, poet, historian, dramatist, essayist and novelist. He is regarded as one of the most important of the French so-called 'Age of Enlightenment' philosophers. His most influential single work is the *Philosophical Letters* (1734, inspired by British and American conceptions of liberty), a collection of very witty, acerbic attacks on the tyranny of the *ancien régime* of France. Voltaire's war cry was 'Ecrasez l'infame' ('Crush the abuses') of religious, political and intellectual despotism, and his writings, with those of ROUSSEAU (with whom he disputed bitterly), are often described as the main intellectual roots of the French Revolution. His other works include several plays and poems, and the remarkable novel *Candide* (1759), which, like Dr JOHNSON'S *Rasselas*, takes a markedly unoptimistic view of human capacity for rational modification of society, concluding with the famous observation that 'we must cultivate our garden'. Voltaire's most famous (attributed) statement of principle is 'I disapprove of what you say, but I will defend to the death your right to say it.'

Vonnegut, Kurt (1922–) American novelist, essayist and short-story writer. Vonnegut's gloomy science fiction fables include

The Sirens of Titan (1959), *Cat's Cradle* (1963) and *Slaughter-house-Five* (1969). This last novel, in which the hero, Billy Pilgrim, travels back and forth in time and place, has a grim base in the reality of the firebombing of Dresden, which Vonnegut experienced on the ground as a prisoner of war, and is generally regarded as his masterpiece. The recurring phrase in the book, 'So it goes', sums up the author's despairing attitude to humanity's folly. The hack science fiction writer 'Kilgore Trout', who appears in many of Vonnegut's works, serves as a fictional alter ego for the author, who was not amused when another science fiction writer, Philip José Farmer, wrote and published a Kilgore Trout novel (*Venus on the Half Shell*, 1975).

W

Walcott, Derek [Anton] (1930–) St Lucian-born West Indian poet and dramatist, who has lived most of his life in Trinidad. Volumes of his poetry include *In a Green Night: Poems 1948–60* (1962) and *Omeros* (1990), a marvellous reworking, in a Caribbean setting, of themes from HOMER's *Odyssey* and *Iliad* and DANTE's *Divine Comedy*. Walcott's plays, e.g. *The Dream on Monkey Mountain and Other Plays* (1971), draw on Creole traditions and imagery, and are highly regarded. He was awarded the NOBEL PRIZE for literature in 1992.

Walpole, Horace [4th Earl of Oxford] (1717–97) English author, noted for his vast correspondence, and for his fascination with the 'Gothic'. His gossipy (rather feline) letters, which have many often highly entertaining anecdotes about his friends and contemporaries, provide an invaluable guide to the manners and interests of the 18th century. His novel, *The Castle of Otranto* (1764), the first major GOTHIC NOVEL, which is crammed with supernatural incidents and violently emotional rhetoric, set high and rarely exceeded standards for succeeding examples of the genre (fearing ridicule, Walpole had it issued pseudonymously, claiming that it was a translation from medieval Italian). He transformed his house, Strawberry Hill, into a Gothic pseudo-castle that attracted admiration and ridicule in about equal amounts.

Walpole, Sir Hugh (1884–1941) English novelist. His best-known work is a sequence of historical novels set in Northwest England, the *Herries Chronicle*, i.e. *Rogue Herries* (1930), *Judith Paris* (1931), *The Fortress* (1932) and *Vanessa* (1933).

Walton, Izaak (1593–1683) English author, best known for his hugely popular work *The Compleat Angler* (1653, revised 1655, 1676), which is both a treatise on the art of angling and a celebration of the quiet life. The work has been in countless editions since the 17th century. The word 'compleat' in the title has also been endlessly reused in imitation of Walton's classic, e.g. *The Compleat Cakemaker*.

Ward, Mrs Humphrey [Mary Augustus Ward] (1851–1920) English novelist. The best known of her many novels is *Robert Ellsmere* (1880), a study of religious commitment that inspired much public debate. She was very highly thought of by her contemporaries throughout Europe (TOLSTOY called her the 'English Tolstoy'). Matthew ARNOLD was her uncle.

Warren, Robert Penn (1905–89) American poet, novelist and critic. The best known of his novels is *All the King's Men* (1946), which charts the progress of a demagogic politician (based on Governor Huey Long of Louisiana) in the Southern US. Collections of his poetry include *Brother to Dragons* (1953) and *Now and Then* (1979).

Warton, Thomas (1728–90) English poet, who was professor of poetry at Oxford University (1757–67) and POET LAUREATE

(1785–90). A prolific poet, his work shows the influence of MILTON, whose early poems he edited (1785). He was a friend of Dr JOHNSON, but is best known for his *History of English Poetry* (1774–81), the first such work of any depth and important for its collection of works by early poets such as CHAUCER, SPENSER and DANTE.

Waugh, Evelyn [Arthur St John] (1903–66) English novelist. His first novels, e.g. *Decline and Fall* (1928), *Vile Bodies* (1930) and *A Handful of Dust* (1934), are brilliant satires featuring, in the main, the brittle, bittersweet pleasures of the postwar 'Bright Young Things' generation of the young upper classes of Britain. He was received into the Roman Catholic Church in 1930, his conversion giving a sharper, less frivolous edge to his satire. His experiences (largely farcical) as a war correspondent during the Italian invasion of Abyssinia form the basis of his novel *Scoop* (1938), which is still regarded as the definitive (and funniest) satire on war reporting. He served in World War II with the Royal Marines, taking leave to write his best-known novel, *Brideshead Revisited* (1945), in which a young Englishman becomes involved with an aristocratic Roman Catholic family. The novel, which includes some biting satire but also displays a growing spiritual concern, achieved immense popularity. Towards the end of the war, Waugh was posted to Yugoslavia to join his equally eccentric friend Randolph Churchill (Winston Churchill's son) with the Communist partisans. Waugh's experiences there resulted in his masterpiece, the *Sword of Honour* trilogy, i.e. *Men at Arms* (1952), *Officers and Gentlemen* (1955) and *Unconditional Surrender* (1961). As in all Waugh's work, the trilogy is shot through with a cruel, dark humour (which is also at his own expense: *Unconditional Surrender* includes a merciless parody of *Brideshead Revisited*), but the sombre, spiritually questioning element is stronger. Two other notable Waugh novels are *The Loved One* (1948), a satire on Californian burial practices, and an astonishing autobiographical novel, *The Ordeal of Gilbert Penfold* (1957). *See also* ACTON, CONNOLLY.

Webster, John (*c*.1578–*c*.1632) English dramatist, noted for two very powerful tragedies, *The White Devil* (*c*.1609–12) and *The Duchess of Malfi* (*c*.1613). Webster's command of the chilly rhetoric of JACOBEAN TRAGEDY is unrivalled by any other contemporary specialists in that narrow, malevolent genre. T.S. ELIOT praised Webster highly, and describes him in his poem 'Whispers of Immortality' as 'much possessed by death'.

Weldon, Fay (1933–) English novelist. Her novels, which belong with the feminist 'consciousness-raising' fictions that began to emerge in the 1970s, include *Female Friends* (1975) and *The Cloning of Joanna May* (1989), the latter being a typical example of the genre in its often leaden satire and paranoid atmosphere. Since the fatwa on Salman RUSHDIE came into force in 1989, Weldon has campaigned vigorously on his behalf.

Wells, H[erbert] G[eorge] (1866–1946) English novelist and short-story writer. His science fiction works include several undisputed classics of the genre, e.g. *The Time Machine* (1895), *The Island of Dr Moreau* (1896), *The War of the Worlds* (1898) and *The Shape of Things to Come* (1933). His novels on contemporary themes generally address their subject matter from a 'progressive' standpoint (Wells was a leading propagandist, with SHAW and others, for Fabian socialism), e.g. *Ann Veronica* (1909), and sometimes have a comic element mixed in with the mildish social satire, e.g. *Love and Mr Lewisham* (1900), *Kipps* (1905) and *The History of Mr Polly* (1910). He was also a short-story writer of rare genius, e.g. *The Country of the Blind and Other Stories* (1910). His last treatise on political and social issues, *Mind at the End of its Tether* (1945), displays a quite stark pessimism about the human future. It should be noted that, like almost all his early 'progressive' contemporaries (e.g. Jack LON-DON), Wells's work, as in *When the Sleeper Awakes* (1899), occasionally includes a brutal form of racism in which Blacks are portrayed as subhumans, whereas Christian novelists and thinkers (e.g. Harriet Beecher STOWE, Lord Shaftesbury) saw them as fellow humans, as indeed (but to a less emphatic degree) did many non-, or barely, Christian right-wingers, such as KIPLING and Rider HAGGARD. Wells, to do him credit, became aware of such disquieting paradoxes of 'rational progressiveness'. *See also* Dame Rebecca WEST.

Wesley, Samuel (1662–1735) English poet and divine, noted mainly for fathering the founder of Methodism, his fifteenth child, **John Wesley** (1703–91; see Richard GRAVES). Another of his children, **Charles Wesley** (1707–88), wrote many very fine hymns, e.g. 'Jesu, Lover of my soul'. Samuel Wesley's other works include a now unreadable and huge epic poem on the life of Christ. His earlier collection of poems, however, *Maggots* (1685), deserves to be better known. This extraordinary (even for a 17th-century divine) volume includes several scabrously funny poems. A characteristic specimen is 'The Beggar and Poet', in which the beggar's words appear in Gothic type.

West, Dame Rebecca [pseud. of Cecily Isabel Fairfield] (1892–1983) Anglo-Irish novelist and journalist, whose novels are regarded as classics of feminist writing for their sharp, fierce wit (H.G. WELLS, who was her lover, nicknamed her 'Panther'). The novels, which include *The Return of the Soldier* (1918) and *The Birds Fall Down* (1966), have never lacked admirers, and her status as a writer has steadily risen. She reported on the Nuremberg Trials after World War II in *The Meaning of Treason* (1947), which she revised in 1964 to include postwar treason trials. Her son by H. G. Wells, **Anthony [Panther] West** (1914–87), was also a novelist, who moved to the US. Following his mother's death, he wrote a bitter account of his relationship with her in *H.G. Wells: Aspects of a Life* (1984).

West, Nathanael [pseud. of Nathan Weinstein] (1903–40) American novelist. His macabre novels have as their main theme the souring of the American dream, e.g. *Miss Lonelyhearts* (1933) and *The Day of the Locust* (1939).

Wharton, Edith [Newbold Jones] (1862–1937) American novelist and short-story writer. Much of her fiction deals with the ironies and tragedies of New York social life, e.g. *The House of Mirth* (1905) and, notably, *The Age of Innocence* (1920). Another well-known work is her (very uncharacteristic) short novel of poverty and vengeance on a New England farm, *Ethan Frome* (1911). Her other novels include *The Custom of the Country* (1913) and *Hudson River Bracketed* (1929). Short-story collections include *Crucial Instances* (1901) and *Ghosts* (1937).

Whichcote, Benjamin *see* **More, Henry**.

White, Patrick [Victor Martindale] (1912–90) English-born Australian novelist. His historical novels, e.g. *The Tree of Man* (1955) and *Voss* (1957), are set in the Australian outback, and describe the suffering and struggles of those settlers and explorers of the wilderness. A central concern of White's is to show how men react to extreme situations, in which they grow or fail spiritually. Other novels include *Riders in the Chariot* (1961) and *The Vivisector* (1970). He was awarded the NOBEL PRIZE for literature in 1973.

White, T[erence] H[anbury] (1906–64) English novelist, whose trilogy on the Arthurian legends, published in one volume as *The Once and Future King* (1958), is the most popular and entertaining of the modern versions of the ARTHUR myth. The first volume of the trilogy, *The Sword in the Stone* (1937), is regarded as a classic of children's literature.

Whitehead, William *see* **poet laureate**.

Whitman, Walt[er] (1819–92) American poet. His collection, *Leaves of Grass*, was first published in 1855; eight subsequent revised and enlarged editions appeared throughout his life, and the book is regarded as the most important single volume of poems in American literature. Its significance lies primarily in Whitman's celebration of America as the land of liberty and democracy, with a concurrent celebration of the poet himself, his sexuality, and the great, honest world of nature. He was a fervent admirer of EMERSON, and was in his turn highly influential on a great many American poets. Ezra POUND said of him, 'He is America.' Whitman's comment on himself should also be noted: 'Do I contradict myself?/Very well then I contradict myself,/I am large, I contain multitudes' ('Song of Myself'). His other poems include 'O Captain! My Captain!' (1865), commemorating the death of Abraham Lincoln, and a superb elegy, also for Abraham Lincoln, 'When Lilacs Last in the Dooryard Bloom'd' (1867).

Whittier, John Greenleaf (1807–92) American poet. Whittier's strong Quaker principles pervade his work, which, like WHITMAN's, celebrates the common people of America. His verse was enormously popular, and his antislavery poems, e.g. *Voices of Freedom* (1846), contributed significantly to the abolitionist cause. Other volumes include *Legends of New England in Prose and Verse* (1831), *Songs of Labor* (1850) and *Snow-Bound* (1866).

Wilcox, Ella Wheeler (1850–1919) American poet, whose prolifically produced verses, in collection *Poems of Passion* (1883), were enormously popular in their day. Her appeal was due to a blend of sentimentalism and everyday 'common sense', exemplified in her best-known lines 'Laugh and the world laughs with you;/Weep, and you weep alone' ('Solitude').

Wilde, Oscar [Fingal O'Flahertie Wills] (1854–1900) Irish dramatist, poet, essayist and wit. He first came to public notice in the late 1870s as a prominent member of the AESTHETIC MOVE-

MENT, and lived gaily up to the 'Bunthorne' image of an aesthete presented in GILBERT and Sullivan's comic opera *Patience*. After the publication of his *Poems* (1881), he made a lecture tour of the US. The tour was highly successful, and Wilde became a household name. In 1888 he published a volume of fairy stories for children, *The Happy Prince and Other Tales* (1888), with his only novel, *The Picture of Dorian Gray*, following in 1890. The first of his great comedies, *Lady Windermere's Fan*, appeared in 1892. The succeeding plays, *A Woman of No Importance* (1893), *An Ideal Husband* (1895) and *The Importance of Being Earnest* (1895), established him as the most important dramatist of the age. The plays are still very popular, with their superbly witty dialogue and flashes of biting satire. His other works include several important essays, e.g. 'The Decay of Lying' and 'The Critic as Artist'. He was jailed for homosexuality from 1895 to 1897, and during his imprisonment wrote *De Profundis,* a bitter apologia addressed to **Lord Alfred Douglas** (1870–1945), the English poet whose relationship with Wilde had led to his imprisonment. It was published in part in 1905 by Douglas. After his release, Wilde fled to France, where he wrote *The Ballad of Reading Gaol* (1898), an account of his experience there. He died in poverty in Paris. YEATS's *Autobiographies* includes a remarkable portrait of Wilde.

Wilder, Thornton [Niven] (1897–1975) American novelist and dramatist. His best-known novel is *The Bridge of San Luis Rey* (1927), a historical novel set in 18th-century Peru. His plays include *Our Town* (1938), *The Merchant of Yonkers* (1938, later remade into the musical *Hello, Dolly* in 1963) and *The Skin of our Teeth* (1942). Wilder's fiction is, for the most part, an optimistic celebration of the lives of ordinary people.

Williams, Charles (1886–1945) poet, novelist and critic, whose highly individual supernatural thrillers, e.g. *War in Heaven*

(1930), *Descent into Hell* (1937) and *All Hallows Eve* (1944) have a devoted following. The novels are written from a Christian standpoint, and feature odd and chilling clashes between the forces of good and evil. *See also* TOLKIEN, NEOPLATONISM.

Williams, Tennessee [pseud. of Thomas Lanier Williams] (1911–83) American dramatist. His plays, lurid melodramas about sexual and social frustration in the Deep South, include *The Glass Menagerie* (1944), *A Streetcar Named Desire* (1947), *Cat on a Hot Tin Roof* (1955) and *The Night of the Iguana* (1962). Other publications include a short novel, *The Roman Spring of Mrs Stone* (1950), volumes of poems, and his *Memoirs* (1975). The best introduction to Williams's life and work is Gore VIDAL's splendidly bitchy essay, 'Tennessee Williams: Someone to Laugh at the Squares with' (in *Armageddon*, 1987).

Williams, William Carlos (1883–1963) American poet, novelist and short-story writer. His early volumes of poems, *Poems* (1909) and *The Tempers* (1913), belong to the Imagist school (he was a friend of IMAGISM's American godfather, Ezra POUND). Later volumes, e.g. *Pictures from Breughel* (1963), use the idioms of everyday speech and concentrate on everyday objects. His most famous poem is 'The Red Wheelbarrow', an eight-line minimalist work, half of which is 'so much depends/upon/a red wheel/barrow'.

Wilmot, John *see* **Rochester, 2nd Earl of**.

Wilson, Sir Angus (1913–91) South African-born English novelist and short-story writer. Long regarded as one of the finest 20th-century English writers, his fictions are sharply observed satires within a wide variety of social settings, and often have a macabre ending. The major novels are *Hemlock and After* (1952), *Anglo-Saxon Attitudes* (1956), *The Old Men at the Zoo* (1961) and *No Laughing Matter* (1967). The *Collected Stories* were published in 1987. He is regarded by many critics as the main heir of the great Victorian writers. *See also* ANGRY YOUNG MEN.

Wilson, Colin [Henry] (1931–) English novelist and critic, whose study of EXISTENTIALIST writers, e.g. CAMUS and SARTRE, *The Outsider* (1956), received extraordinary praise from the critics on publication. The work appeared in the same week as OSBORNE's *Look Back in Anger*, resulting in both writers being classified as ANGRY YOUNG MEN. Subsequent volumes received a much more muted welcome, and Wilson's work began to be savaged by the very critics who had earlier hailed him as a great writer. As has been pointed out, the most unnerving aspect of the affair was the virtual unanimity of the critical establishment, first one way, then the other. Wilson's critical reputation remains low; his very many nonfiction works, e.g. *A Criminal History of Mankind* (1984), show signs of being under-researched, and his novels, e.g. *Ritual in the Dark* (1960), are pot-boiling studies of alienated 'Outsiders' with heavy doses of sex and violence that are of little interest. As a popularizer of major writers, however, Wilson's influence has been both very wide and largely unrecognized.

Wilson, Edmund (1895–1972) American critic, poet and dramatist. Wilson's main critical work is *Axel's Castle* (1931), an influential study of such SYMBOLIST writers as W.B. YEATS. His other principal works are *To the Finland Station* (1940), a history of European socialism, and *The Wound and the Bow* (1941), a collection of Freud-inspired studies (MARX and FREUD were the two main influences on him). Another fine work is his *Patriotic Gore: Studies in the Literature of the American Civil War* (1962), a very useful and much quarried study of the writers of the period. His third wife was Mary McCARTHY.

Wilson, Harriette (1786–1846) English author and courtesan. Her *Memoirs of Harriette Wilson* (1825) created a public scandal by naming and discussing her various 'protectors', associates and acquaintances, many of whom were among the most prominent men of the day. The work is not a totally reliable narrative: advance publicity for each edition of the work was designed to extort hush money from those due to be named, the Duke of Wellington responding famously with 'Publish and be damned.' The book is written in a lively, restless prose that often modulates into captivating pastiches of contemporary prose styles; for example, her meeting with BYRON is described in a suitably 'sentimental' manner. The opening sentence of the book is itself a small masterpiece: 'I shall not say why and how I became, at the age of fifteen, the mistress of the Earl of Craven.'

wit 'what oft was thought but ne'er so well expressed' (POPE, *An Essay on Criticism*). The term has had many meanings and shades of meanings down through the years, and can denote either the thing itself or a notable practitioner of it. The main shifts of meaning to bear in mind are: (a) Elizabethan usage, meaning intelligence or wisdom; (b) early 17th-century usage, meaning ingenious thought, 'fancy', and original figures of speech, as in DONNE's verse and METAPHYSICAL POETRY; (c) the period relevant to Pope's definition, roughly from the mid-17th century to the last half of the 18th, which is discussed below; (d) 19th-century to modern times usage, meaning an amusing, perhaps surprising observation, usually involving paradox.

Wit as defined by Pope must be distinguished from what we now regard as humour: wit can be malicious, humour is benevolent amusement. SWIFT is witty, ADDISON and STEELE, who set the pattern for the future, are both witty and humorous. Wits tended to congregate in groups of like-minded intellectuals sharing similar political, social and religious views, e.g. the debauched circle around George VILLIERS, 2nd Duke of Buckingham, which included ROCHESTER, SEDLEY and WYCHERLEY, or the Tory quasi-Jacobite circles around Pope and Swift.

By the late half of the 18th century, the term largely ceased to be used to describe intellectual groups, implying as it did either heartless frivolity or political faction. Intellectual groupings became looser, although certainly no less formidable: a literary gathering in 1780 London, for example, could include figures as diverse as SHERIDAN, Dr JOHNSON, BURKE and Edward GIBBON, all of whom could be described as sharp-witted heavyweight thinkers and controversialists, although not 'wits' in the previous sense of the term.

Wodehouse, Sir P[elham] G[renville] (1881–1975) English novelist and short-story writer, who became a US citizen in 1955. He wrote amiable accounts of aristocratic life, featuring such characters as Lord Emsworth and the Empress of Blandings (a prize pig), but his most famous creations are Bertie Wooster, a giddy young upper-middle-class man who spends his large amount of spare time flitting about getting into situations with which he can't cope and doesn't understand, and his butler, Jeeves, a shrewd and immensely competent man who can cope with anything and understands everything. Representative volumes are *My Man Jeeves* (1919), *The Inimitable Jeeves* (1923) and *Carry on, Jeeves* (1925). Wodehouse also wrote many lyrics for musicals in collaboration with composers such as Jerome Kern and Irving Berlin. Interned by the Nazis during World War II, he foolishly made some innocuous broadcasts from Germany, which led to his being branded (even more foolishly) a traitor. Both Evelyn WAUGH and George ORWELL wrote spirited defences of him, effectively disproving the treason charges.

Wolfe, Thomas [Clayton] (1900–1938) American novelist. His major achievement is a huge four-volume series of largely autobiographical novels, i.e. *Look Homeward, Angel* (1929), *Of Time and the River* (1935), *The Web and the Rock* (1939) and *You Can't Go Home Again* (1940). Wolfe's novels were very popular in their day, despite critical complaints that they lacked form or structure (the first draft of *Look Homeward, Angel* was said to have filled suitcases, and the role of his editor, **Maxwell Perkins** (1884–1947), was crucial in the development of his fiction).

Wolfe, Tom [pseud. of Thomas Kennerly Jr] (1931–) American journalist and style guru. Wolfe's studies of American culture, e.g. *The Electric Kool-Aid Acid Test* (1968) and *Radical Chic and Mau-Mauing the Flak Catchers* (1970), are important and entertaining analyses in the non-objective mode of 'New Journalism', a term immortalized in the title of Wolfe's anthology of his contemporaries' writing, *The New Journalism* (1973). His first novel, *The Bonfire of the Vanities* (1987), a nightmarish yet brilliantly witty study of the disintegrating social order of New York, achieved great popular and critical success in the late 1980s.

Wollstonecraft, Mary *see* **Shelley, Mary Wollstonecraft**.

Woolf, [Adeline] Virginia (1882–1941) English novelist, critic and short-story writer. She married the novelist and social reformer **Leonard Woolf** (1880–1969) in 1912, and their home in Bloomsbury in London became the centre of the so-called 'Bloomsbury Group' of writers and artists, of whom the most important was Virginia Woolf herself. Her novels are written in a fluid, poetic style, and are recognized as being among the most innovative of the 20th century. They are particularly noted for their use of 'stream-of-consciousness' narration (*see* William JAMES), and include *Jacob's Room* (1922), *Mrs Dalloway* (1925), *To the Lighthouse* (1927), *Orlando* (1928), *The Waves* (1931) and *Between the Acts* (1941). Her literary criticism was collected in several volumes, e.g. *The Common Reader* (1925, 1932), and is often enthralling and lively, if occasionally a bit intolerant (*see* BENNETT), as are her *Letters* (six volumes, 1975–80) and *Diary* (five volumes, 1977–83). She also wrote several important feminist works, e.g. *A Room of One's Own* (1929). She suffered greatly from mental illness, and drowned herself. *See also* Vita SACKVILLE-WEST.

Wordsworth, Dorothy (1771–1855) English writer, sister of William WORDSWORTH. She lived with William from 1795 until his death, and kept journals which were not published until after her death. The most famous of these is the *Grasmere Journal*, which contains many superb passages describing people and landscapes, which her brother used as the basis for some of his poems. She is now recognized as one of the finest prose writers of the early 19th century.

Wordsworth, William (1770–1850) English poet. Like many young men of his generation, he was a great admirer of the French Revolution, and became disillusioned with revolutionary principles when the Terror began in 1793. He met COLERIDGE in 1795, and they published their great joint volume *Lyrical Ballads* in 1798. Wordsworth's contributions to the volume reflect his view (in the preface to the 1802 edition) that poetry should be plain and accessible to all men, and be written in the everyday language of men (poetry is defined, famously, as 'emotion recollected in tranquility'). The book is regarded, with BLAKE's works of the 1790s, as the first great flowering of English literary ROMANTICISM. Other great Wordsworth poems include 'Resolution and Independence' and the 'Intimations of Immortality' ode, and such sonnets as his stirring tribute to Toussaint L'Ouverture, the Haitian revolutionary leader, and 'The world is too much with us'. Wordsworth's masterpiece is the long narrative poem *The Prelude: or, Growth of a Poet's Mind*, the first version of which was finished (but not published) in 1805. Wordsworth toyed with the poem over the years, and a revised version was published in 1850. Few other poets have so successfully blended into a coherent whole the personal with the natural and social worlds, as

Wordsworth does here, whether in questioning his motives while picking up stones from the ruined Bastille, or in remembering a dark vision from childhood of the 'unknown modes of being' of nature. Wordsworth became POET LAUREATE in 1843, succeeding his friend SOUTHEY. Like Southey, he had become a staid conservative, much vilified both by contemporaries such as BYRON and by the new wave of radical poets (e.g. Robert BROWNING, who attacked him in 'The Lost Leader'). KEATS, SHELLEY and Blake, however, while disagreeing radically with Wordsworth in many ways, were definite about his significance as a great new voice in poetry. As Keats put it in one of his letters, his thought reached 'into the human heart'. After Wordsworth, English poetry was never the same again. *See also* Dorothy WORDSWORTH.

Wyatt, Sir Thomas (1503–42) English poet and diplomat. He spent most of his adult life in the dangerous diplomatic service of Henry VIII, when he was not being imprisoned by him. Wyatt was very probably the former lover of Anne Boleyn, Henry's second wife, and how he avoided execution is still a mystery. Wyatt's main claim to literary fame rests on several striking love poems, e.g. 'They flee from me that sometime did me seek', and his role as popularizer of the sonnet form in English (he translated and imitated PETRARCH's sonnets). He was a powerful and original poet, with a vivid turn of phrase, e.g. 'Drowned is reason that should me comfort'.

Wycherley, William (1641–1715) English dramatist. His two best-known comedies are *The Country Wife* (1675) and *The Plain Dealer* (1676), both of which have had many modern productions. Wycherley's plays were regarded as being among the most licentious of RESTORATION drama, but have grown steadily in reputation in the 20th century. Wycherley's relentless, sardonic mockery of social conventions and hypocrisy works very well on the stage.

Wyndham, John [pseud. of John Wyndham Parkes Lucas Benton Harris] (1903–69) novelist and short-story writer. Wyndham's best-known works are the science fiction novels *The Day of the Triffids* (1951), *The Kraken Wakes* (1953), *The Midwich Cuckoos* (1957) and *Trouble with Lichen* (1960). He preferred to describe his works as 'logical fantasies' in which a highly improbable event occurs, e.g. the world is suddenly invaded by giant, mobile carnivorous vegetables (as in *The Day of the Triffids*), and the consequences are explored in a naturalistic manner. The most notable of his other works is the short-story collection *Consider her Ways* (1961), a rare example by a male author of a common feminist fable, the future all-female world.

Yeats, W[illiam] B[utler] (1865–1939) Anglo-Irish poet. He studied art for three years at Dublin (his father and his brother, Jack Butler Yeats, were well-known artists), but became a writer in the early 1890s. His early works include several very important collections of poems, e.g. *The Wanderings of Oisin* (1889), *The Rose* (1893) and *The Wind Among the Reeds* (1899), which reflect the poet's concern with Irish myth and legend. He also edited two noteworthy editions of BLAKE in the 1890s. The influence of Blake upon Yeats was profound; Yeats followed Blake in establishing a private, arcane mythology in which to express his ideas, and, like Blake, his lyrical gift, e.g. the magical 'faery' poem, 'The Stolen Child', was as evident in the early work as in the later. It should be noted that Yeats's later complicated, arcane system of 'gyres' and occult symbolism, as in *Michael Robartes and the Dancer* (1921), can be safely ignored; like MILTON's equally esoteric mechanisms in *Paradise Lost*, the structures are only of relevance to dissertation-hounds and are no real barrier to the uninitiated reader; it should also be noted that Yeats admired Blake so much he gave him an Irish father, a piece of whimsical myth-making that is still repeated as fact in reputable works of reference. Several of Yeats's plays, first performed at the ABBEY THEATRE, which he helped to found, are also of great importance, particularly *Cathleen ni Houlihan* (1902), a celebration of Irish patriotism which he later feared had sent men to their deaths against the British. Many of his poems, e.g. 'Easter 1916', 'Among School Children', 'The Second Coming', 'Coole Park at Ballylee, 1931', the 'Crazy Jane' poems, 'Lapis Lazuli' and 'The Circus Animals' Desertion' are among the greatest poems in the English language. His prose works are also of great importance, notably the remarkable collected *Autobiographies* (1955), which includes many valuable portraits of his contemporaries. Yeats's politics are too complex to explain briefly; he certainly flirted with Fascism (*see* ORWELL's essay 'W. B. Yeats'), but became a highly respected member of the Irish senate (his speech in the senate in defence of divorce and of the Anglo-Irish heritage is a masterpiece of political rhetoric). His relationships with other writers, and with artistic movements, especially SYMBOLISM, are equally complex. Yeats was very much his own creature, and too conscious of the great literary heritage of the English language to take modern movements too seriously; he paid tribute to innovators such as JARRY, but wondered what could follow: 'After us, the Savage God'. He was awarded the NOBEL PRIZE for literature in 1923.

Yonge, Charlotte M[ary] (1823–1901) English novelist. Of her many novels, the only one that is still regularly printed is *The Heir of Radclyffe* (1853), a study of the influence of a good-natured (but bad-tempered) man upon his apparently good (but actually devious) cousin. The dominant theme in Yonge's fiction is her strong belief in the transforming power of Christianity. She was a High Anglican, and part of the profits of *The Heir of Radclyffe* went to fit out a missionary ship.

Yorke, Henry Vincent *see* **Green, Henry**.

Z

Zamyatin, Yevgeny Ivanovich (1884–1937) Russian novelist, short-story writer, dramatist and critic. His best-known work is the grim anti-Utopian (*see* Thomas MORE) novel *We* (part publication 1920–21), the influence of which was acknowledged by ORWELL (on *Nineteen Eighty-Four*), and unconvincingly denied by HUXLEY (on *Brave New World*). The novel, like *Nineteen Eighty-Four*, was read as a diabolical fantasy by Western readers and as virtually pure naturalism by its Soviet readers. It was first published in its full version in the mid–1920s, outside the USSR, by which time Zamyatin's position had become a highly dangerous one. Stalin let him emigrate, and he died in Paris.

Zangwill, Israel (1864–1926) English novelist, dramatist and journalist, best known for his novel of Jewish life in the London slums, *Children of the Ghetto* (1892). The most notable of his plays is *The Melting Pot* (1909), which describes America as 'God's Crucible, the great Melting-Pot where all the races of Europe are melting and re-forming!'

Zola, Émile (1840–1902) French novelist, regarded as the most prominent exponent of NATURALISM in the novel (*see* MARX). His huge sequence of 20 novels, entitled the *Rougon-Macquart* series, describes the history of the Rougon and Macquart families within the setting of what he called the 'natural and social history' of Second Empire France, *c*.1850–1870, 'natural' in this context denoting a deterministic view of human nature and the pernicious effects of hereditary faults. The novels include his masterpiece *Germinal* (1885), a moving account of the brutalized lives of miners and their families, which ends with a superb evocation of future revolution. Zola's works had an enormous influence on other naturalistic writers (e.g. DREISER), but few of his imitators produced anything as good. Zola was a highly able propagandist for socialism and for social justice in France; he had to flee France and take refuge in England for almost a year following the publication of his letter 'J'Accuse', a brilliant defence of the Jewish officer Alfred Dreyfus, who had been falsely accused of treason.